PRAISE FOR

The Uncrushable Rose

"...spellbinding, reads like the Chinese *Gone With the Wind*...."

— Radio Taiwan International, Paula Chao

"Of special interest in this world of divided nations is the political background of the 1940s and 50s. Shen's childhood was spent in pre-revolutionary French Indochina, Chinese but not ever living in China, as her father was retained as a diplomat of the Taiwan government in various postings. It gives insight to a uniquely traditional Chinese culture in a time of worldwide change."

— US-China Review

"The title of the book comes from her time in the concentration camp where her father planted two rose bushes. His lesson was: "These rose bushes are also in the concentration camp, but it makes no difference to them. Their nature is to bloom no matter where they are planted. We must learn from them and not allow any outer circumstances to keep us from being what we were born to be."

— Evolving Magazine

" An empowering advice of letting go came from her nanny:'...shake off hurtful words like the ducks shake off water from ⟨...⟩ That's how Bambi overcame her mother's ⟨...⟩ always be a day late, a measure short, a be⟨...⟩ success to serve others."

— University O⟨...⟩

i

"...You are as engaging and motivational in person as you are in print....Our culture tends to dwell on how circumstances make us feel like victims. At every stage of Bambi's life she has defied that mentality and regarded adversity as a learning opportunity."

—*Daniel Boone Regional Library*, Patricia Miller

"The lessons in your book are valuable to women as well as to men. You have used them for greater personal and spiritual growth."

—Robert Brumet, Unity minister, teacher, author of *Birthing a Greater Reality, Finding Yourself in Transition*

"It's a fine piece of work, and I found the parts of the book where you speak in an intensely personal voice to be especially effective.....Best wishes for the success of your splendid and very touching memoir."

—Charles Gusewelle, author of *Rufus Chronicles, A Paris Notebook, The Cabin: Away From It All....*

"What a sweeping panorama of life you have lived--history, personal and emotional hardship, strength...such intelligence, learning, work, endurance, growth, becoming, and leadership."

—Emma Curry, advocate, manufacturer of *UbiDuo* (communication device for the deaf) Sedalia, Missouri

"Your book greatly influenced me. You were brave to share your life experiences."

—Theresa O'Dell, I.T. specialist, Harrisonville, Missouri

"...a colorful account of a lifetime in China's worldwide diaspora."

—Robert Gamer, Professor Emeritus of Political Science, University of Missouri, author of *The Politics Of Urban Development in Singapore and Understanding Contemporary China*

ii

THE UNCRUSHABLE ROSE

To Ruth,

THE UNCRUSHABLE ROSE

*A Memoir from Concentration Camp to
Becoming a Free Woman*

Bambi Nancy Shen

*Thank you
for your interest;
Wishing you Peace
in Every Step!*

Bambi 沈
September 17, 2014
Gardner, Ks

How High The Moon Publishing
Kansas City, Missouri U.S.A.

Cover by Kelly Ludden Design and Dustin Maberry
Cover art by Bambi Nancy Shen
Interior design by Mike Walker and Dustin Maberry

ISBN 978-0-9743606-1-4
LCCN

Published by
How High The Moon Publishing
9826 James A. Reed Road
Kansas City, MO U.S.A. 64134

Third Printing
Printed in the United States of America

DEDICATION

This book is dedicated

to the empowerment of women

of all ages, all times, and all cultures.

May we take the courage to realize our potential

and achieve our dreams.

Acknowledgments

I have many people to thank for helping me share my life story in a memoir.

First, I thank my husband Gene Foster who listened to my story on our first date and encouraged me to put it in writing for others to experience. He said, "This should be a book! I'll help you with it." Up until that point, I was not one to reveal much about myself. I am grateful to Gene for seeing the value in my life and giving me the title of the book. Gene blesses me with his love, support and the many roses he has left to surprise me—on my pillow, bathtub or somewhere in my kitchen....

I am deeply indebted to my extraordinary writing coach and co-editor, June Holte, who tirelessly polished my language, line by line, while allowing my voice to come through. She helped me clarify, and re-sequence sentences, asking me to juice things up—to add more details to paint a better picture for readers. Without her weekly encouragement and assistance this book would never have seen the light of day. I thank her for staying with me, helping me believe in the importance and possibilities of my stories, and giving me the push I needed.

Much appreciation goes to my other writing coach, Pat Berge, especially for lending her compassionate ear. She allowed me to tell her the painful stories from the difficult periods of my life. She drew them out even when I wanted to stop. There were wounds deeper than tears, buried, hidden, which I had never expected to unearth. Her mantra became, "If you don't tell the whole truth, then there is no need to tell your story at all."

Many thanks to my co-editor, Jo Hoffman, who meticulously whittled away the unnecessary words, further refining the story. For her contribution to journalism she was inducted, in 2010, into the Hall of Fame of the Missouri Press Association. A mutual friend introduced us suggesting that she help me. Jo didn't know whether she wanted to take on such a large project. After reading just three pages of the first chapter, she accepted. I replied, "I need to know whether I can afford you." Her answer surprised me to no end: "I don't need to be paid." So I said, "OK, I'll cook for you and will bring several dishes over on Wednesdays." What a wonderful exchange!

I am grateful to my Wednesday evening potluck group of friends, who patiently listened to passages I wrote, asked helpful questions and provided a regular supply of encouragement. They got me to express my feelings more candidly, transcending my early training to keep my emotions in check. I thank Christine Colbert, Bill Logan and Dillard Eubank for giving me advice along the way. Special gratitude goes to Wei Huang, the Chinese student sharing our home—my in-house "techy" who saved my sanity when I didn't know what to do with the computer. My hair might have been all pulled out had he not been there.

I offer my greatest admiration and appreciation to my friend, David Westbrook, who is blind. He took time to listen to me read from my manuscript, giving me many invaluable suggestions. He holds the vision of a bright future for my book.

Special gratitude goes to my Uncle Richard Shen, author of *The Yellow Riding Jacket,* a meticulously researched historical novel. It is the saga of the Lindleys, father and son, revolving around events that led to the Opium War of the 19th century. We had lost touch for years. Thanks to the internet, I found him! We have been able to renew our family ties, and he gave me counsel on accuracy of historical events.

Also, I thank Mike Walker, of *How High the Moon Publishing,* who helped pull everything together for publication. I especially appreciate his expertise, his patience, the many hours of work he did, and the much-needed encouragement he offered early on.

To my proof-readers Lynn Snyder, Bill Langsdorf, and Jane Hatch, many thanks for your careful scrutiny and suggestions.

Lastly, I thank the pioneering women journalists and writers association, AMMPE (*Asociación Mundial de Mujeres Periodistas y Escritoras*), for blazing a trail for women writers everywhere. In advance, I thank them for providing translations of the book to enable my story to be told in other cultures, thereby inspiring and empowering women across the world.

Special appreciation goes to Mike Bonderer and Nancy Jochens—truly the hands and heart of *Homes from the Heart,* the not-for-profit charitable organization we co-founded with others. They kept the mission of building homes for those in need going, even when we ran into financial snags.

Contents

Foreword

The Uncrushable Rose is a moving and heart-rending memoir—
the story of a girl born in 1939 to a Chinese diplomat in Saigon
(now Ho Chi Minh City), Vietnam. Author Bambi Shen offers
vivid memories of the concentration camps she lived in during
the five-year Japanese occupation of then Indochina, in World
War II. Her memoir also paints a clear picture of the mother/
daughter conflict predictable in a culturally patriarchal society
and male-dominated family system. It is a story of challenge and
survival, and of the struggle to be freed from the limitations of
centuries-old tradition and cultural boundaries.

Bambi's story is that of a Chinese woman with boldness and
spiritual strength gained from her Catholic education, along
with her understanding of Unity theology and of Buddhist and
Confucian ethics. She has beautifully articulated her compelling
life journey, filled with lessons learned through experience,
bringing her to long sought-after self-empowerment and freedom.

In the way she lives her daily life, Bambi herself demonstrates
the interconnectedness of humankind and the opportunity for
each of us to grow, to serve society, and to participate in the
healing of our world. This is exemplified in the fact that, despite
extreme differences with her mother, Bambi spent years caring
for her until her death. Bambi's memoir demonstrates that even
under the most difficult circumstances *anyone* can find countless
ways to engage in the world to be a beneficial presence. Bambi
Shen is a true model to give us lessons in action, involvement,
and support for the creation of a peaceful global community.

Manouchehr (Manny) Pedram, Ph.D.
Professor of Philosophy and History of Education, Retired
Founder of Global and Muliticultural Education (GAME)

PREFACE

On the hundredth day after my mother's death—the end of the deep mourning period in Chinese tradition—I picked up my pen intending to reclaim my freedom by writing down my life story. Had mother been tolerant and kind, my story would have been very different.

Death does not end a relationship. It only changes the way we live our days and nights. I did not know that it would take much longer than the hundred days to heal—it took more than the hundred days just to begin to find my voice. Four years later, on my seventieth birthday, I vowed to write some of my many stories to share in a memoir, thinking: "If I don't recount the events as I saw them, these tales will die with me."

My journey began in 1939 when I was born in Saigon, capital of French Indochina, now Vietnam. The fact that my father was a diplomat for the Republic of China, led by Chiang Kai-shek, has shaped my life profoundly.

Do you recall anything from the time you were three? My memories from that age are so vivid, perhaps because my environment was so unusual. I lived in a concentration camp next to an aboriginal village where I saw elephants used as beasts of burden. That was during the five-year Japanese occupation of Southeast Asia in World War II. The war ended in 1945, three months before I turned six.

My childhood was spent in French schools in Saigon. During that time I learned to speak several languages and to navigate the wide variety of expectations of different cultures, sometimes conflicting.

My academic success enabled me to receive a Catholic scholarship, which brought me to the U.S.A. in 1958. Who would have predicted that my journey was to continue in this country for more than five decades? A rich life has unfolded for me, one step at a time, as a student, teacher, wife, and mother, public speaker, interpreter, businesswoman, and co-founder of a charitable not for profit organization. I have harvested a lifetime of lessons from my challenges and victories. By sharing these stories, I hope to inspire women to have the courage to stand up for their self-image, health, education, legal rights and finances.*

I wish you courage and peace in every step of your journey,

Bambi Shen
Kansas City, Missouri U.S.A.
August 1, 2010

*S.H.E.L.F. Women's Issues Forum, University of Central Missouri, March 14-15, 2006, Community Engagement Assistant Director Karen French, Conference Chairwoman

Chapter 1
WRONG, WRONG, WRONG

According to my mother, everything about me was wrong, wrong, wrong—beginning with my birth: I was born the wrong gender. I was her first-born so I was supposed to have been a boy (photo 2). She prayed for a male child because, as a Chinese Confucian, her most important duty was to produce a son to carry on her husband's family lineage. The duty of an adult son is to maintain the ancestral altar in the home and lead the family in carrying on customary rituals and offerings on holidays and anniversaries of birth and death. In so doing, the spirit of the ancestors would be remembered from generation to generation. At the same time it is the male child's duty to support his parents in their old age, therefore having a son has always been "Social Security" for a Chinese family. Tradition and popular belief are slow to die.

I have been in the United States for more than 50 years now, so I realize how difficult it is for a Western person to understand the seemingly unreasonable preference a Chinese couple has for a male child. It is shocking to see the lengths to which some parents will go to ensure that the baby a woman is carrying will be born a male. One of the strange practices is to have a relative's baby boy sleep, play, bounce, and urinate in the couple's marriage bed. This baby boy must be "lucky," which means both of his parents and all four grandparents are alive and in good health. The future mother must eat nutritious and special food that is supposed to give her strong male "chi" (life-force), such as a stew made with ginger, wine, sesame oil, and a whole silkie black chicken—a type of chicken that has black skin and bones and grayish meat, purportedly with curative and fortifying properties.

The invention of the sonogram machine has enabled the decision to abort many baby girls simply because they are the undesired gender. A daughter does not count as a permanent member of the family. She is considered her father's property. Upon marriage, she becomes the property of her husband and his family. That is a fact of life for a Chinese woman. Since I was not the son my mother wanted, time and time again she reminded me that I was her greatest disappointment. Throughout my life she often told me she cried for weeks after I was born. The nearly constant reminders of her non-acceptance gave me much to overcome in my self-image.

According to mother I was also born at the wrong time. China and Japan were once again at war—the eight-year-long Sino-Japanese conflict had begun two years prior to my birth, with the Marco Polo Bridge incident in Beijing on July 7, 1937. It was also a time of world war. In Europe, the conflict started three months before my birth, with the German invasion of Poland on September 1, 1939. Mother often lamented, "How inconsiderate could you be?"

Worst of all for a girl, mother saw me as all wrong because she considered me to be very ugly—my face was too round, my eyes too small, and my skin too dark. Her ideal pretty girl would have a face the shape of a "melon seed," big eyes, and porcelain white skin—all the qualities *she* had, making her a "Chinese Beauty." I remember clearly the moment she looked right at me when I was about five and said, "You were born ugly as a monkey! What did you do in your past life to deserve such ugliness?" She held no hope that any man would want to marry me and believed I was destined to live the life of a spinster. This would be a fate almost worse than death because I would be viewed as a useless mouth for my parents to feed. I was born on December 26—one day after Christmas. According to my mother, I would always be "one day late, one measure short, one beat behind."

Instead of being blessed in my cradle, I was cursed. Mother repeatedly made negative prophesies over me. From the time I first understood language, her words sounded like the gong of my seemingly doomed destiny—w-r-o-n-g…w-r-o-n-g…w-r-o-n-g. Because my father was a diplomat, I grew up in a French society where many positive words were spoken about all little girls—cute, sweet, lovely…. I wondered why others said I was good, while my mother, whose love and opinion were most important to me, considered me so worthless.

According to a Buddhist teaching, the most difficult person in our life often is our most valuable teacher. In this light, mother's constant belittling forced me to rise above her criticism and make something of myself. Ultimately, it was my father's words of encouragement and my academic success, along with the teachings of Buddhism and Unity's Practical Christianity, that enabled me to do so. My dear nanny, who was an illiterate peasant woman from Guangzhou, in southern China, taught me my early lessons in Buddhism. In my 30s I was introduced to Unity, a new-thought movement founded in 1889 by Charles and Myrtle Fillmore, in Kansas City, Missouri—the very center of the United States of America.

I first drove into Kansas City when I was 34 years old. All my worldly possessions were packed in the trunk and back seat of my old 1963 tan Chevy Impala, with its distinctive six round tail lights that looked like red doughnuts. At first sight of the skyline of tall buildings, I felt I had come to the Emerald City, like Dorothy in *The Wizard of Oz*. Even though I had gone through some heartbreaking experiences during the preceding 12 years, I still had great expectations for my life. I was making this move to enter the master's program in French Language and Literature at the University of Missouri Kansas City campus, UMKC.

At the time I arrived in this Midwestern city, some people may have considered me "tainted" because I had gone through a divorce. According to the Catholic Church, in which I was baptized at 13, my divorce made me a "fallen" Catholic. I would be excommunicated if I were to remarry, and would not be allowed to receive the sacraments or be buried in a Catholic cemetery. Not surprisingly, according to my mother's old-fashioned Chinese thinking, it had to be my fault that my marriage had failed. I had "lost face" because I could not "hold on to" a husband. If I were to remarry, I would be said to "carry two oil bottles"—a demeaning way the Chinese would refer to my two sons, who would then be stepchildren. I was judged by my church, by the people of my culture, and by my mother, but I knew I had made the right choices for my life.

Prior to Kansas City, I had lived in Warsaw, Missouri with my husband, Simon, and our two sons (photo 41). It became clear that Simon had no interest in supporting a family. Also, he was actively pursuing a gay lifestyle. I chose to get a divorce when he repeatedly brought his lover home to spend the night, a situation I could not tolerate in front of the children.

Immediately after the divorce, Simon filed for bankruptcy over a $5,000 debt that included some medical bills and the price of a car that he had wrecked. He bought the car locally and, since we were married, I had co-signed the note. I consider my signature to be my bond, therefore I was responsible for the debts. I agreed to pay them in full. This meant I needed to work two jobs.

During the school year I taught second grade by day and added evening work as a waitress at the Hill-Top barbecue restaurant. I had to hire a babysitter for the afternoons and evenings. My boys hated the situation. I did not know how to drive—Simon had forbidden me to learn—and I did not own a car, so I had to ride the school bus with the students to get to my teaching job and walk to the restaurant for my second job. I felt humiliated. How could the school kids have any respect for me? I had little for myself.

After the school year ended, I continued evening work at the restaurant and was hired as the bakery manager for the local IGA grocery store because I knew how to decorate birthday and wedding cakes. I was always so tired that I was afraid I would oversleep and be late for one of my jobs. Sometimes I even took the alarm clock to my kitchen and slept on the floor so I would not get too comfortable in the bed and miss my alarm; I set the stove buzzer as a backup alarm. In a town of 1,400 it was not easy to get a job, so I considered myself lucky to be able to hold on to two!

My position at the bakery was a blessing, but childcare became a nightmare. There was no way I would drag my eight-year-old Gregory and five-year-old Michael out of bed at 4:30 in the morning. We would have to walk the hilly, unpaved country road of the Warsaw Blue Branch development for 20 minutes to get to the store. So for the first weeks I had to leave my boys to sleep on the sofa of my neighbor, Gail Knox.

I did not have to work at the restaurant on Sundays because it was closed. One Sunday afternoon I saw a tan car pull into my driveway. Out came my tall, slim friend of seven years, Dr. Don Hinshaw. We met when I lived with the boys and their dad in Butler, Missouri, a town 65 miles south of Kansas City. I had gone to his clinic with a terrible toothache. Following Don was his blue Cadillac, driven by another man. I opened my front door. As they came in Dr. Hinshaw handed me two keys. "This is your car," he said with a huge grin. "Ron will stay with the boys. You come with me—I'm going to give you your first driving lesson!"

"Dr. Hinshaw, I can't accept that!" I declared firmly.

"I knew you wouldn't accept it as a gift, so I bought it and had it registered in your name. Here are the bank loan papers. I co-signed them for you. It is $750 for two years, so your payments will be only $35 a month. You have to have a car. It will solve a lot of your problems." I will always be grateful for his generous and compassionate help.

Gail Knox quickly taught me to drive. The car allowed me to take my boys to the bakery—wrapped in their blankets so that they could sleep on the floor of the little office. Their babysitter would pick them up later. As an inexperienced driver, I was thankful that I was driving mainly when most people were sleeping. When I arrived at the grocery store the parking lot was usually empty. We were at the store by 5 a.m. because I had to fry the doughnuts before the morning rush. I had the key to this big store and it was always a little spooky to be the first person there, leading my sleepy boys in clandestinely. I felt guilty that I had to put them through this interrupted sleep.

It was not a good situation. I agonized, "How could I make life easier for my boys?" Their father was not working and I knew I could not expect any support from him. Eventually I discussed the situation with their paternal grandparents. We came to agree that the best solution was to let my sons go live with them. Their home was in West Plains, Missouri, about four hours away by car. One Sunday they came to get Gregory and Michael, along with their clothes, books, and toys. My heart dropped as I watched my boys ride away with them. It was the saddest day of my life. I knew I would miss out on their growing up and many of their big moments. I felt my babies were slipping away. Someday they might understand that it took more courage to let them go than to keep them close to me. I was aware that I was in some ways losing them. I wondered if they would ever forgive me.

Some people condemned me for letting my children go to be reared by their grandparents, questioning me, acting as if I had abandoned them. But under the circumstances it was the best solution. Gregory and Michael had fun living in the country with a stay-at-home grandmother who was a good cook and loved caring for them. Shortly after the move, their grandfather, a brakeman on the Frisco Railroad, died of a heart attack in Springfield, Missouri. It was a shock because he had never had any sign of heart problems. Nana Sue became a 48-year-old widow who found that my children gave purpose and meaning to her life. They became her saving grace.

Not having the expense of a babysitter helped me speed up the repayment of my debts. After two and a half years of working two jobs, I saved enough money to begin my master's program. I continued earning extra money to subsidize my children's expenses, which helped Nana Sue live a more comfortable life. I knew my decision was creating a win/win situation, especially in light of my Chinese belief that grandparents are often better care-givers than parents. They have more time and patience along with experience gained in raising their own children.

Nevertheless, when I arrived in Kansas City in late August 1974, I felt like I was "alive in a bitter sea"—a Buddhist expression referring to the struggles and sufferings of life. When UMKC accepted me in its master's program, I remembered that Dr. Hinshaw had some rental property in Kansas City. I called to inquire if he had an apartment near the university. He was happy to let me rent a studio, just two miles from the school. He spent his weekends in the larger apartment across the hall. After I moved in, knowing that I had a Catholic background, he offered to show me the way to the nearest Catholic Church. I said, "Remember, I am divorced. I don't want to go to there—they consider me a reject."

He replied, "Then would you like to come with me to my church this Sunday? It's just down the street. It's a very open-minded, all-encompassing spiritual center. It does not dictate any dogmas. It is a Christian church, but no one there will ask you if you are 'saved.' You are free to choose your own spiritual path—I know you were born a Buddhist. Unity even encourages you to examine the spirituality of other religions. After the service, we could grab a bite of lunch somewhere."

Eager to make friends and find a spiritual home, I replied, "Thank you, Don. I would love to visit your church. Afterwards a simple lunch would be lovely." I intended to pay my part, and I was concerned that he might take me to an expensive restaurant. I didn't want to become indebted to him beyond our landlord/tenant relationship.

We went to Unity Temple on the Plaza. The congregation sang a hymn called "Confident Living." When I heard the lyrics "… Confident living rights every wrong…" I felt as if I had received a flash from the Light of Intelligence. That phrase became my daily affirmation, my lifeline, and my guiding light. By my choosing to live confidently I could overcome my mother's negative judgment and prophesies. My reaction to that day's lesson by the minister, Dr. Ernest Wilson, was, "He seemed to speak directly to me. How did he know I needed to hear that? Where has this church been all my life?" At Unity, over the years, I have learned to minimize my concerns about what other people think and to concentrate on living my own truth. At long last, I had found my spiritual home. I have attended Unity Temple ever since—for 36 years. I have participated in many classes there that provided opportunities to deepen my understanding of my mind, heart and soul.

A few days later, my French Language and Literature classes began, along with my duties as a teaching assistant in the language laboratory. The chair of the department, Dr. Jon Beeker, had assigned me to teach French 101, a five-hour-a-week course. I reported to him often. I was always in high spirits and so enthusiastic about my work and my studies that one day he said, "How can you be so happy all the time? You wear me out!" We developed a great working relationship.

Having good command of the language, I was very comfortable teaching French 101. On the first day of class, some students who were about to enter my classroom took one look at my Asian face and exclaimed, "Oops, wrong classroom!" To catch them before they moved on I quickly said, "If you want to study French, believe it or not, I am your teacher." Subsequently, on the first day of each semester I would leave my belongings on the teacher desk and sit in a student's chair until the bell rang. Then I walked up to the front to announce that I was the French teacher they were waiting for. I usually spent the first few minutes of class telling my students the story of how all my elementary and secondary education had been in French schools, in places with names like Tahiti, Saigon, and Vietnam. I also explained that, even though I am Chinese, I consider French my mother tongue because it was the language of my formal education.

My other memorable professor was Dr. Raymond Riva, an American who had lived in France. His was the first class I attended on my first day back to school after 12 years. I was in such a state of euphoria and gratitude that day that I just listened to him lecture without uttering a word. During the second class, Dr. Riva posed a few questions on our reading assignment and suddenly spoke to me, *"Mademoiselle Shen, que pensez vous de ce que les américains disent que les français ont une terrible attitude de supériorité et refusent de parler anglais quand on leur demande des renseignements dans la rue?"* (Miss Shen, what do you think about Americans saying that the French have a terrible attitude of superiority and refuse to speak English whenever one asks them for some information on the street?)

"Le titre de votre cours est 'L'histoire et la culture françaises.' En partie je crois que c'est une question de culture. Les américains sont souvent trop directs. Si seulement ils apprenaient a commencer leur questions par une petite phrase de politesse—par example, 'Monsieur, excusez-moi de vous déranger, mais s'il vous plait, pouvez-vous me dire de quel cote se trouve le Musée d' Orsay?'—tout irait beaucoup mieux. Il est vrai que la

plupart des français ne parlent pas bien l'anglais et ils le savent. Donc une attitude de supériorité souvent cache un sense d'infériorité." (The title of your course is French History and Culture. In part I believe it is a question of culture. Americans are often too direct. If only they would learn to preface their inquiries by using this little phrase of courtesy—for example, 'Sir, excuse me for disturbing you, but could you please tell me which way is the Musee d' Orsay?'—all would go much better. It is true that most French do not speak English well, and they recognize it. Therefore, a posture of superiority often hides a sense of feeling inferior.)

Dr. Riva looked at me with surprise and said, *"Et mademoiselle, d'ou venez vous?"* (And miss, where did you come from?)

"De Warsaw, Missouri, Professeur."

"Vous savez bien que ce n'est pas ce que je veux dire; ou avez-vous appris votre français?" (You know very well that's not what I meant; where did you learn your French?)

From then on Dr. Riva and I made a game of challenging each other. When he lectured, he spoke French only, without incorporating any English words. I especially appreciated that because my father taught me that it is rude to mix languages when speaking to someone who might not understand the second language. Papa also taught me that mixing languages might also make you appear to be incapable of expressing yourself fully in the first language.

During my first year of graduate school, I worked as a translator for a professional publication called *Modern Jeweler,* where I took care of their correspondence in French with Swiss watch making companies and jewelry houses in France. With the salary I received from *Modern Jeweler* combined with US $5-a-week savings from having worked as a waitress, I planned to visit mother. Finally, in the summer of 1975, I had gathered $1,200 for a round trip ticket. I flew to Taipei, my first time in 17 years, since I had left for college.

Mother picked me up at the airport that evening. She barely spoke to me in the taxi on the way to her apartment. Right after we arrived she unleashed her furry. She ordered me to kneel down and confess my unforgivable sin of having divorced. I protested, "Should I have stayed in a marriage where I was constantly humiliated and risk being beaten?" Instead of showing any compassion, she hissed, "Who told you to choose him? You deserve what you got! You're causing me to lose face among the relatives." On my knees, in that posture of submission, I felt worthless. I stiffened and refused to shed a tear. Mother abruptly walked away.

I stood up in disbelief and made my way to my room. After I climbed in bed and turned the lights out I sobbed, missing father, his love, and support. Suddenly, across my bed something fell with a bang! I turned on the light to see. Father's photograph had fallen off the dresser onto the floor, and the glass had broken. I knew papa heard me. The next day I went to his grave site in Yang Ming Shan. A white butterfly landed on my shoulder briefly, then hovered and followed me until I boarded the taxi. Again I knew that papa was watching over me.

After an awkward two week visit, I was relieved to be able to return to my life and my studies in Kansas City. It took two years to complete my master's degree. They were two years of pure joy, studying the old masters of French literature I had first read in childhood. On the day of my oral exam I felt that the four professors who made up the panel were not really testing me. Each one seemed to be showing off to the others what I had learned in his courses. I was told to expect two hours of questions. After about one hour Dr. Beeker said that I could go get some coffee and take a break while the professors conferred. A few minutes later he walked over to me, extended his hand and said, "Congratulations, you pass. We don't need to question you anymore. We are convinced you deserve the degree. Do come back and visit us from time to time. *Au revoir.*"

Completing my degree fulfilled my reason for moving to Kansas City. Now that I had achieved it, I would be able to get higher paying positions and take better care of my boys.

Chapter 2

DEVIL'S BARGAIN

For many years I had relied on teaching French for a living, in schools in Memphis, Tennessee, and in Springfield and Republic, Missouri. And in Warsaw, I had to teach second grade because the position of foreign language teacher was already filled. So I expected that after completing my master's degree, I would use it to get a better paying teaching job. But—surprise of surprises—two weeks before my master's oral exams, Don Hinshaw, my former dentist, present landlord, and thoughtful friend asked me to marry him! What was I to do with such an invitation?

I knew immediately this was not a romantic proposal but a very calculated bargain. In our seven years of friendship, Don had told me the story of his life and never hid from me the fact that he was gay. As a dentist in a town of 4,200, he considered remaining "in the closet" to be essential. He had graduated from the Kansas City Dental School in 1950, married a nurse and bought a dental practice in Butler. He and his wife had two daughters and a son. They divorced when their children were teenagers. When his ex-wife and children moved away, he remained in Butler because, after nearly three decades, his practice was well-established.

Shortly after I moved into Don's apartment building in Kansas City, he told me he wanted his daughter Nancy to meet me. I was glad he suggested it, so he called her right away: "I'd like to introduce you to my new tenant across the hall," he said. "She is a graduate student at UMKC. Her father was a Chinese ambassador to three African countries (photo 42). She is very interesting. Would you and Gary join us for lunch Sunday after church?"

When Nancy first met me she was intrigued by my name. "Is Bambi your real name?" she asked.

"Well, it is now my legal name, but it has nothing to do with Walt Disney's *Bambi*," I told her. "I was six when my mother registered me at my first French school. She told the administrator that my name is *Lu-zhu* and that *zhu* means 'bamboo' in Chinese. The French lady did not think it was a good idea to give me such a foreign sounding name because all my classmates would be French kids and I might be teased. She suggested 'Bambi' because her mother was Italian and had called her *Bambina*. Mama preferred to name me after the friend she admired most in college, Nancy Yu Huang, who later became the founder and publisher of the first English language newspaper in Taiwan, *The China Post*. So during my years in French schools I was known as 'Nancy,' but with the French pronunciation."

"Then we have the same name," Don's daughter replied with some surprise. "But what made you change it to Bambi?"

I told her that when I was in college in Kentucky, there was another Nancy in the dormitory. To make it easier for people to distinguish us I asked to be called Bambi. I wanted to honor the name 'Bamboo' because my father had given it to me.

"In Chinese culture the bamboo tree symbolizes the virtues people seek. The bamboo tree will bend in a storm but will not break because of its flexibility. The knots on the trunk represent determination. The hollow center symbolizes two virtues: humility, for not being full of oneself; and open-mindedness, for keeping an open mind for further learning and growth. These are the virtues my father wanted me to incorporate into my life."

"How very interesting—flexibility, determination, humility, and open-mindedness," Nancy repeated. "I would love to know more about Chinese culture. Dad is so fond of anything oriental."

"You are correct," I praised Nancy. "You know that 'oriental' describes things, like an oriental carpet, and 'Asian' refers to a person from the orient."

"Oh, really, I wasn't aware of that distinction. I am glad you pointed it out."

In no time, Nancy and I became close friends. She was a pediatric nurse at Children's Mercy Hospital in Kansas City. We had many common interests so we got together often. At 25, she was only nine years younger than I. Even so, she saw me as a good companion for her father and for herself.

A few days before Thanksgiving, Don's widowed mother came from Sand Springs, Oklahoma, to spend the holiday with him, his daughters Nancy and Linda, and their husbands. Don wanted to introduce me to her, so he invited me to join them for Thanksgiving dinner. He told me his plans: "Since most restaurants are closed on Thanksgiving," he said, "we can eat in the Alameda Plaza Hotel dining room. I love that place." As usual, Don had planned every detail completely. The Alameda Plaza is adjacent to Kansas City's famous Country Club Plaza, America's first outdoor, suburban shopping center, which had gained national attention for lighting building outlines with multicolored lights each holiday season. Don intended to park on the top level of the Swanson store parking garage. That way, as we walked back to our car after dinner, we could attend the annual lighting ceremony—or, if the weather turned too cold, we could view the event from inside his car.

This trait of thinking through all the steps toward what he wanted to accomplish was characteristic of Don. Realizing that he was not comfortable cooking for that many people, I offered, "Would you like for me to cook Thanksgiving dinner? I would really enjoy doing it. It will be fun to eat at home. You brought back such a beautiful set of Noritake china from your trip to Japan. Just the other day you said you regret that you haven't used it yet."

He seemed pleased, "That sounds wonderful! Let's write out the menu and then you give me a full list of everything you need. I'll help you in the kitchen, maybe even learn something! I love to entertain. You can be my 'hostess with the mostest!'"

He shopped and brought everything I wanted to work with, so it was easy to show that I knew how to turn out a feast. I cooked a completely traditional Thanksgiving dinner. Everyone was surprised that I had so totally integrated into the culture of the United States. We went to the holiday lighting ceremony as planned. I seemed to have worked myself into Don's family and his life.

During Christmas that year, the Mid-Century Dental Club,

which had been created by Don's graduating class, held its annual holiday party. This was an elaborate dinner-dance at a country club. He asked if I would be his date for the evening.

Embarrassed, I said, "I never got to participate in social life during my nine years of marriage to Simon. These last two years have been nothing but work. I really have nothing proper to wear."

He laughed, "That is the least of your worries. I want you to look nice so I am going to take you shopping. We will choose your clothes together. I want you to accentuate your Chinese features. You will be my 'China Doll.' Now that your hair is longer I'd like you to wear it up. Go to the beauty shop next door. They rent from me. I'll pay your bill."

As I listened to his detailed staging, I wondered if Don was what I'd heard described as a "sugar daddy." By this time I had gotten to know him well enough that I was not surprised by his elaborate plans. I paused for a moment, then said, "Don, it doesn't feel right to let you do so much for me."

Then Don cleared up my puzzlement, "Bambi, let me clarify my position. I only want you for a 'front.' So if you are willing to be my date at social events, I will dress you. Your looking good will make me look good. But we both know all this won't lead to romance since I'm gay. I don't want my friends in the dental club or my patients in Butler to know this part of my life. That's why I keep this apartment in the city."

"Yes," I said, "I can accept being your date in this way. I'm not looking for romance anyway. My happiness comes from my studies and teaching. I am making enough money to take care of my expenses and to send some money to Nana Sue for my sons. I had managed to save enough tuition money for four semesters before I started my master's program, to prevent running into any financial snags—that was very important to me."

In reality, because I needed to send money to support my children, I was living on a shoestring. I only allowed myself about ten dollars a week for food. I got pretty tired of ramen noodles! They cost a dollar for ten packages when I could catch them on sale. I only drove from the apartment to the university and back, once a week to the grocery store, and nowhere else. I could make a tank of gas last six weeks.

Don and I rarely saw each other except on Sundays. We would go to the Unity Temple and then enjoy a good lunch out, most of the time at the Princess Garden Chinese restaurant. Even though I offered to pay for my lunch several times, he never allowed me to do so. Finally he insisted, "Don't offer again. It's my pleasure to treat you." After lunch we would go to flea markets. Don enjoyed searching for collectibles and visiting with dealer friends.

On one of these Sundays I met Cass White at her booth at the Westport Flea Market, where she carried many astrology-related items. Since there were no other customers, we started a conversation on how our signs and the stars affect personalities and lives. She commented, "I see you came in with Don Hinshaw. I've known him for a long time. He has many friends here. How do you know him?"

"He is my landlord. Our apartments are across the hall from each other. We are friends."

I could tell she was trying to figure out our relationship.

Quickly she added, "May I call you? Would you like to go out to dinner and take in a movie sometime?"

"I don't have a phone at the moment," I replied. "Don allows me to use his phone to call my kids at their grandmother's. I am very busy with school and teaching, so leisure time will have to come later. But thank you for asking."

My finances did not allow me to spend for my own enjoyment, but I appreciated her friendliness and directness. At that first meeting I would not have predicted that we would become close friends. Over 36 years later we are still friends.

I saw many beautiful things on our trips to the flea markets. They were only there for me to admire. The one frivolous thing I bought was a small gold butterfly pin that I treasure to this day. I spotted it among many other expensive pieces of jewelry at the Waldo Flea Market in Joseph Candioto's booth. He had been in the antique business for years and from whom Don had bought many beautiful decorative pieces over the years. Joseph remains my dear friend. The pin was delicately made with antiqued variations of gold hues. To my eyes it looked very French. When I found out it cost forty dollars, I saved for two months. I did not choose to put it in lay-away because I did not want to let Don know I liked it. I knew he would have bought it for me and I did not wish that to happen. Instead, I took my chances that the pin would still be there when I had saved enough money. I believed that if it were gone by then I was not supposed to have it. This little butterfly became my symbol for the transformation I was going through—gaining confidence in myself, going through my master's program with high grades, and making new friends.

From that time on, I wore it regularly on my left shoulder, the side of my heart, the seat of compassion. It serves to this day as a reminder of the presence of my angel I named "Butterfly." Later, I found another pin, a dragonfly, which I sometimes wear on my right shoulder. It reminds me of a second angel whom I named "Dragonfly," which embodies the courage to take action and the willingness to let go of things I cannot control. I think of a dragonfly diving down to take a sip of water or catch an insect, then quickly flying away—this reminds me to practice the concept of non-attachment.

Don and my arrangement worked well for both of us until spring break in 1976. His son Doug was getting married in Indianapolis, the home of his bride-to-be and family. Don wanted me to fly there for the wedding with his elderly mother and daughters. Don's older daughter Nancy met her grandma at the Greyhound bus station and brought her to Don's apartment. When I got home from school I joined them for lunch. Bluntly Nancy asked her father, "How am I to introduce Bambi? Is she your girlfriend or is she your fiancée?"

To my utter amazement, Don answered, "Introduce her as my fiancée."

I was too flabbergasted to protest or question.

Nancy, who had long suspected that her father was gay or bisexual, pushed, "Let's go get her a ring! Bambi has to have a ring before we go to Indianapolis." That very afternoon, the three of us went to choose a ring for me. Actually the two of them chose it—a beautiful marquis diamond, over a carat in size, which any woman would be proud to wear.

We arrived in Indianapolis just in time to go directly to the restaurant where the rehearsal dinner was held. Nancy could not wait to announce, "Dad is engaged! This is his fiancée Bambi." I felt terrible for the young couple. We stole the show. I had an uncomfortable feeling when I was introduced to Don's former wife, Joy. She must have known the truth about him. For a while I thought she was going to take me aside to warn me. Fortunately it did not happen. What could I have said to her?

I felt I had been thrown into a whirlwind. My future life with Don looked like a *fait accompli*. Nevertheless, I believed our "engagement" could last indefinitely without ever setting a wedding date. I thought Don and I would simply continue our sweet, platonic relationship.

With a ring on my finger, Don's thinking started to change. He explored the idea of my moving to Butler three months later, after my graduation.

I protested, "No, I will not move to Butler if we are not married. It's too small a town for us to do that. You, who are so concerned about public opinion—you want us to appear 'shacked up'? What would your patient, Cleta York, think? She is my friend, a business owner, and the mayor's wife. I couldn't face her or anyone else. Let's be real—Butler is not *that* liberated."

"OK, OK, I've got it! Let me think it through," he replied.

I told Don that I agreed to remain his "fiancée" if I stayed in Kansas City. I had planned to get a teaching job and have my children come live with me. Gregory would be twelve in August and Michael nine. I had recently written them a letter asking if they wanted to come to live with me in Kansas City. To my disappointment, but not to my surprise, they said they wanted to stay with Nana. They had developed their routines and loved living in the countryside with a barnyard of chickens, ducks, and peacocks. Their hunting dogs and fishing holes were special to them. They had made friends in school and participated in sports. It would be too hard for them to leave all that for a city life. I suppose they also remembered that it hadn't been fun to live with a mother who had to go to work at all hours as I did in Warsaw. I had to come to grips with the fact that my sons would not be coming to live with me. Every mother will know what a loss this was to me.

Because I had protested to Don about moving to Butler without being married and because he really wanted me to be part of his life, he decided we should get married the Saturday after my graduation. I agreed to this. He invited his mother and children to come to both events. We planned a very simple ceremony in the clubhouse at Unity Village, with the associate minister from Unity Temple on the Plaza, Jerry Thompson, performing the ceremony.

Don was exceedingly courteous during this time. After he had asked me to marry him, he called my mother in Taiwan to invite her, "We want to be married two days after Bambi receives her master's degree." He said, "We would love to have you come. If you can, I'll send you a round-trip airfare immediately."

To Don's surprise, but not mine, her reply was, "What's your big hurry? Are you sure you want to marry her?" He thought it was a strange response. "Of course I want to marry her. We are meant to be together," he exclaimed. "Here, talk to Bambi." He handed me the phone. She let me have it in Chinese: *"Ni zhen bu yao lian!* (You really want to lose face!) Don't you know it's shameful to remarry? You have already failed at one marriage. What can you offer him? He is 17 years older than you are. Maybe he just wants you to be his nurse in his old age. You make me so ashamed! You are so far away that anything I have to say is of no use. You will do as you please, with no regard to family honor. Again and again, you make *ME* lose face. What are the relatives going to say?"

I responded, still in Chinese, "Mama, can't you just be happy for me? *Zui shao yo ren yao wo.* (At least someone wants me.)"

As I got off the phone Don asked, "What did she say?"

"Oh, the usual good wishes. She is not coming. She said to take good care of you and that I am very lucky!" I lied. I could never tell him what she had really said.

Six years before, Don had met mama when she came to visit me in Warsaw. Because Don was scheduled to go on a dental mission trip to Taiwan not long afterward, he wanted to meet her so she could later show him around during his visit. On that trip mama helped him find several lovely pieces of hand-carved Chinese furniture, which he bought and had shipped to Kansas City. They later became part of our home furnishings.

Mama had always prophesied that no one would ever want to marry me—but here I was, getting ready to marry for the second time. Even if under false pretense, I was still going to be a married woman in the eyes of society. Yes, I was marrying a gay man for the second time in my life. With Simon I had not known he was gay prior to our marriage, nor did I understand the secrecy of that lifestyle. But now, I would be getting into it with my eyes wide open. Mama had so drilled into my head that I was not worth being chosen as a wife that I actually believed I did not deserve to have a true husband, one who wanted to marry me simply because he loved me.

The evening before our wedding, Don came to my apartment. We had another long talk about how we could live together in harmony.

He said, "Be assured that I will always take care of you. It is good for both of us to be married. I love you, in my own way, and I will give you affection in the measure that I am capable. I promise you an easier life. In Kansas City, you will retain this studio apartment. In Butler, since, as you know, I live behind the dental office in the adjoining building, I am setting you up in a separate studio apartment across the hall from me, with a king size bed and a remodeled bathroom. I have a housekeeper who comes in once a week to do my cleaning, laundry and ironing. I am very fussy about my shirts because my patients see me under very bright lights, so I change shirts at least twice a day. I will keep her working for me so you really will have no housework to do. But I would like for you to take charge of the kitchen. I like your cooking so I would like to eat more at home and less at the country club in the evenings. I want my lunches very simple because I like a short nap before I see my patients in the afternoon. I will respect your closed door as I expect you to do the same with mine."

"I really appreciate the way you spell everything out to avoid any misunderstanding," I replied. "I can easily accept this idea of our arranged marriage because it is similar to earlier practices in China. Both my paternal and maternal grandparents' marriages were arranged by their families. The bride and groom never saw each other before the ceremony. There was no romantic love. Their love for each other grew out of commitment, mutual respect, and learning to adapt to one another's personality and preferences. My grandmothers, in particular, believed they had to surrender to their destiny and their karma. Historically and culturally, marriages had been used to create alliances for political, social, or financial reasons. I don't expect any romantic love from you. I have never known the pleasures of sex, so that makes little difference to me. I promise you my devotion. I accept your sexual preference. I would like to ask that, out of respect for our marriage, you promise me never to move a sexual partner into our home. What you do behind the closed door of your bedroom is for you to decide. If I am to be your 'wife,' I claim the right to be the only mistress of our home. Your respectful attitude and your affection toward me in public will be more than enough for me."

Just as my grandmothers had done, I was marrying for financial security and social approval, not for love. Some may consider it hollow, but at that time I thought that the ultimate goal for a woman was to have a home with a husband—even if it was in name only. At 36, I still believed that I needed a man to validate my existence.

Immediately Don replied, "Yes, I can promise you I will never move a man into our home. After all, we are getting married for the sake of appearances. I am not going to cut off my nose to spite my face!"

I continued, "You have also said that you don't want me to get a job. You want me to be free and at your beck and call. But you know I need money to support my children at their grandmother's. Their father has never sent one dollar toward their needs. Since I agreed to let them continue to live with their Nana, how could I contribute to their support if I don't have any income?"

Without hesitation he replied, "I am glad you brought it up.

I've thought it through and already instructed Effie, my office manager, that on Fridays, when she writes the paychecks for my staff, she also give you a check for $250. This money is solely for your personal expenses. I will never ask what you do with it. Over a thousand dollars a month should be ample money for you to take care of your kids."

In 1976, a thousand dollars was a significant amount of money. I felt very grateful for his generosity, and relieved that my boys would be well taken care of.

Don continued, "You'll have no household bills of any kind to pay. You can buy all your groceries and anything else you need that is available at Jennings' Grocery Store in Butler. Just sign the bills and Effie will pay them at the end of each month."

I replied, "Don, you are so thoughtful and more generous than I could hope for. I don't know what to say."

"My dear Bambi, you don't have to say anything. We are serving each other. For some reason, ever since I first met you, I felt I owed you a karmic debt. I don't know what it is. I wish I did."

I realized it was the right moment to tell him what I thought I knew about us, "The first time I went to your dental office seven years ago, I was in a lot of pain. You were so very kind. You took me as an emergency. I was your last patient that day, remember? When you leaned over me, I had a flashback that almost took my breath away. I saw a bamboo screen behind you, and I saw myself squatted on the ground, washing a pot of rice for you. I did not know what to make of it because there was no bamboo screen in your office. I thought I recognized you from a past life. I prayed to understand our connection. Shortly afterward, I started having a recurring dream. I thought it might be a revelation of our past, but it seemed so fantastic that I hesitated to consider it real."

"I want to hear it!" he exclaimed. "Maybe it can explain to me why I feel the way I do about you. I have a need to make something up to you. I feel I owe you plenty."

"OK," I continued cautiously, "I will tell you my dream, the way I have seen it several times. I have no idea how accurate it is. Since both of us believe in reincarnation and karma, maybe we can

41

gain some insight about what we should be for each other. Accept what you can and let the rest go."

Due to my Chinese culture and Buddhist background, my belief about reincarnation and karma is that my soul can live many different times in different bodies in order to learn what I need to learn. The quality of each life is determined by our good or bad behavior in a previous life or lives. Thus, it makes sense to me that our lives are largely the result of past deeds. We alone are responsible for our actions.

I was seated on the couch with my legs curled under me. Don was in a chair facing me. I knew I had his total attention. Hesitantly I began, "In my dream, I saw us on a battlefield. My father was the leader of one camp. You were with the enemy. Father's side had lost the battle. He was on his knees with his hands tied behind his back. He was condemned to be beheaded. To make the sentence worse, I, his daughter, was given the sword and ordered to do the beheading. I fell on my knees, cried, and refused to do it, begging to die instead. You stepped forward and said to your commander that this was too inhumane. You added that, even if I tried to do it, I would not be strong enough to behead in a single blow. So you did it for me. 'You killed my father!' I screamed. Afterward, you took me to your home and had me work as your maidservant. Then I saw myself washing a pot of rice, squatting on the ground, feeling deep hatred for you. Next, I was burning up with fever, dying. You held me close to you, with my left arm against your chest. I remember feeling your heartbeat. I heard you say, 'Forgive me for having caused you so much pain and suffering. I wish that we shall meet again. I will repay you in kindness.' I was not able to reply but I understood your sincerity, and I too wished with all my heart that we would meet in a future life. Then all seemed to fade away in a fog. The way we were dressed looked as if we belonged to ancient Japan."

I started to tremble as I recounted my dream. I reached for the patchwork quilt from the back of the couch and wrapped myself with it. I fell silent. Neither one of us spoke. Slowly Don came and sat by me, took me in his arms and held me for a long time. Before he broke away, he kissed me lightly on the forehead and said, "It is right for us to be together. Tomorrow we will be married. Good night, sweetheart. Thank you for allowing me to serve you."

He walked out of my apartment closing the door gently. As I climbed into my ornate white iron bed, I wondered whether I was fulfilling a karmic destiny or making a devil's bargain.

Before I fell asleep I looked back at how far I had come in the 36 years of my life. It was 1958 when I arrived at Saint Catharine College in Kentucky armed with a two-year scholarship from the alumni of that school. It was obtained for me by Chinese archbishop Yu-Pin, who had been expelled from China in the early 1950's by the communist government. At that time in Taiwan, Father's monthly salary was only (New Taiwan Dollars) NT $1000 which equalled US $25. How could he afford to send me to college! He talked mama into selling the diamond ring he had given her to raise funds for me, with the promise of replacing it with a larger stone. My parents scraped together enough money to give me a one-way plane ticket to the U.S. and five hundred dollars in American Express Travelers checks, which I carried in my purse. They told me that was all they could ever do for me financially, and that I would have to earn the rest of my college expenses on my own. From then on their extra money would have to be saved for my younger brother's higher education, coming in three years.

Thus began my journey of thousands of miles, filled with hope, but also with so much fear: fear of going hungry again, and fear of being thought to be worthless. Both were remnants of my mother's hatred of me combined with years of growing up in four concentration camps in Vietnam, when the Japanese invaded Southeast Asia during World War II.

On the eve of my second marriage, I felt blessed. How far I had come! Nevertheless, I knew I was participating in a façade. Some may think I was going into a marriage with no heart, but I knew I was marrying a caring friend who had already done so much for me. My heart was filled with gratitude. Still I wondered what would father think if he knew the truth about the choice I had made? I already knew mother considered it scandalous that I would re-marry at all after being divorced. I realized I must learn to live with my secrets. I was demoting myself to the rank of a kept woman; and there was no pride in that. Yes, I was choosing to limit my world. But considering the hunger, poverty, and sense of worthlessness of my early years, my hard work to pay debts that hadn't been mine alone, my inability to be with my sons as they grew up, and my limited means even as an adult until this time, did I not deserve an easier life? And isn't life full of trade-offs?

Now that I had made the decision to share my life with Don in a marriage of convenience, I felt like Scarlett O'Hara, standing on her devastated land, defiantly swearing, "With God as my witness, *I will never go hungry again!*"

Everything in life has a price—even the piece of paper I received the day before that represents my master's degree. For my sons' and my own security, I was paying a calculated price, a devil's bargain.

Chapter 3

HOME IN TAHITI

As I lay awake in bed, contemplating the price, I continued thinking about my life and also about how my parents had fallen in love, married, and remained married to each other all their lives. The last time I had seen both of them was in 1962, four years after leaving home to go to school in the United States. As a graduation present they gave me the gift of a three months' stay with them in beautiful, exotic Tahiti. Papa had written during my third year in college to tell me he was assigned to Tahiti as Consul General for the Chinese government in Taiwan. I could hardly believe the words in his letter. I was so excited about the news of his future post that I wrote back immediately and shared with him everything I knew about Tahiti based on reading I had done over the years.

Tahiti had been my dream destination since the summer of 1952, after my sixth grade. I had received several beautiful coffee-table books as awards at that year's *Distribution des Prix,* an event in the French education system in which good students are recognized in an elaborate ceremony. It is attended by important government officials, mayors, and ambassadors from countries that have students in the school. Distinguished students' academic accomplishments are read aloud and awards are given to each of them in form of books. That year my two most memorable award books were a thick *Larousse Gastronomique,* the source of my love for cooking, and an erudite treatise on Tahiti that included its history, geography, geology, art, and culture, along with intriguing pictures of tattoos and impressive photography of the people and landscapes. Not only did I devour the book, I carried it with me to Hong Kong for our family vacation, where mama, my younger brother Max, and I spent most of that summer. (photos 12, 13)

I shared this Tahiti book with mother's cousin whom I met for the first time shortly after we arrived. According to Chinese custom, I was to address him as "Uncle Siaoti." He was only six years older than I, but he enjoyed acting like an uncle, and treated my brother and me to movies and swimming outings at the famous Repulse Bay beach. Having grown up and been educated in France, he spoke French fluently, whereas few of our other relatives or his friends did. Thus he quickly felt close to us—we could relate and joke with him in French, the language of our feelings and our formal education. All three of us functioned better and with greater ease speaking French than we did using Chinese. This was a common phenomenon among "embassy brats," who typically are schooled in the language of their parents' host country.

It is difficult for people who do not speak several languages to understand the sense of closeness we felt when we could use our "mother tongue." Imagine the sense of comfort one feels returning home after having lived for years in a country where a different language is spoken. It was sharing our more familiar language that made us feel at home with one another.

Every Sunday Siaoti took me to Catholic Mass, even though I was not yet baptized. He was in his second year at the University of Hong Kong, so he carried a book and read en route when he took the bus to visit us. We always had heated discussions on whatever he was reading. We also discussed French literature and read many other books together, including my award book on Tahiti. As we read it, we talked and dreamed about Tahiti as if we would someday visit there. Siaoti had a fabulous memory and I loved to listen to him quote from books. The way he could recite poetry reminded me of *Cyrano de Bergerac* in Edmond Rostand's play. I admired Siaoti tremendously. Even though I was only 12, secretly I had a huge crush on him.

I recall that when I spoke French with him I was not bashful in voicing my opinions, but when I spoke Chinese my personality seemed to become more timid and submissive. My French education had taught me to think for myself and had given me the freedom to express my views, but when I went home, I took on the Asian cultural expectation that women are to be quiet and accommodating.

Siaoti's family and mine had developed a deep connection, especially during World War II when Japan took over French Indo-China, now called Vietnam. His father, Kuo Tse-fan, was mother's uncle and also the second in command at the Chinese Embassy in Paris. It was Uncle Tse-fan's responsibility to keep in touch with the Chinese Consulate in Vietnam, which was then a French colony. During that difficult time in our lives he paid close attention to our well-being, even more so because mother was his niece.

At the end of my summer vacation that year Siaoti gave me a list of books in French that he wanted me to send him when we returned to Saigon. I gladly purchased and sent them with eager anticipation of his reply. I was disappointed that I didn't hear back from him. We lost touch with each other for six years. In 1958 I would see him again in Hong Kong on my way to the U.S. for college. I was there for two weeks with mother and Max to have some winter clothes made. We had none because we had lived for over a decade in the tropics. Siaoti happened to drop by the home of his uncle where we were staying. He was astonished at how I had grown, exclaiming, "My, oh my! You are no longer a little girl with pigtails!"

"I am so happy to see you. You must have graduated from the University. What are you doing now?" I responded, hiding my pounding heart.

"I am teaching French and Portuguese at Maryknoll Catholic School," he replied. "I love sharing the languages I know with these high school kids."

"I knew you had lived in France and Portugal. I would love to be in your class. I bet your lessons on cultures are super interesting," I offered.

"You don't know how strict I can be. I would make you work harder just because you are my niece," he joked. "Anyway, yesterday was our last day of school. Tomorrow will be our teachers' picnic at the beach. You want to go with me?" he added, casually.

"Sure, if it's okay with mama," I replied as I hastily glanced over at her, eager for her nod of approval.

The next day Siaoti picked me up and we went directly to the Hong Kong Yacht Club, where the father of one of his students hosted the faculty and staff on his fancy motorboat. We were taken to an outer island where we swam, chatted with his colleagues, and were served a lavish picnic by the crew of the yacht as the sun set. Under the starry sky, Siaoti and I reconnected as if our hearts could beat in unison, understanding each other as only soul mates do. We fell in love. We saw each other every single one of my remaining ten days in Hong Kong. On August 1, 1958, two days before I was to depart for Taiwan to see my father, we went to the beach at Repulse Bay. Lying on the warm sand I received my first kiss from Siaoti. My heart melted. I was his from that moment on. I would remember the sweetness of that kiss the rest of my life and cherish it as an incomparable treasure.

For the next four years, twice a week, throughout my time in college, we wrote to each other in French. He gave me love, support, and encouragement. We became one in heart, soul, intellect, education, religion, language, and culture. We felt we were meant to join our lives together. Yet we also knew there would be objections from our families. Given that Siaoti was my mother's cousin, and he was considered my uncle, such a marriage would be frowned upon.

Nonetheless, during my last year in college, we were so sure of our feelings toward each other that we took steps toward marriage. Siaoti consulted several older relatives in Hong Kong who had one foot in old China and one foot in the modern world. These elders confirmed that a marriage between us would go against Chinese tradition; but they also acknowledged that times and customs were changing. They thought that, given that many ancient traditions had disappeared since communism had come to China, our union might be accepted.

Meanwhile, I sought my parents' blessing. Since they had lived outside of China for decades, they still adhered to the social customs of old China and had not kept up with the changes rapidly taking place in their homeland. Therefore, they remained more traditionalist than their relatives in Hong Kong. They told us they were concerned that our blood line would be too closely inter-mingled. How could we risk producing a child with mental or physical impairment? I had seen many people with such severe limitations that they became burdens to their families and society. During my last two years in college, I had volunteered on Saturday afternoons for the Easter Seal children with disabilities, and the unfortunately named Home for Incurables in Memphis. So my parents' objection weighed heavily on me.

In the end, I was the one who made the final decision not to go live with Siaoti in Hong Kong—breaking our relationship and our hearts.

We went our separate ways but we both knew that, emotionally we would be attached to one another forever. Our love was deep. We agonized over the decision. We managed to rise to our culture's expectation of stoic conduct even when in distress. Ceremoniously, we placed our love in the evening sky, on Venus, for safe-keeping. For the rest of our lives, no matter where we might be, all we would have to do to reconnect our thoughts would be to look at the evening star and be reunited. Many years later, one scene in the movie *E.T.* caused me to sob my heart out. This scene showed young Elliott struggling to say goodbye to his new, but already much-loved, extra-terrestrial friend. Both gestured that it was a major "ouch" to their hearts to part, but we sensed that they would keep each other in their minds. Then E.T. boarded the space ship that took him back to his home in the stars. The French poetically call Venus *l'Etoile du Berger*—the Shepherd's Star. When it appears in the evening sky, the shepherds gather their flocks to go home. Venus was the place where Siaoti and I could reconnect our hearts.

In 1962, ten years after Siaoti and I read the book on Tahiti together, I actually had the chance to go to this magical island. Even better, it was to be more than just a vacation spot—I was going to my parents' new home. What an incredible blessing! My parents mailed me a ticket to fly from Los Angeles. It arrived through the postal service a couple of weeks before graduation. I would fly over on the second jet plane ever to land at the brand new Faa'a International Airport, built on a human-made peninsula on top of a coral reef. Until that summer the runway could accommodate only small planes. I recognized that the arrival of jet planes would dramatically change the face of tourism in Tahiti, so I felt fortunate to be making the trip at that time.

As I completed my course work, I began to plan my travel by bus from Memphis to Los Angeles. On my limited budget I was thrilled to discover that Greyhound Bus Company was offering a "special"—one could travel one-way to any place in the U.S. with unlimited stops for only $99. Even though this seemed like a lot of money back then, it was far less than airfare, and it enabled me to see a little more of the country.

Working backward, I planned my trip to fit the number of days before my flight from Los Angeles. I mapped my route based on places I had heard about. My first destination was Atlanta, Georgia, in remembrance of the burning of Atlanta as depicted in the movie *Gone with the Wind*. Then it was on to Daytona Beach, Florida, where Connie Francis was filmed in *Where the Boys Are* in 1960. I chose to travel by the most southern Interstate 10, which took me through New Orleans, Houston, Tucson, Phoenix, and finally on to Los Angeles.

With little money to spend, I enjoyed simply riding through these cities, getting off the bus only at the depots. I would stretch my legs and eat light meals, chiefly buttered toast and jelly. I did not mind having limited funds because the journey itself was a most memorable adventure. Skimping on food allowed me to save for the highlights to come. One of the most striking moments of the trip was waking up early one morning and seeing the desert for the first time—so flat and dry, with little visible vegetation. Having lived most of my life in the tropics, this sight was unfathomable.

I had done enough travel book research to know that I could go to L.A. International Airport, store my luggage in a locker for a dollar a day, and take a bus to one final U.S. destination—*Disneyland!* There I bought a day pass which gave me numerous rides—all of which I fully enjoyed. I spent the entire day there, staying until after dark. Disneyland workers indicated that it was the first time that Tinker Bell had ever "flown" from one tower to the other amid the nightly fireworks that illuminated the California sky. As with many people all over the world, the Disney characters were among my fondest childhood memories. They came to life for me as they roamed the streets of Disneyland: Snow White and the Seven Dwarfs, Peter Pan and Wendy, Pinocchio and Jiminy Cricket, Mickey and Minnie Mouse, and especially my favorite, Dumbo the elephant, who had enough courage and faith in himself to fly!

The new-found skills I mustered in planning that trip foreshadowed a later occupational path. In the 1980s I would plan and guide pilgrimages to European Catholic shrines and trips throughout mainland China, when Chinese tourism was in its infancy.

My day in Disneyland remains a fond memory. It was a great way to transition to my summer in Tahiti. Some ten hours after departing from Los Angeles, I landed mid-morning in Papeete, the capital of Tahiti. To see the island for the first time after such long anticipation brought tears to my eyes. My thoughts were of Siaoti. As my heart called to mind the deep love between us and the book about Tahiti that we enjoyed when we first met, more than anything I would have liked to share that moment with him. But I couldn't and, deep down, I knew we would never see Tahiti together.

It was a joy to be reunited with my parents after a four-year separation. Immediately I noticed they had both aged a little. It did not surprise me that Papa was wearing a suit instead of adopting the very casual Tahitian shirt, similar to what is more widely known as the Hawaiian shirt. Mama wore a light blue Chinese dress with a white cardigan sweater, reminding me that she would get cold at the slightest drop in temperature. Several leaders of the Chinese community were with my parents when I arrived—men and women with garlands and more garlands of fresh flowers that they draped around my neck, before kissing me on both cheeks. What a warm welcome! I was no longer the short-of-money, struggling student. As had happened on many occasions throughout my life, I felt suddenly promoted to V.I.P. status, riding on Papa's coattails (photos 36, 37).

During my days in Tahiti my parents talked to me more than any other time in my life. I gathered that, at 22, they finally considered me an adult. They also knew that I would go back to Memphis to teach and it would be many years before they could see me again. Little did I know that at the end of the summer, when I left, these would be my last in-person conversations with my father.

Throughout my stay, I took advantage of the fact that papa's office was on the ground level in the same building as our living quarters. I visited him often when his workload was light. I wanted to learn everything I could about my parents' past, the stories of their lives.

On my first visit there, I commented, "It's wonderful that your office is so close to your living quarters. Whose idea was it?"

"It was set up this way from the beginning. This consulate is unlike any other location of Chinese embassies or consulates, where our government buys or rents the premises. Here in Tahiti, at the end of World War II, the Chinese community (photo 38), led by the Chinese Chamber of Commerce, bought this property and had the building constructed. The Chinese leaders here requested that the government send representatives to open a consulate. So we use this facility rent-free, only paying the utilities. As you know Chinese like to live near their workplace. Have you noticed that many of their stores in town have living quarters upstairs? The Chinese population here is much smaller than in Vietnam, so you see that I only require a small staff here—my assistant, Mr. Wong Qui-sang, who is a local Chinese, and my chef Lao Pu. Since the yard is so huge, about the size of a football field, it is ideal for the celebration of our national day. Last October, I decided to hold a garden party here, catering food from different Chinese restaurants and featuring Lao Pu's *dim sum*. Tahiti's style of living is more casual than at any other foreign post. Even so, it was a surprise when the French governor arrived driving himself in his convertible and wearing a Tahitian shirt. Can you imagine the *chichi* (fussy) French acting like that anywhere else? We both laughed. Papa added, smiling,

"Of course one of the Tahitian policemen who was here to direct traffic immediately took over his car to park."

I loved chatting with papa. He was my champion and my encourager. I have always described him as the parent who "praised me to excellence."

I continued, "All the years we were in Saigon you were so busy with work and I with my school. Now that we have some time together I would like to hear all about our family."

Papa replied, "I've been thinking the same thing—while you are here with us I want to share many stories with you."

"Wonderful! Could we begin with how you and mama met?"

"I was already in my last year of undergraduate school when your mama started as a freshman at Yenching University (photo 5), in Beijing, the second most prestigious college in China. Our families are related. Her brother and parents had moved from Beijing to Shanghai, so she was told to look me up. I took her under my wing and showed her around. We both lived in the university dormitories—she in the women's, I in the men's."

Puzzled, I asked, "I thought your family was from the South. What made you choose Yenching University?"

Papa explained, "I was interested in international affairs and Yenching had a strong reputation for this major and also its foreign language department. Thanks to my high score on the college entrance exam I was accepted.

"Had you met mama before she went to the university?" I asked.

"Yes, we had met when we were children. My father had taken me to Beijing on a business trip when I was about ten years old, shortly after my mother had died. He was a government official with the Bureau of Salt Taxation in our southern city of Fuzhou. He knew your *Waipo* (maternal grandmother), so he parked me at your mama's home for a few hours while he attended to his business."

He came to sit by me and continued, "I remember that the first time I saw your mother she was crying and throwing a fit about something. She was then about six and seemed so spoiled. She looked like trouble so I got as far away from her as I could. Later that day, her mama gave us some snacks so we ate together and played for a while. I felt like a country boy compared to her because I spoke Mandarin with a heavy southern accent, which I am still trying to lose thirty years later."

I added, "I remember that when I was learning to speak Mandarin you often told me, 'Don't say it my way—use your mother's pure Beijing accent; it sounds so much more cultured.'"

Papa chuckled, "You are lucky to have had her for a model because your Mandarin accent is perfect, like hers." He continued, "I was so impressed by the opulence of her home. It was like a palace, much larger than where I lived. Her type of house was called a *syh heh yuan*."

"What do you mean by a *syh heh yuan?*" I asked.

"Your mama can explain better than I. Ask her later."

As we were talking, we heard Mama drive up to the front of the consulate. She had gone shopping because we had seen a French ship arrive early that morning from our upstairs window. If you live in Tahiti you know that when a cargo ship docks in the morning by early afternoon the items it carried will have been unloaded and placed on the shelves of the grocery and other stores. From papa's office I could see Lao Pu open the car door and carry away her purchases. Mama walked in and announced, "I bought some wonderful things for our afternoon tea, you'll see."

She sat down and inquired, "What are you two up to?"

Quickly I replied, "Papa was telling me that the first time he saw you he was dazzled by the house you lived in. He said to ask you to explain a *syh heh yuan*."

Proudly she answered, "It's a large compound, with several courtyards in the middle, and each have elaborate fountains, gardens, statues, porcelain garden stools, and fish ponds. One especially unique feature is rocks and stones arranged to look like a mountain scape. These courtyards are surrounded by many rooms, corridors, and banisters like those you have seen in Chinese period movies. In the American movie *Love Is a Many-Splendored Thing*, there was a scene that showed the main character, Han Suyin, in her uncle's home. That was a *syh heh yuan*—a courtyard house. By the way, did you know that Han Suyin, the author, and I lived in the same dormitory at Yenching University?"

"Wow, I didn't know that," I said.

"We were just acquaintances, not friends, since she was in pre-med and I was in foreign languages and history. Han Suyin is her pen name; her real name is Chou Kuang-hu. Because she was Eurasian she felt ostracized by her classmates. That's why she left Yenching to continue her studies in Europe." Mama commented that her father was Chinese and her mother was from Belgium. "Mixed marriages cause problems for the children and they are bad for society. It's the children who suffer."

I was quite familiar with her opinion that races should be kept "pure." Papa expressed a different view, "Mixed marriages may produce the most beautiful and intelligent children because they often reflect the strongest genes of both races. Sometimes these children are even described as the golden race.'"

Mama threw a glance of disapproval toward him and continued, "Anyway, in a *syh heh yuan* many members of the same family live together with the elder son as head of the clan. In my case, he was my uncle, my father's elder brother, Kuo Tse-yun. Beginning in 1909 Kuo had held several national government positions. He was secretary general of the Imperial Archives when the last emperor was still on the throne. Later, he became the head of the Examination Ministry, which administered the eligibility tests for the country's civil servants. His office also conferred awards and promotions throughout the government. In the early years of the Chinese Republic, after that examination board was abolished, he became the Minister of Transportation for all of China."

"Mama, I knew that your uncle was a government official, but I didn't realize that he was of such high rank." I was unaccustomed to her speaking that much to me.

Mama seemed to sit straighter in her elevated mood as she proudly gave me more information, "Oh yes, we were the elite. He had a large household. His wife, my aunt, was in delicate health, so my mother ended up with the responsibility of running this assembly—relatives and staff, cooks, men and woman servants, nannies, coachmen, stable boys, and even horses. It was a complicated role that required tact, but also a firm hand."

Just then Lao Pu walked in with a platter of French cheeses—Brie, Camembert, and our favorite, Roquefort—along with an apple and a pear that had been peeled and cut into bite-size pieces, and some little Melba toasts—the treats that mama had just purchased. He also brought a pot of freshly brewed tea with china cups and saucers. He poured a steaming cup for each of us and passed the tray of treats.

After serving us, Lao Pu addressed mama, "Is there anything else, Ma'am?" Mother gestured "no," with a wave of her hand. I added, "*Xie, xie* (thank you) Lao Pu." He smiled at me and bowed slightly as he turned and walked out.

I was delighted at the sight of these goodies and exclaimed, "All these French delicacies remind me of our life in Saigon. Thanks Mama, for getting them for us."

Deep down, I felt left out. She hadn't asked if I'd like to go shopping with her. I had been reading in the living room when I heard her leave. It would have been so simple for her to have taken me along. I ventured, "The next time you go shopping, may I please go with you?"

Unconvincingly, she answered, "All right."

I shifted my attention to take in the familiar aromas and tastes of these French cheeses. "Papa," I said, "thanks to the career you chose, you enabled all four of us to master French and to appreciate French culture. You don't realize how much being able to speak French fluently helped me throughout my college years."

"How so? Tell us," Papa said.

"The first semester at Saint Catharine College, as part of my scholarship program, I was assigned to clean five classrooms and the toilet stalls of one floor every weekday after class. Hoping to improve my assignment, at the beginning of the second semester, when I was more comfortable speaking English, I went to Sister Jean Marie, the Dean of the college. I said to her, 'With so many students you may not remember that I received my primary and secondary schooling in the French education system. French is my first language. Do you think Sister Paracleta might like to have me as her assistant? I can help her correct papers and even make some language tapes for the oral exercises that she assigns.'"

Mama interrupted, "It is unbecoming for a young woman to be so forward and aggressive!"

Papa diverted the conversation, "Well, did you get the job as a teaching assistant?"

"Yes, I did," I replied, "and I continued in this position for all the remaining semesters at St. Catharine and for both school years in Memphis." Then turning to mama I said, "Mama, why should I have cleaned toilets if I could use my knowledge of French to earn my education?"

The moment I had said the word "toilet" mother gasped and rolled her eyes—appalled. Cleaning school toilets had felt as demeaning to me as hearing the word apparently did to her. Until I left home to study in America, my nanny had done everything for me. I never even made a bed or had to wash so much as a handkerchief.

Father interjected, "Well, no scholarship is totally free. It is customary to return some labor to the school."

"I know Papa, but I still wanted to get out of it. I hated it, but I suppose cleaning toilets is more honorable than selling your body. What wouldn't I do for an education?" I joked.

Mama chastised, "Don't say such stupid things! You always have a way of twisting everything to your advantage."

"Tai, don't put her down for her ability. Remember, I was the one who told her to learn to do something so well that someone is willing to pay her for it." Turning toward me Papa continued, "I am proud that you were able to earn your college with your knowledge of French."

"Thanks, Papa. I went to college in the U.S. to study, but I learned a lot more than what was in books."

Addressing mama he continued, "If you had not studied French so well during your schooling, my work as a diplomat would have been a lot more difficult. You are a great helpmate and hostess in our social relations. You are part of the first generation of Chinese women to graduate from college. You would be very capable of getting a job if you had to. The ancient system of inheriting a position has disappeared. This is the age of meritocracy. In America B-be (my nickname) is a foreigner in a foreign land. She will have to be better than her competition if she hopes to be chosen for a job."

Mama nearly always found fault with everything I said or did. Papa, realizing this, made it a point to lavishly praise her and give her strokes, hoping this would smooth the tenor of our interaction.

Papa changed the subject, "B-be wants to know how we met and more stories from our lives." He paused and handed me his cup to warm up his tea.

Still directing his gaze on mama, he continued, "So I started to tell her that during your first year in college, we began seeing each other on campus and that on weekends we went to my uncle Jin E Shen's home, near the university."

Turning toward me he said, "You must know, B-be, that in those days it was not considered proper for young people to date un-chaperoned. Ours was the first generation that had the freedom to choose our own spouses. Before us, our parents' marriages were arranged by the families according to social and economic class, *men dang hou dui* (matching doorways). Your grandparents had never even seen each other before their wedding ceremony. Similar to European royalty and nobility, there were a lot of inter-marriages among elite Mandarin families like ours."

Slowly I added, "I know that was the tradition, but it is difficult for me to understand how you can marry someone when you have never met him. I never really pictured *Waipo* and *Waigung* (my maternal grandparents) that way."

Papa replied, "Times and customs are changing. It is said that in the West you marry the one you love, but in China you commit to love the one you marry. There is wisdom in this kind of arrangement. It may go against your notion of romance, but quite often parents recognize an ideal match better than young people."

Turning to mama I said, "Papa mentioned you lived in the dormitory at the university. I thought your family resided in Beijing, so why the dormitory?"

Mama answered, "By the time I went to the university, my brother, who was older by seven years, had graduated from Qin

Hua University in Beijing. He was very proud that he attended the top university in the country—it is comparable to Harvard in the U.S. After graduating he got a job with the British-American Tobacco Company, married and moved us to Shanghai—including your grandparents and me. I entered high school at Bei Mann's, a Christian school. Attending a formal school was an eye-opening experience for me."

"Oh, I see, you had moved to Shanghai when you started high school," I said.

"Right, but keep in mind that I never went to grade school in Beijing. Families of our social status have tutors and governesses at home for the children. We didn't go to school with the common people. At Bei Mann, for the first time in my life, I was introduced to the story of the birth of Jesus, Christmas trees with decorations and cotton balls to simulate snow, and the idea of exchanging Christmas presents. Every day I came home with stories to tell my mother. She was as fascinated as I was. Then one day, my sister-in-law took mother and me on our first trip ever to a modern international department store in Shanghai. I couldn't believe my eyes for all the beautiful things I saw. What a big, wonderful new world it was!"

I smiled hearing about mama's childhood experiences. Going to a department store had transported her into a new world; whereas, I had to fly across the Pacific Ocean alone and put myself through college before I could call it my new world.

I commented, "Mama, you were really sheltered in Beijing, weren't you?"

Papa sat back and was happy to let her do her favorite thing, talk about her past.

Wistfully mama continued, "I rarely left the compound in Beijing because I was home-schooled with my two male cousins. We had the same male tutor. He had his own quarters in our *syh heh yuan*. He was always stricter with the boys than with me because they were boys and they were older. Their mother was my father's younger sister. Her husband had died, so she had come home to live with us. She had brought her boys with her, which was very unusual, because customarily boys in this situation would have remained at their paternal grandparents' home; they belonged to that family." I was noticing as she was telling her story how, here again, one can sense the older cultural idea that male children were an economic asset and a means of support for parents or grandparents in old age.

Trying to picture mama in her home-school setting, I asked, "You suppose your uncle's social standing carried enough clout to overrule the cultural expectations of male children, so that her boys were allowed to be with their mother?"

Looking away as if she were reliving that time, mama said, "I think so, and there was some kind of financial compensation to the boys' family. It was a whispered item of conversation in the compound. I sure didn't like those boys because they bullied me. I was very intimidated by the intelligence of the younger one. Our tutor often made us learn passages of literature by heart; afterwards, we had to recite them. This cousin never studied. He would play with his pencil box or carve little animals out of his erasers during our quiet time. When our master asked him to recite, he would say with a smart-aleck tone, 'I'll give it to you both frontward and backward. Which way do you want first?' He could truly recite without studying, as if he were reading from his mind, character after character. That just wasn't normal. I felt I could never measure up. I still have never met another person like him."

Seeing that mama was on a roll, I asked, "Did you have any other brothers and sisters other than *Jiu-Jiu* (Uncle), who moved to Shanghai?"

"No, I was my mother's sixth and last child. All four babies between my brother and me died very young, including twin boys who only lived a few days. My parents spoiled me because they were always afraid that I, too, would die. I was the youngest one in the whole compound. They even bought me a *ya tou* to keep me company."

"What! You mean you had a slave girl?" I exclaimed.

"Oh, don't make it sound so bad. I was about eight years old when a poor harvest caused wide-spread famine in northern China. This farmer brought his daughter to sell. My mother decided to take her in. It was out of compassion. She was well-fed in our home and she even received some education because when she did not have other household duties, she could sit in during my home-school time. She might have starved to death if she had remained with her parents."

"Did your mother ever free her?" I anxiously asked.

"Yes, of course! She was about three years older than I. So, when we were moving to Shanghai, she was of marrying age. My mother arranged for her to marry our coachman's son and stay as a housekeeper in my uncle's household."

"Did you have any other playmates?"

"Yes—just a few. When I moved to Taiwan in 1958, I was lucky to reconnect with two of them. One was Irene Chang's mother, whom you call *Ba Gu* (Eighth Aunt), and Lu Bai Shen's father, whom you call *Syh Da Yeh* (Fourth Uncle). You had met both of them during your short stay in Taipei, do you remember them?

"Yes I do, but I remember Irene and her sisters, Margaret and Linda, better. They admired my foreign clothes and thought it was wonderful that I could go study abroad. Please mama, tell me more about you and papa."

I glanced over at papa. He caught my eyes and we both smiled. He knew mama was in her element. She loved being the center of attention. She continued, "The summer after my sophomore year, your father got a job in the office of the City of Qing Dao. He lived at the YMCA (Young Men's Christian Association) to save money for his second year of graduate school, even though he had already been awarded a scholarship for the next year. Unexpectedly, his uncle Jin E received from the Ministry of Foreign Affairs the assignment of opening the first Chinese consulate in Saigon, capital city of Annam. Remember that Annam was the older name for Vietnam, and Annam, Laos and Cambodia, together were called French Indochina. Knowing that your father was studying French and France's policies toward its colonies, Uncle Jin-E sent a cable to your father offering him the chance to become his assistant.

Your papa accepted, gave up his scholarship, and prepared to leave China."

I looked over at papa. He commented, "That's why I never completed my master's. I don't really regret it because entering the Foreign Service quickly and being assigned to Saigon was an opportunity I couldn't pass up. Many people wait several years before getting a post in a foreign country. Had I delayed one year to finish my master's, all foreign assignments would have been frozen until years after World War II ended."

"When papa left with Uncle Jin E, Mama, did you go with him?" I asked.

She replied, "Of course not. Your papa was very insistent that I graduate before we married. Our courtship continued through letters for almost three years."

"How long did it take for your letters to get from Beijing to Saigon?" I asked, silently thinking of the seven-to-ten days it took Siaoti's and my love letters to go between the U.S. and Hong Kong.

"Usually it took about three weeks because at that time the mail traveled by boat. Don't forget, it was in 1936. I finally graduated in the summer of 1938. Then in January 1939, your papa got special permission for a leave to travel to Shanghai for us to be married on February 1 (photo 1). Two days later we boarded a *Messagerie Maritime* ship to take me from Shanghai to Saigon, with a day-long layover in Hong Kong. On the boat I felt like a fish out of water. Every communication with the staff had to be in French. I really understood what papa meant when he said that studying a language from books was not enough. Everyone seemed to talk so fast! And all our meals were served with knives and forks—there were no chopsticks in sight. It all seemed so strange and foreign." Mama sighed, "Oh, how I missed my good life in China! I am tired. I am going upstairs. I told Lao Pu to serve dinner later, since we have snacked so late. You two, don't delay too long before coming up."

"Okay mama, I'll gather the dishes for Lao Pu," I said as she left the room. After she was out of earshot I remarked, "It isn't easy to make mama happy, is it?"

"Her childhood was like that of a princess," papa said with a wry smile. "She likes to compare the present with her glorious past. She forgets that it was her uncle's position that put her in such an elite social class—she did nothing to earn it. I feel I can never measure up to her ideal of a high government official. In a way, I have you to thank for giving me the chance to become chief of mission."

Astonished I exclaimed, "How can that be? What do you mean? What do I have to do with your position now?"

After a moment of silence, papa switched chairs because a ray of sun was coming through the window and shining in his eyes. "I came from a very large and complicated family of old China," he said. "There were three mothers, and nine children—six girls and three boys. I was the first-born son with an older and a younger sister. Our mother died of tuberculosis when I was only eight. Shortly after, my father married my mother's younger sister. That was common practice in those days. She told me to continue to address her as 'Aunt Six' because, she said, 'You are old enough to remember your mother. Although I am taking the role of mother in this family, I can never replace her in your heart. When you have children they can call me *Nai-nai* (grandmother).'"

"Not having lived in China, I did not understand all the ins and outs of your family," I responded. "The only time I remember seeing them was shortly after we got out of the concentration camp, when we flew to Shanghai. I was only six, and I met so many new people that my memory of them is sketchy. We stayed with mama's parents and went over to *Nai-nai's* (paternal grandmother's) only a few times."

Papa continued, "Unfortunately, my father made our family even more complicated by having a concubine. This woman was none other than my own mother's *ya tou* (slave girl). She was brought to the Shen family when my mother came as a bride. She was the one who took care of me after my mother died. Nevertheless, I very much disapprove of this ancient custom that allowed a man to take as many wives as he could afford. This system created much discord in families. She had two girls, and my stepmother had two boys and two girls. So, with the three of us from my mother, made nine."

"Papa, I always knew you didn't want a large family. Now I can understand why. So you were in Saigon for three years before you went back to Shanghai to marry mama?" I asked.

Papa replied, "That's right. Anyway, before your mama and I boarded the ship to go to Saigon, my father took me aside and reminded me of my obligation as first-born son. I promised him that I would take care of paying for my brothers' and sisters' education in case anything should happen to him. Well, during the eight-year Sino-Japanese war, there was so much upheaval and so many changes that my father lost his job at the Bureau of Salt Taxation. Around 1942 he went to Hong Kong to teach college chemistry and died there of a heart attack the next year. It was during the time we were kept in protective residency by the French government at the Moi village. It was such a bad time for all of us. I felt cut off from my homeland. The war was going badly for China."

As I looked at the sadness on papa's face I remarked, "You may be surprised but I truly remember the day you received the news of *Yeh-yeh's* (paternal grandfather) death. We were in Kon Tum, in our house that was on stilts, with a veranda and an outside wooden staircase. You read a letter that came from Shanghai and gave mama the news. I remember she cried and lamented that she didn't even have proper mourning clothes to show her respect to *Yeh-yeh*. I recall your saying that in time of war all of those rituals become unimportant, that survival was the first order of concern. Your worry was how your two stepmothers and siblings were going to live and eat. I still have a distinct memory of mama using some white yarn to make a bow for her hair to indicate that she was in mourning."

Incredulously, papa remarked, "You had to be about three years old. I had no idea you were so aware of what went on around you. I was so worried about my family in Shanghai. My fourth younger sister, whom you call Auntie Yo-Yo, was the only one out of school and working. Thanks to her they were able to eat."

I interjected with a memory, "I remember Auntie Yo-Yo best because she took me to a movie once, and she was the one who gave me a coloring book of *Snow White and the Seven Dwarfs* with a beautiful box of colored pencils made by the French company *Conte'*. She showed me how to color and stay in the lines. I had not gone to school yet and had never owned a coloring book. She made me feel special when she came to stay with me after I injured my eye."

After taking a sip of tea, papa continued, "Fortunately, after the war, in 1945, I was reassigned to the consulate in Saigon where I stayed until the year you went away to college. I chose to remain in an overseas post because I received a much larger salary, allowing me to afford to pay for my brothers' and sisters' education, fulfilling my promise to my father and my duties as eldest son. In 1956 Minister of Foreign Affairs, Yeh Gong-chao (George Yeh), came to Saigon on an inspection tour. Privately he said to me, 'You are very deserving to be chief of mission, but you must do a stint back at the Ministry in Taiwan before I can assign you to be the head of a post. I understand you have family obligations. When will you be free of them?' I told him at the end of 1957. He did not forget. Shortly after Chinese New Year, I received my transfer orders to Taipei, for April 1958. I had promised your mama I would concentrate on my own career after fulfilling my promise to my father.

I realized that my mother had desired the status of being an ambassador's wife, so this promise made sense to me. I knew that, in her consideration regarding the welfare of family members, I would be a very low priority for her. I simply thought that was my lot for having been born an unwanted child and that there wasn't anything I could do about it.

"I want to apologize to you, B-be. I took care of my siblings, but, when your turn came to go to college, you had to fend for yourself. It was a blessing that you were such a good student. If you had not been capable of earning your scholarship I would still be working as a second-in-command."

I was stunned by father's revelation. "I remember you told me when I started seventh grade that it was absolutely essential that I be an excellent student, deserving of a scholarship, if I wanted to go to college. I worked hard during all my years in school—but I enjoyed studying and learning. Success built up confidence in me, but mama calls me too aggressive. You must not feel guilty about not paying for my college. I am sure I learned more by having to depend on myself. Thank you for speaking so candidly with me. I also have something to tell you about George Yeh."

Papa said, "I remember you wrote that Ambassador Yeh took you to the White House. Your mama and I were amazed at your opportunity. Tell me more about how that happened."

"It was in 1959, a few days before Christmas. I traveled by train to spend the holidays in Flushing, New York with your former classmate, Auntie Pearl. Since I had worked the summer before in Washington, D.C., I had friends there and decided to spend a couple of days visiting them on my way to New York. I stayed with my friend Suzanne Tihon. She had a car, so she drove me to visit our mutual friends. Afterward, she had some other errands to run, so I asked if we were anywhere near the Chinese Embassy. Since it was close by, she dropped me there while she took care of her own business.

"I walked into the Chinese Embassy and was greeted by an older woman. I learned later that she had been the receptionist for many years.

"Timidly I asked, 'May I please see the ambassador for a few minutes?'

'Do you have an appointment?' she inquired sternly.

'No Ma'am, I don't. But I am here to bring greetings from my father. When Ambassador Yeh was the Minister of Foreign Affairs he visited my father in Saigon. He assigned my father to be the director of the Asian Division at the Ministry. My father's name is Tsu-hsun Shen and I am Bambi Shen.'

"Reluctantly, she called the office upstairs. Almost immediately the ambassador's secretary came down and walked me to his office.

'Hey, little girl, you're all grown up!' the ambassador greeted me warmly. 'You must be a college student now. What are you doing in D.C.?'

"I replied, 'Happy holidays, Uncle Yeh. Yes, I am in college in Kentucky and on my way to New York for Christmas. I just wanted to stop by and bring you my good wishes. I appreciate your giving me a few minutes. Thank you for visiting us in Saigon three years ago. Papa is very happy to be in Taipei. He has reconnected with former classmates, friends, and relatives who are living there.

'It is sweet of you to visit me,' he replied. 'Do you have a Chinese gown in your suitcase?'

"Puzzled by his question, I responded, 'Yes, I do. I carry one with me whenever I travel because father told me to always wear a Chinese dress if I go to any function of consequence.'

"What he said next thrilled me: 'Good, good. This evening is President Eisenhower's last Peace Pageant. He and Mrs. Eisenhower will light the Christmas tree on the White House lawn. I would like to take you with me as my guest. Can you come?'

'Wow! Really?' I replied in awe. 'Of course I can come!'

'It's settled then. Give my secretary the address where you are staying. My driver will pick you up at 4:30. Be ready in your Chinese gown. We'll visit over dinner at my residence; then we'll go to the White House,' he added as he stood up to acknowledge my departure.

"As soon as I got back into Suzanne's car I said, 'I am sorry, but I'll have to change our plans for this evening. The ambassador is taking me to the White House. I need to go to your apartment now to get ready.' I explained to Suzanne my family's relationship with the ambassador. I tried to wrap my mind around what I was about to experience. At my friend's, I showered and dressed in my burgundy red silk Chinese gown embroidered with roses in shades of charcoal and silver grey.

"At 4:30 on the dot, the driver arrived to take me to the ambassador's residence for dinner, then on to the White House. I felt like Cinderella—being chauffeured through the gates of the White House of the United States of America. We were ushered to our assigned seats. I was thrilled to see the Eisenhowers in person, instead of on some small television screen. Even though the ceremony was short, I was delighted to watch President and Mrs. Eisenhower pull the switch that turned on hundreds of lights. The First Lady wore a bright red suit with a small red hat. I wondered what they were thinking and feeling on this last Christmas in the White House. I supposed their emotions must be very mixed about leaving the highest position in the land. I thought they probably regretted leaving but also felt relief that the responsibility would be passed on to the newly-elected president. Many people eagerly anticipated the changes that the youngest ever president-elect, John F. Kennedy, would bring."

"What an incredible experience you had!" papa commented with delight.

"Papa, there is more. After the ceremony, Ambassador Yeh took me for a walk on the National Mall and along the reflecting pool adjacent to the Washington Monument, to see the elaborate display of holiday greetings that had been sent to the U.S. by embassies from all over the world. Some of them were small Christmas trees decorated with themes associated with the donor countries; some were replicas of famous landmarks, such as the Eiffel Tower and the Taj Mahal. The one from Taiwan was a message of good wishes from the citizens of Taiwan to the people of the United States, carved on native Taiwanese green marble. It was particularly special to us because Ambassador Yeh had commissioned the carving to replicate his own calligraphy. Later, I remembered you had told me in a letter that in Taiwan he is a renowned calligrapher."

Papa smiled with pride, "You're a lucky girl! You took the initiative to visit the ambassador—and look what you got in return. You know, he was Minister of Foreign Affairs for the first ten years after the Chinese government moved to Taiwan, before President Chiang Kai-shek sent him to represent our country as ambassador to the U.S. He is an astute diplomat. You really have some story to tell your grandchildren.

"Let me give you some details about Ambassador Yeh's residence where you went for dinner. There is a lot of history connected to this estate. It is considered the largest privately owned estate in Washington, D.C., a 26-room Colonial style mansion on more than 18 acres. Just a month before Japan started the war with China in 1937, Thomas C.T. Wang was appointed ambassador to the U.S. from the Republic of China. He was sent by Chiang Kai-shek's government in Nanking. After he arrived he presented his credentials to President Franklin Roosevelt. Ambassador Wang found the Chinese embassy's quarters on 19ᵗʰ and P Street too cramped for his wife and two young daughters, so he decided to rent a home on the estate known to locals as Twin Oaks. It belonged to the Hubbard family, who established the Smithsonian Museum. Over the next decade, he continued to rent it to Wang and his successors: Hu Shih, a leader in the renaissance movement of modern China, and Wei Tao-ming, famous for signing a treaty which did away with extraterritorial rights the U.S. had enjoyed in China for nearly 100 years."

I interrupted, "Oh yes, I remember, the chauffeur drove through a large wooded area after we went through the gate. The house was a mansion, decorated with beautiful Chinese landscape paintings, porcelain vases, and carvings of ivory and jade."

Papa added, "A couple of years after the Second World War, the Hubbard family sold Twin Oaks to the Republic of China, at that time represented by Ambassador Wellington Koo. Remember, during the war when his post was in France, he refused to go to Vichy after the Germans captured Paris in 1940? This resulted in Siaoti's father becoming *charge' d'affairs* at the Chinese embassy in Vichy. After the war ended, Koo was promoted from Paris to Washington, D.C."

Enthralled, I commented, "My dinner at Twin Oaks means much more now that you've added the history of the place."

Since we were dining later than usual, Lao Pu took time to make two different kinds of special dumplings—one with ground pork and napa cabbage, that mama liked; and the other meatless, with scrambled eggs, black mushrooms, and bean threads, which were my favorite. The Chinese look on chefs as having higher status than other laborers because of the training and skill required for their work. They are addressed with a word that indicates the mastery of an art, *shi fu.*

I loved Lao Pu's cooking. During dinner I asked, "How did you find Lao Pu to be your chef? Was he happy to travel to Tahiti with you?"

Mama answered, "Before we left Taipei we interviewed and tasted the cooking of a couple of chefs who were registered with the ministry as being willing to go abroad. When my cousin *Da Yi* heard that your father was looking for a chef, she suggested Lao Pu, who was the cook for her kindergarten and child care center.

He had learned his kitchen skills in the Chinese army. Your papa said, when he decided to choose Lao Pu, that his cooking may be less refined than that of the other highly trained chefs, but he has the devotion of an army *aide-de-camp* toward his general. Papa knew he not only would cook but also would be willing to be a jack-of-all-trades. He takes on other tasks in support of the overall well-being of the consulate, such as mowing this huge lawn. As a veteran he is proud that his daily duties include raising the flag over the consulate each morning and lowering it at sunset. Before we moved here he packed and nailed our wooden crates and even traveled with them by boat via Australia while we took a plane. Since he is single, he was happy to have the chance to see the world this way. He is a good man and has made our lives here easier and more comfortable."

"Mama, Papa, I appreciate your telling me so much about your lives. I missed you a lot when I went away to college."

Chapter 4

Rumbles Of War

During those three months in Tahiti, along with enjoying the pleasures of the island, I shared many conversations with my parents. I learned much more about their lives, and I was able to verify the accuracy of my childhood memories and fill in gaps in my understanding.

One afternoon while mama had gone to play *mah jong*, Lao Pu asked me if I wanted anything special for afternoon tea. I replied, "I love your fried bananas with crackled spun sugar. If father is not busy, please serve us in his office."

He responded, "Good, I'll use some of our own bananas. Did you see me cut a big bunch from our tree outside the kitchen? I left it by the gate for the Tahitian children to take."

Recalling the knowledge of Tahiti that I had gained from reading my award book with Siaoti, I asked, "Do you know that it is a local custom that we are supposed to share all fruits and flowers that grow in our yard? It is believed that the more we share, the more the plants produce." I explained because I was aware that Lao Pu didn't speak French or Tahitian and couldn't have heard of the local tradition.

A big smile came over his face, "Now I understand why the kids feel so free to come into our garden, climb the trees, and pick mangoes and pomelos. I'd thought they were stealing, but since the trees put out more than we can use anyway, I've pretended I didn't see them. Thank you for explaining this custom. I feel better about those kids."

At tea time, about 4:30, I stuck my head in papa's office and asked, "Are you busy? If not, may we have tea served here? Mama is out playing *mah jong*."

"Sure," papa answered, as he put his desk in order. "Mr. Wang just left for the post office. We are finished for today. Come in and sit down."

"I asked Lao Pu to make something special for us. I'd like to hear more about what happened when you first went to Saigon," I requested.

"Well, remember I told you that Uncle Jin E gave me the chance to be his assistant? The ministry had already assigned two other men to the Saigon consulate, so I became the most junior official there. The three of us were bachelors, so we rented a house together and hired a Cantonese housekeeper, who later became your nanny, as you know, Ah Jie. She did our laundry the old fashioned way, by hand, on a washboard. She also prepared the meals we ate at home. On work days we ate lunch at the consulate, because Uncle Jin E brought a Chinese chef with him who cooked for staff lunches as well as for his home. The chief of any mission was allowed to take a chef with him whenever he was sent to a foreign post," papa explained.

"Does the ministry pay for the chef? That is quite a privilege," I commented.

"Yes, it is considered a necessity for two good reasons," papa replied. "First, Chinese cuisine is reputed to be among the best in the world. So when we entertain, it's a good idea to serve our food as an important way of sharing our culture. Second, we Chinese can't get used to foreign food day in and day out, so it is just sensible to have our own chef. In our case, as you know, mama does not cook at all and is not interested in learning, so we absolutely need Lao Pu."

I said, "Do you remember when I went to Kentucky for college, you wrote to one of the bachelors, Chou Er-Hsun, to let him know I was coming to the U.S.? He sent me a train ticket to visit his family in Silver Spring, Maryland, for the spring break of my freshman year. During my visit he reminisced about the period when you three bachelors lived together. He said you were very dedicated to improving your French, and that you spent every evening at your desk, either writing to mama or studying."

"Yes," he confirmed, "I did spend a lot of time at my desk. One of the smartest things I did was to engage a tutor named Jacques. His father was a rich Chinese merchant, his mother a French young woman. When he was a teenager his parents sent him to an exclusive boarding school in France, where he learned all the proper etiquette of French high society. That enabled him to not only help me learn French, but also teach me a lot of what I needed to know, culturally, to be a diplomat in the West. I felt that the Ministry of Foreign Affairs was weak in preparing future diplomats to function elegantly in the wide variety of social situations we were likely to encounter."

I said, "You've always said that Max and I are 'embassy-trained.' Now I see we also inherited some of your training from Jacques. You know, Papa, both colleges I attended in America were run by Catholic nuns and were known as 'finishing schools.' So, in addition to our academics, we were taught all the proper manners of American society. The sisters were very strict about how we dressed and behaved. They said that when we left them we would know how to act should we be invited to dinner at the White House. I appreciate very much all the refinement I learned from you and mama and also the extra polishing from the nuns."

Lao Pu brought in a tray with a pot of tea and a dish of fried bananas.

I addressed Lao Pu, "Thank you for taking the time to make the bananas; I know they took several steps."

With a slight bow he answered, "No problem, Little Miss. I am happy to do it."

After he left, papa said, "I am glad to see you treat him with respect. He is very devoted to me. You remember the time I gave you Dale Carnegie's book *How to Win Friends and Influence People* to study? It certainly taught me a lot about how to relate to people; showing respect is an important part. It's always good to know how to act in society: it gives you confidence."

Papa had a faraway look as he continued, "I am happy you had a chance to meet Uncle Chou in Washington. The other bachelor who had lived with us was not so lucky during the war. His name was Juo Huan-lai. His knowledge of English was better than mine, so he was transferred to the Chinese consulate in the Philippines. During the Japanese occupation there, the entire staff of the consulate was rounded up, put in prison, and condemned to death. They had to dig their own graves and stand in front of them while they were shot."

"That's awful!" I exclaimed. "It's against international law!"

"You're right, but during the war the Japanese had no regard for international law. We heard that the consul general, who was an older man, had difficulty digging. A Chinese onlooker was ordered to do it for him. The Chinese community of Manila was forced to watch the execution. They had a memorial built for the staff of the consulate after the war. We were luckier in Vietnam. Even though we had to live in concentration camps, we survived. How miraculously we have been served by my simple choice to study French at the university; otherwise, our destiny would have been very different."

"You said the Sino-Japanese war started in Beijing, a year after you left. Mama was still studying there, so weren't you worried?" I asked.

"Of course I was worried," he said. "The younger students had to transfer to another city because of the escalating violence. Mama and her classmates were close to finishing their course work, so they were allowed to stay until completion. Actually, your mama was on summer vacation at her parents' home in Shanghai on July 7, 1937, the day we call *Qiqi Shibian* commemorating the incident that started the war. In the West it is known as the Marco Polo Bridge Incident."

"Papa, please tell me more about what caused that."

"Well B-be, at the turn of the 20th century several foreign nations had embassies in China; at that time embassies were called 'legations'. Guidelines for the presence of these legations were set forth in a document called the Boxer Protocol of 1901, signed between the Qing Empire of China and the Eight-Nation Alliance—Austria-Hungary, France, Germany, Italy, Japan, Russia, the United Kingdom, and the United States—after China's defeat in the intervention to put down the Boxer Rebellion. Under the terms of the Boxer Protocol, China had to pay 450 million taels of silver as indemnity, over 39 years. China also had to allow foreign nations with legations the right to have their own guards. These foreign guards were placed at twelve points along the railroad between Beijing and the port of Tianjin. This was to ensure that the route was kept open and secure for transporting trade goods. Gradually in the 1930s, Japan expanded its armed force to 15,000 men—several times the size of other European delegations, and greatly in excess of the limits set by the Boxer Protocol. In June 1937 these Japanese troops began carrying out military training maneuvers. The Chinese government requested that advance notice be given in order to minimize disturbing the local population, and the Japanese agreed to this condition."

Puzzled, I said, "That sounds so complicated. What gave foreign nations the right to have troops around Beijing?"

Papa continued, "In order to understand the situation in China at that time, we have to go back in history, to the 16th century, when direct maritime trade began between China and Europe. Europeans developed a strong taste for Chinese goods, like tea, silk, and porcelain. In contrast, there was little Chinese demand for European goods. European exports at that time were primarily cheese and wine, but the majority of Chinese were lactose intolerant, and they preferred their own liquor made from fermented grains rather than fruit. Therefore, this created a huge trade imbalance between China and all European countries.

"In order to balance this trade deficit the Spanish began to sell opium, tobacco, and maize from the 'New World' to China. They, like all European merchants, had to purchase Chinese goods with silver, because it was the only commodity the Chinese would accept.

"This caused a special difficulty for Britain's trade with China. Since it had no direct access to the silver required by the Chinese, Britain had to use gold to purchase silver from other European countries, thus incurring transaction fees, and aggravating their trade imbalance. To find a solution Britain began to import opium from India into China in the 18th century.

"The addictive nature of this drug caused it to quickly become popular, so in the short term it solved Britain's trading problem with China. However, it was a detriment to all who used it and Chinese society at large. In 1729, realizing that opium was a scourge, Emperor Yongzheng issued an edict prohibiting the sale and smoking of opium, allowing only a small amount to be used for medicinal purposes.

"Along with the flood of European merchants entering China for trade, unprecedented cultural influences were streaming in as well. Faced with this, the Chinese government tried to limit contact with the outside world by allowing trade only through one port, the port of Canton, now Guangzhou, in the south.

"In 1773, the British East India Company obtained the monopoly on production and export of Indian opium. Considering that the importation of opium into China was illegal, this company found a way to buy tea in Canton on credit and sell opium at auction in Calcutta to Chinese merchants, who smuggled it into their own country. In 1810, the Chinese Empire issued a new decree against opium, but given how far north the capital Beijing was, the law had little effect on the ports of the southern provinces, through which the substance made its way in. By 1820, an estimated 900 tons of opium were imported annually. In 1838, the government sentenced a number of native drug traffickers to death. Listen carefully. This is where our family history comes into play. By that year, the British were selling some 1,400 tons of opium to China each year. In March 1839, Emperor Dao Guang appointed a strict Confucian commissioner, Lin Zexu, to stop the opium trade at the port of Canton. He is our ancestor."

"Excuse me for interrupting, but how are we related if his family name is Lin and ours is Shen?"

Papa explained, "Both the Lin and Shen families were high-ranking Mandarins from the city of Fuzhou. Lin Zexu's third daughter married our ancestor, Shen Baozhen. That's another part of Chinese history. For now let's focus on Lin Zexu. After he arrived in Canton, he had more than 1,700 Chinese opium dealers arrested, and many of them were executed. His most important initiative was to permanently stop all opium shipment into China by enforcing the imperial edict of 1810.

"When the British refused to end the trade, Lin imposed an embargo on all British ships—carrying opium or not. Backed into a corner, the British Superintendent of Trade, Charles Elliot, demanded that all British merchants turn over their opium. Lin Zexu confiscated 2.6 million pounds. It took 500 workers 22 days to destroy this massive amount of the drug, mixing it with water, lime, and salt then dumping it into the ocean."

"That's incredible!" I gasped. "500 workers, 22 days! The ocean must have been a mess!"

"Imagine the harm that was done to the marine life in that area," papa sighed. "Lin Zexu, who had a reputation for being a righteous and forceful man, above all temptation of bribery, had earned the nickname of 'Lin Blue-Sky.' Most history books don't mention a previous order he had issued weeks before the confiscation of the opium. It was *that* order which caused the foreign merchants to fear Mandarin Lin—he dared challenge their sense of superiority and disregard for Chinese law."

"What did he do that got their attention?" I asked.

"He had first sealed off the area where the foreign merchants did business and lived, called the 'Factories', and forbade all entry and exit. Then he ordered the withdrawal of all Chinese servants and shopkeepers from that enclave—including houseboys, cooks, gardeners, couriers, and laundrymen. Lin's soldiers boarded up all tea and wine houses, as well as all shops and stalls, with wooden planks and sealed them with a paper tape stamped with the official order. Anyone disobeying could be decapitated."

"What a strong intervention," I said. "It's an interesting strategy that he isolated the foreign merchants, hitting them in their daily life and comfort. I remember some of your friends were opium smokers in Saigon, and that this was always spoken of in hushed tones."

"Yes, B-be, that's true of friends, but as you know, in our family, we never, never touched opium. It is such a bad and expensive addiction—almost impossible to break. As descendants of Lin Zexu, we shouldn't even smoke cigarettes!"

"What happened next?" I asked.

"The British merchants accused Lin of destroying their property. When the British government learned what had taken place, they sent a large British Indian army, which launched the first Opium War. Their ships wrecked coastal towns, occupied Canton, and sailed up the Yangtze River. There they captured the barges that were carrying tax revenue to Beijing. This was a devastating blow to the imperial treasury.

"This forced the Qing Dynasty to sign the Treaty of Nanjing in 1842, which required China to pay an indemnity to Britain, open five ports to trade, and cede Hong Kong to Queen Victoria. A second Opium War was fought from 1856 to 1860, with other European countries also participating. Europe had stronger firepower, so China was again defeated, resulting in our being forced to give still more extra-territorial rights to Britain and other European countries. The Chinese found these agreements humiliating and the people's dissatisfaction contributed to the Taiping Rebellion, the Boxer Rebellion, and—ultimately—the fall of the Qing Dynasty in 1911."

"Papa, you were born the year before the fall of the empire. You have seen so many changes." Here I contributed something I had heard in my French school, "China's recent history is full of humiliation and defeat. But do you know that Napoleon said of China that it is a sleeping dragon which, when awakened, will rule the world?"

Papa sighed, "I remember reading his prediction. Our beloved China is going through a lot more changes since 1949 because of the communist regime. In the 19th century, Lin Zexu's forceful policy against opium failed, and China lost the two wars. Lin became the scapegoat for those losses. He was demoted and exiled in remote Xinjiang. Nevertheless, because of his fight against the trade that caused drug addiction he is now celebrated as a national hero. In Taiwan, June 3 is celebrated as Anti-Smoking Day, in remembrance of the day Lin Zexu confiscated the crates of opium."

After this long history lesson papa fell silent. Neither of us spoke for a few moments. Eventually, I said "There is such a gap in my education because I did not get to go to a Chinese school. The little Chinese reading and writing I know is from the days you taught me while we were in the concentration camps, before I turned six."

Papa lamented, "We couldn't send you back to our homeland because of the communist takeover. Otherwise it would have been good for you to go to college at our wonderful alma mater, Yenching University."

"Even though China is closed off now, I believe I will someday visit Beijing and climb the Great Wall," I replied, both expressing my true intention and attempting to console him.

Papa patted my hand. "Losing my homeland to communism is my most bitter cup of sorrow," he said. "I hope you get your wish. I will probably not live long enough to see that day. I want you to know that I have never been completely well since the concentration camp. Mama will surely outlive me. I can see that you are a very capable person. You have the initiative to put yourself into position to take advantage of serendipitous opportunity, as when you went to the White House with Ambassador Yeh. You have the courage to do well in unfamiliar situations. I am sorry that mama does not appreciate your strength and your courage."

"You know," I said cautiously, "she has never loved me the way she loves Max. Do you remember the summer when I was 15 and had a terrible case of malaria? I lost so much hair that you could see my scalp, and my eyebrows were gone too. *You* were the one who took notice. One afternoon, you gave me some money and said, 'Go get an eyebrow pencil and draw them in.' I was so touched by your paying attention to me, even though sad that mama *never* did.

"I went that very afternoon on my bicycle to the *Pharmacie de France,* on the fashionable *rue Catinat* in downtown Saigon." At 15 I was a little embarrassed to ask for an eyebrow pencil because, in Asia, girls of good families customarily don't wear makeup until after they are married." When I approached the French saleslady, of course she could see my need and softly asked, 'What happened?' At that time only black and brown pencils were available. She advised me to use black and to be careful to not draw the line too dark.

"I had had malaria many times but that summer I was so sick

that one evening, when I was delirious, you and Dr. Wang sat up with me all night until the fever broke. That was the last time I had malaria. You may not know that, after I recovered, Ah Jie had a fruit merchant deliver two bushel baskets full of mangosteens. Every afternoon she made me eat three of them until they were all gone." Years later I learned that research into Eastern medicine has confirmed the curative properties of that fruit.

"At a party a few days after I got the eyebrow pencil, you mentioned the condition of my hair to a friend, May Ong. She volunteered to have her French beautician cut my hair and give me a permanent so that the curls would hide my scalp. That was the only time I have ever had a permanent."

Papa looked at me. "B-be, you have the most amazing memory. How do you remember so much?"

"I really pay attention to what goes on around me," I said. "After I came home with the permanent I remember overhearing you fuss at mama. You said, 'The way you hardly ever pay attention to her, if I didn't know better, I'd think you hadn't given birth to her yourself.' Papa, do you know that until I overheard your remark I had wondered, at times, whether she was my real mother? Ah Jie tried to explain to me that I must have owed mama a karmic debt, one which would have to be paid sooner or later."

"I am sorry she is so hard on you, B-be. She is not an easy person to get along with most of the time. I hope she will mellow with age. She is already better than when we were first married. I absolutely cannot see her being capable of living in harmony with a daughter-in-law. I know this is a lot to ask of you: Can I count on you to care for her in her old age?"

I paused and took a deep breath. After reflection I slowly responded, "Yes, I promise you I will take care of her. You can be assured that I will keep my word." Even at 22, I knew this was something that had weighed on his mind. I thought to myself, "Perhaps this would be my opportunity to repay my karmic debt." As it turned out, it would be many years before I was called on to fulfill that promise

I remember his look of relief when I committed to caring for mama. He smiled at me gratefully and said, "I am so sorry that your mama has been so stubbornly set in her preference for a first-born boy, and that she placed the blame on you for disappointing her. I don't think anything could change her mind. I have tried to soften this many times. You were lucky to have been in Ah Jie's care during your childhood. I know she was more of a mother to you than your own mama. So this is a very meaningful promise you are making to me, that you will watch over your mama. Again this shows me just what a strong woman you have grown to be. Thank you B-be."

I smiled and held his hand for a moment, "Papa, even though I have been brought up in Western culture, I do understand something of the demands and the sacrifices of filial piety. I will figure out what I need to do for mama when the time comes. Don't worry."

Changing the subject, I said, "Please tell me more about how the war between China and Japan started. I know my childhood was so entwined with it."

Looking out the window as if to erase his pain, he said, "In Beijing, on the night of July 6, 1937, the Japanese soldiers carried out night maneuvers without prior notice. The local Chinese forces were alarmed, thinking they were under attack, so they fired a few shots, leading to a brief exchange of fire. When a Japanese soldier failed to return to his post that night, his commander thought that the Chinese had captured him and demanded to enter the Chinese sector to search for the missing man. The Chinese general refused because the Japanese had violated China's sovereignty by conducting maneuvers without advance notice. The next day both Chinese and Japanese reinforcements arrived. A bloody exchange on the Marco Polo Bridge caused severe casualties on both sides. The missing Japanese soldier was later found, unharmed. This incident escalated into an eight-year long war between China and Japan. It later became a contributing factor in the Far East theater in World War II."

"I am a little confused about something mama told me. She said that she took me to Shanghai when I was six months old and we stayed until I was one (photo 3). Does this mean she traveled while the country was at war?"

Papa sighed, "Yes, your mama did—much to my disapproval, considering the world situation. She left Saigon with you and your nanny a few days after the Germans entered Paris in June 1940. I had no idea how we would be affected, as we were living in a French colony. But she said she was homesick and had to go see her parents. Only three months later, on September 22, while you were still in Shanghai, Japan claimed Vietnam without any resistance from the French, by taking over the administration of Radio Saigon."

Puzzled, I asked, "Why didn't the French resist the Japanese take-over?"

"The French had signed an armistice with Germany. Since the Nazis only wanted Paris, northern France, and the Atlantic seacoast, they governed those areas from Paris. The French formed what was called the Vichy Government to oversee the parts of France that did not interest Hitler, along with the colonies. Germany and Japan were allies, therefore the Vichy Government was not going to fight the Japanese. Considering that Japan was at war with China, I worried about Japan's plans for the Chinese consulate in Saigon. I was really concerned that the war could separate us for a long, long time, so I cabled your mama to come back right away. In spite of this, she delayed another three months—until early January 1941."

"Fortunately, the war did not separate us," I said, "but I remember seeing Mama cry many times when we were in the concentration camps. She complained that you made her come back only to suffer a life in prison. I don't remember either of you talking much about it after we were freed."

Papa said, "You're right, we have seldom talked about that time because I follow an old Chinese maxim: 'That which is done, there is no need to speak about; that which is past, there is no need to blame.'"

I was touched by papa's response—a pearl of wisdom that anchored deep in my consciousness. I smiled and said, "Allow me to share a little Western wisdom as written by Goethe, 'One ought, every day at least, to hear a little song, read a good poem, see a fine picture, and, if it were possible, to speak a few reasonable words.'"

Papa chuckled, "Well said, well said. We are definitely speaking a few reasonable words now."

"Yes, Papa, thank you for taking the time to talk with me and give me this history lesson. I want you to know that I remember many things about the time we spent in the four different camps, but I would like you to fill in some gaps about the war. Tell me, why was Vietnam important to the Japanese?"

"Strategically," papa explained, "Vietnam was important because its long seacoast made it easier for Japan to dispatch its naval forces to the rest of Southeast Asia. Vietnam was also rich in tin, rubber, and rice—which were all essential for the maintenance and support of the Japanese army. The tin mines were controlled by the French colonialists. The rubber plantations, used for the production and distribution of the famous Michelin tires, were also in the hands of the French. The Vichy Government gave the Japanese access to the tin and rubber. However, the rice that was planted and harvested by the Vietnamese was controlled by Chinese merchants. They resisted turning it over to the Japanese, given China and Japan had been at war since 1937. The Japanese decided that, in order to force the surrender of the rice, they needed to capture the government officials on staff at the Chinese consulate in Saigon. That's why we were put in the concentration camp. After the war, I defended the reputation of several rice merchants who were dubbed *han jian* (Chinese traitors) because they let the Japanese take their rice. What could they have done? Members of their families were held for ransom in order to force their hands. I felt bad for them."

Just then we heard mama's car drive up. Papa stood up and said, "Let's go greet mama. We'll continue this conversation another day. By the way, thanks for ordering the fried bananas—they were delicious. You are truly the child of my heart."

Chapter 5

CONCENTRATION CAMPS

In Papeete we were blessed with an idyllic South Seas island vista—eleven miles from our windows, across the Sea of Moons, rising from the ocean was Moorea. Polynesian creation mythology holds this island to be a gift from *Ruahatu*, king of the ocean, so that the Tahitians would have something beautiful to look at every day. According to the myth, *Tane*, the god of beauty, bordered the azure waters of its lagoons with white sand beaches and planted fragrant white Tiare Tahiti blossoms under the majestic coconut trees.

Scientists say that Moorea is shaped like a triangle. Romantics believe that it represents the heart of a mythical lover after his heart had turned into a butterfly. Polynesian legend has it that the island was created when an enormous magical fish swam from the lagoons of Raiatea and Tahaa and laid down, becoming the island of Tahiti— and its dorsal fin grew into the eight mountain ridges of Moorea.

At times, when sunlight comes from a different angle, the jade-colored velvety peaks can look like the spires of a cathedral, or *Sleeping Beauty's* castle, or the serrated jaw of a shark. These volcanic peaks of Mou'a Roa (Long Mountain) are the most photographed wonders of the South Seas and are often pointed out to visitors as "Bali Ha'i" from the movie *South Pacific*. The song made it sound like *bali hai* means "come to me," but actually in Tahitian it should be *haeri mai ia'u.* In reality that movie was not filmed in Tahiti nor did the book indicate that the story took place there. In fact, the Hotel Bali Hai on Moorea was named for the movie. The hotel staff claimed the connection to boost tourism and a new legend was created.

I made a ritual of partaking of the beauty of Moorea from our upstairs living room window at dusk each day. I was mesmerized by the colors of the setting sun melting into the water, in shimmering shades of blue, golden yellow, orange, and red. I often observed Tahitians stopping their bicycles or their chores to behold the sight and savor it. It seemed they were reveling in their gifts from the gods. In the modern world we often miss out on such beauty, anaesthetized as we are by too much information and too many impressions bombarding us from all sides, keeping us from enjoying the present moment.

As the sun sank into the ocean and the starry night traded places with the day's clouds, the salty air quickly filled with rhythmic, distinctive Tahitian drum beats, guitar music, and melodious voices. One evening as I savored this treat from an upstairs window where I had a view of the beach, I asked Mama, "Do the Tahitians sing like this every evening? They sound so beautiful."

She replied, "Yes, they often do. They have been doing this every evening for a month now. You will hear them each night for the next few weeks because they are practicing for the Bastille Day island-wide music and dance contests on July 14. In a few days you will see many stalls being built on the waterfront as beer and food bars, along with stages for performances and amusement booths. The celebration lasts for two weeks. Your papa already informed the governor's office that you are here and that we need three seats in the grandstand for the military parade, as well as at the soccer field, where the cultural events will be held.

"Performers and competitors from all the neighboring islands gather in Papeete for the big annual contest of music, dance, javelin throwing, and other sports. Many strict rules keep the traditions pure, such as that the *tamure* dancers have to wear real grass skirts."

"Oh, I know about the Tahitian national dance," I said. "It's hard to believe they can shake their hips so fast—it's amazing. I've read that the dancers' undergarments have to be of *tapa* cloth, made from beaten bark. They are not supposed to use any factory-made cloth or thread."

Mama continued as if I had not spoken, showing off her knowledge of Tahiti, "Their choir music is unique and beautiful. It's totally *a cappella*. What is especially unusual is that some of the singers use their voices to imitate the sound of instruments, which are not allowed. Men and women all dress in white outfits—the women wear long, full-cut, white muumuus, an invention of the Christian missionaries to cover the bare-breasted natives. The javelin-throwing is really impressive because the target is a coconut on a big pole at least 15 meters high. Wait till you see how the javelins quiver through the air before they pierce the coconut. Each contestant's javelin is marked and the winner is the one whose javelin pierces closest to the center of the coconut. There is also a foot race with men carrying big bundles of bananas and other fruits.

"I enjoy these people. They remind me of the Mois in the Vietnam Highlands," she said finally glancing at me, "but you wouldn't remember them."

"But I *do* remember them and also the village of Kon Tum. I remember when papa was sick with jaundice, the French Army doctor, Dr. Porte (photo 11), came to see him several times on horseback. He tied his horse on the wooden handrail outside our house, and he always had a piece of candy in his pocket for me. Once it was a *sucette* (lollipop), which was especially wonderful because it lasted a long time."

"You can remember that? I had forgotten. What else do you remember?"

"I remember that every afternoon after my nap, nanny Ah Jie took me for a walk. One day we met a Moi riding on the back of his elephant. We watched as the animal used its trunk to move some tree branches. I was fascinated. The Moi asked Ah Jie if he could give me a ride. She told him she had to get your permission. She was a little afraid of him because she considered him a savage."

"That's right, I said no because it's too dangerous and you'd get dirty. But your papa was more adventuresome and allowed you to ride."

"Papa thought I should take advantage of such an opportunity. He said, 'How many little Chinese girls have the chance to ride an elephant?' He also corrected Ah Jie and told her not to call the Moi a savage, because it was disrespectful—instead to call him an 'earth person.'"

"It was hard for us to get used to the Mois not wearing clothes, only little loin cloths. The women wore absolutely nothing to cover their breasts," Mama said smiling, embarrassed at the thought of this.

Delighted that for once I had been able to engage her in conversation, I continued describing my memories of that time, "I could hardly wait for my afternoon walk the next day. Ah Jie and I met the same Moi again. He had his elephant kneel, he stooped down, pulled me up, and set me in front of him. We began to ride bareback. Right then I understood what you meant about my getting dirty because I felt his sweaty chest against my bare arms and noticed that he smelled bad. Quickly he gave a tap on the elephant's backside and it stood up. We rocked back and forth, but I felt safe as the Moi held on to me. Suddenly I could see such a big world, so far away! I could see the pond where I liked to watch the ducks and I could touch the leaves on the trees as we passed under them. I giggled with excitement as the elephant swayed when it walked. In an instant, I grew from a short little three-year-old to the height of an elephant. I felt so special and grown-up. I was disappointed when Ah Jie said it was enough—that was only after a short while. I thought it was worth getting a little dirty. Ah Jie gave me a bath when we came home and I couldn't stop talking about how much fun it was. After that, I often begged to ride on papa's shoulders, calling it 'riding the big elephant.'"

"Yes, I remember. Your papa spoiled you," mama replied, shaking her head.

Trying to divert her attitude of disapproval, I continued by putting the attention back on her, asking, "I've heard you call the time we spent in Kon Tum 'protective residency.' Would you tell me why we lived there for two years?"

It worked. She stopped being critical and replied, "At your papa's insistence, two weeks after your first birthday, in January 1941, I left Shanghai with you and Ah Jie and returned to be with him in Saigon. The war with Japan was not going well in China. The Japanese had entered Vietnam the previous September without firing a shot, by taking over Radio Saigon. Your father believed we would be better off together with the uncertainty of war and

Japan gaining power everywhere. They were becoming bolder and bolder throughout Southeast Asia. During the week-long boat trip back, I questioned your father's decision and resented having to leave my parents.

"A month after we got back, in mid-February, a Chinese rice merchant went to the consulate to warn that Japanese soldiers were coming to capture them. He piled the staff of seven men in his rice transporting truck and drove them to Dalat, a resort town in the northern highlands, some six hours away from Saigon. He left them in a Chinese laundry. The shop owner cooked dinner for them and stood guard at his window while they ate. When he saw soldiers approaching, he hid the men in the big barrels used for boiling large pieces of laundry, such as sheets. The Japanese arrived, blocked the street on both ends and searched door to door. Suddenly a soldier from one side called out that they had found no one. The opposite trooper called out the same. Both sides missed the middle house where your papa and his colleagues were hiding.

"After the soldiers left, your papa's superior, Consul General Yin Fong-tsao, decided that it was not right to put the laundry owner in danger of angering the Japanese—he would have surely suffered severe punishment if they had been discovered in his shop. So that night, all seven men checked into a French hotel in town where they gathered to strategize. Consul General Yin explained that since the Japanese were already in control of the country, trying to evade them was not a permanent solution. Yin had been educated in Paris to be an attorney, so he was well-versed in the French and international laws under which diplomats were to be protected. He knew he could negotiate with the French government because it was still administering Indochina. The next morning he contacted the French governor in Saigon and asked him to put the staff of the consulate and their families under his protection. Yin strategically made the request official and on record, so the governor could not ignore us. That governor was under the directives of the new Vichy Government, set up after the Nazis took over Paris. The Vichy

Government oversaw the French colonies and the interior parts of France that the Nazis did not occupy.

"Marshal P'etain, a French hero from the First World War, had signed an armistice with the Nazis in June 1940. The terms dictated that Germany would control three-fifths of northern and western France, as well as the Atlantic coast. The rest of France and the French colonies in Asia and Africa were to be administered by P'etain, as Chief of State, from the City of Vichy. This government was pro-German, therefore allies of the Japanese. The Chinese ambassador, Wellington Koo, protested this alliance and refused to move from Paris to Vichy, as a public sign of disapproval. Instead, he went to London, leaving my uncle, Kuo Tse-fan, in charge of the Chinese embassy in Vichy. For political reasons, it was necessary to retain a presence in France for the sake of the Chinese people who lived in that country and the colonies."

My heart skipped a beat, "Kuo Tse-fan, you are talking about Siaoti's father, aren't you? Was he your father's brother or cousin?"

"They were cousins," she said. "My father and his father had the same grandparents. Uncle Tse-fan did us the greatest favor of our lives during that time. He received news that the French governor in Saigon had ordered the closing of the Chinese consulate and had put us in 'protective residency,' a diplomatic way of saying 'house arrest.' So he sent the governor a telegram discreetly worded as a personal inquiry: *'Ou se trouvent ma nièce, Madame Shen, et bébé?'* (Where are my niece, Mrs. Shen, and baby?) Consul General Yin thought my uncle was brilliant because, by his phrasing it without mention of the political situation, Uncle Tse-fan called the governor's attention to our fate without potentially antagonizing the Japanese. Until he received that telegram, the governor had not yet decided what to do with the consulate staff and families. He then personally negotiated with the Japanese to allow us to be moved to Kon Tum (photos 4, 6). Simply because of Uncle Tse-fan's inquiry, we were guarded by French and Vietnamese soldiers in the service of the French army. We were allowed to move about in the village, just not to cross its perimeters, which was why it was called 'protective residency.' Had we been guarded by Japanese soldiers, it would have been called *'residence forcee'* (forced residency), a euphemism for concentration camp."

"All together how many were we in Kon Tum? I remember our house on stilts but not the houses of the others."

Mama said, "The other families and servants stayed in smaller bungalows. There were seven men, five wives, five children, and five female servants. Before we were moved to Kon Tum, the servants, not being staff or family of the consulate, were given a choice to leave or to stay with us. Yin's chef was the only one who decided to go his own way."

"I remember many people came to our house for lunch and dinner. Why was it that way?" I asked.

Mama continued, "We were the only family with two servants. You had Ah Jie as your nanny, and we had Mei Jie as our house-keeper. The other families only had one servant. The consul general's wife was French and did not speak Chinese, so she was not comfortable socializing with the group, who naturally conversed in Chinese. Since Yin's cook had chosen to leave, Yin assigned cooking duties to Mei Jie for himself, his wife, and the two men who did not have their wives or servants. So, Mei Jie cooked for all of them as well as for us and we all ate together. Yin gave our family the larger house to accommodate the daily gatherings."

Amazed, I inquired, "You must have been busy all the time with so much company. Did you feel you had no privacy?"

Mama smiled, haughtily, "Remember that I came from an elite family with a whole entourage of people. I had seen how my mother handled servants and social situations, so I knew how to entertain and keep things moving smoothly. Your father calls me an 'armchair cook.' I am good at directing even though I've never had to do the work, given I've always had good servants."

"Yes, you have been very lucky that way. When Yin's chef left because he was not a member of the consulate, Ah Jie was afraid that she would not be allowed to continue to stay with us. She wanted you to learn to care for me. She tried to teach you to carry me by tying me to your back with a sling made of a rectangular cloth with long straps," I reminded her.

"You remember that? You had to be only about three years old. I told Ah Jie that I couldn't carry you. You were already too heavy. Shortly after that I became pregnant."

"Yes, you told me I was going to have a little brother and you allowed me to feel your growing belly and the baby kicking. How were you so sure it was a boy?"

She retorted, "Surely Heaven would not be so cruel as to disappoint me another time. This baby just had to be a boy." Her tone made it clear no further discussion was permitted. She continued the story, "The last week of November 1943, the French authorities ordered us to move to Phu Luong, a town north of Hanoi. Consul General Yin objected strongly, explaining that I was about to give birth and it would be unsafe for me to travel. Nonetheless, after some negotiation, we still had to leave the first week of December, accompanied by a French army physician, Dr. Henri Mole, in case I gave birth on the train."

"Oh yes, I remember him," I said. "He continued to be Papa's doctor in Saigon after the war. He even traveled with you to France in 1951 when papa was so sick with amoebic dysentery."

Mama continued, "Anyway, that train trip took many hours. We ate and slept on the train. The railroad kitchen staff was all Chinese from the island of Hainan, typical for the trains in Vietnam in those days. They felt bad that we were traveling under lock and key, with armed Japanese guards in our car, to be taken to a concentration camp, so they gave us extra food and treated us well. When they bid us goodbye, several had tears in their eyes. They were afraid we were going to our deaths. We, too, were afraid because the soldiers tied the men's wrists and roped them to one another. We felt so powerless!" Mama started to cry as she recounted these events.

I gently spoke to her, "How terrible that had to be for you. That's one part I don't remember. I wasn't aware of your fears. I was too young. I was simply enjoying the new experience of a train trip. I remember watching out the window, seeing beautiful green rice paddies for a long time. There were black birds flying over them.

I fell asleep, and when I awoke there was not a single rice paddy. I asked Ah Jie where they went. She explained, 'We are on a train. We keep moving forward and the rice fields stay where they are. It is like your life, nothing stays the same.' Of course I was too little to understand what she was talking about, but I remember what she said. I recall that I felt both disappointed and puzzled."

Even though Ah Jie was illiterate, I learned a lot from her. Papa always said that she had a high degree of integrity and he greatly appreciated her devotion to us. She was always teaching me something.

As mama and I were talking, papa stepped into the living room. Immediately, I stood up to greet him, as I always did whenever a grown-up entered, still practicing old-fashioned formal good manners. Mama filled him in, "We were reminiscing about our life in Kon Tum. It's amazing that B-be remembers so much about that time—that was before she turned four."

Papa sat down to join us. With him present, I felt I could have more of a voice, so I opened up with more memories. "I remember that when we arrived in Phu Luong, we were taken to a big house with many rooms. All the grown-ups went into the house and the children stayed in the courtyard. The ground was covered with pebbles which became our toys. I saw some workers adding bricks to the existing walls to make them taller. Others were breaking glass bottles—green, clear, and brown—and embedding the broken pieces into wet cement, making the top of the walls jagged. They also sank metal rods into the cement, then strung barbed wire. On the corner of the front wall they had installed a look-out tower. I watched some men place a search light there that went around and around. At night, from my bed, I could see its beam at regular intervals. I saw a soldier suddenly run to open the gate. A jeep came in carrying a Japanese officer and three soldiers. All of them had guns.

"Someone blew a whistle. Ah Jie came into the yard, gathered up the children, and rushed us into the grown-ups' dining hall. All twelve adults were standing, lined up facing one side of a long wooden table. Seated on the opposite side was the Japanese commandant. Behind him were five armed soldiers, three of whom I had seen arrive in the jeep and two more who had come in from the guardhouse next to the front gate. We filed in and stood in front of our parents. One of the guards walked by us counting—he asked for our age and marked in his notebook. I held onto Ah Jie's hand tightly. We were told that any time we hear the whistle we had to gather there to be counted. From then on, randomly, it happened at least twice a day, sometimes as many as five times a day. Looking back, I know now, they did it just to intimidate and terrorize us.

"The commandant motioned to Consul General Yin to stand next to him. Then I saw them write to each other in a notebook. I never understood why they did that."

Papa said, "You seem to have recorded all this in your mind like a movie—I am absolutely amazed! We have hardly ever talked about the concentration camp since we were freed, so I know you did not get any of the details from us.

"The reason Consul General Yin and the Japanese commandant communicated by writing was because, even though they did not speak one another's language, the written characters of both languages are similar enough to understand. The Japanese language is derived from Chinese, just as the Romance languages are derived from Latin. That commandant was the best-educated of all the Japanese who had anything to do with our concentration camp. In Japan, he had been an elementary school principal. He came to see us far less often than the officer under him. That man was cruel—he liked to brag that he was one of the officers who entered the city of Nanking in December 1937 and massacred many Chinese with his own sword. He threatened us by boasting that his sword shone so brilliantly because it had been bathed in Chinese blood. Every time he came, he sat and propped his boots on the dining table, took his sword out of the sheath and polished it, saying, 'I may need some more Chinese blood to keep it shiny.' He was despicable."

I could see the pain on papa's face as he recalled that oppressive time. I responded slowly, "I was terrified every time that officer came to count us. I remember seeing and hearing the metal cleats on the bottom of his boots. All the Japanese soldiers had boots like his, so the sound of their footsteps came to represent danger to me. To this day any similar sound still gives me a chill. Even as young as I was, I knew that putting your feet on someone's dining table was rude and demeaning. I remember your telling me, sternly, never to whine or cry because that could make the soldiers angry and they could kill us. Because of that I have learned not to show my emotions. Even now, I hardly ever cry for any reason."

Papa nodded and said, "I remember instructing you to go *immediately* to the dining hall whenever you heard the whistle and to the bomb shelter as soon as you heard the air raid siren. I appreciated that Ah Jie never had to chase after you. Wasn't it awful to hear parents and servants running around and screaming at all the children several times a day, just to round them up?"

"Oh yes, Papa. I remember the bomb shelter in the front yard. We had the room closest to it. When we first arrived in Phu Luong, I saw the workers dig the big hole to build it. It had a little mound over it. The doorway was so low even the children had to duck down to go in, nearly crawling, one by one. I remember that the ceiling was barely high enough for your heads after you sat down on the wooden benches. I always carried my little leather cushion to sit on the dirt floor and a goose feather fan to chase away the many mosquitoes. It always smelled terribly musty. I was so frightened listening to the bombing by the Allies and feeling the vibrations. The only light was what came through the entrance, and if we had to be there at night there was no light at all. After the air raids were over, I would take the cushion and fan back to my room and keep them by the door."

Recalling and retelling all of this, I had to take a deep breath. We paused, silent. After a moment I continued, "Papa, the only beautiful things of that time were the two rosebushes you planted in front of our room. Please, tell me—how were you able to get them?"

"You actually remember them? I am amazed," papa said. "The first evening after we arrived in Phu Luong, I consulted with Consul General Yin about the codebook that I had used back in Kon Tum for our occasional telegraphic transmissions. I thought it unwise for me to hang onto it now that we were in a Japanese concentration camp. Until then our belongings had never been searched, but I could foresee it happening soon in this camp. Yin concurred. The next morning I got up very early and went to the kitchen after the cook lit the wood fire for the day. When his back was turned, I quickly pulled the book out from under my shirt and tossed it in the stove. To cover up my reason for going to the kitchen, I took some money and asked *bep* ('cook' in Vietnamese) to buy two rosebushes for me to plant. Surely he was aware of the smell of burning paper—you can't bother a chef's fire and go un-noticed—but he seemed to ignore it. I always thought he was trying to protect me, but I guess I'll never know for certain. He probably felt caught in the middle. He was employed by the Japanese, the conquerors, to cook for us, the prisoners, but I supposed his sym-pathy was with us."

Recalling how important those rosebushes had been to papa, I could hardly wait to say, "I will never forget the lesson you taught me while we watched those bushes grow. You told me that they, too, were in the concentration camp, but it made no difference to them—their nature was to bloom, and they would do so no matter where they were planted. You said that we needed to learn from them, that we must not allow our outer circumstances to keep us from being what we were born to be. You told me I must learn to bloom wherever I am planted, or even transplanted, because your career as a diplomat would mean that I would grow up in foreign countries rather than in China. You said there was nothing we could do about being in the concentration camp, but we could take heart and place our hopes on the roses, believing that by the time they were in bloom we would be freed. Of course they bloomed many times before we got our freedom. Nonetheless, the roses came to symbolize our hope for freedom. I knew roses were your favorite flowers. Even though they were said to be difficult to grow, you thought that by tending them with care at the initial planting, their life force would become *uncrushable*. The lesson I learned from you was to face difficulties in my life with uncrushable courage."

Papa walked over to me and gave me a long hug—very unusual

for him. Chinese parents are normally undemonstrative toward their children. There is little hugging or kissing between them after babyhood. I treasured this brief moment of closeness between my father and me. At the same time, I was aware that this would not sit well with my mother. I have always had the feeling that she thought I robbed her of her honeymoon because I was born too soon, only eleven months after they were married.

Papa tried to steady the emotion in his voice and said, "I see that those years in the concentration camps left an indelible mark on you. I am sorry I was so unaware of what you were going through, what you were feeling. I mistakenly thought you were too young to understand or remember. But I am convinced that you became a stronger person because of that experience."

I really let that apology soak in because it is a very big deal for a Chinese father to admit a failing to his child. Gratefully I responded, "Yes Papa, it did make me stronger. And I thank you for the lesson you taught me. It helped carry me through those days and gave me hope. Another one of your important lessons was about getting things done. I will never forget the way you told me, 'Do it and finish it in one breath, because you are not sure whether you will see the sun rise tomorrow.' I do work at putting your sense of urgency into whatever I do, and that has served me well in my schooling. Also, while we were in the camp you made a game out of teaching me to read Chinese characters. Do you remember? You wrote them on small squares of white paper you had meticulously cut with a knife. In American schools they are called 'flash cards.'"

Papa smiled and said, "I do remember. You were always so willing to come for your lesson and you were so easy to teach."

I was delighted to be speaking of a happy memory. "In your room you had a table that you used as a desk. It was made out of two planks of wood, side by side, with a small crack in the middle. You had me sit under the table, then you read each character out loud and passed the card down to me through the crack. I repeated it, studied it, and passed it back up to you. After teaching me a few words this way, you mixed the cards up and passed them down for me to read by myself."

Papa interjected, "Oh, I remember, that was fun for me, too. You learned some 300 characters that way, before you turned six."

I continued, "I took great pleasure in learning and understanding something new. Do you know that, to this day, I can still recite the short Tang Dynasty poems you taught me as well as the long epic *Mulan Goes to War?*"

Papa laughed and said, "You were like a little sponge!"

Realizing that I had been speaking exclusively to papa, I suddenly wanted to include mama and said, "I also remember the day you gave birth to Max. I saw Ah Jie and Mei Jie carry a rectangular table out of the kitchen and scrub it with soap, a coarse brush, and water they had boiled. Then they carried it to your bedroom and stayed with you. Then another French army doctor arrived, Dr. Levi. I heard you screaming many times. I was so scared because I did not understand what was happening. Hao Jie, Auntie Da Hung's maid, noticed how frightened I looked, so she put me on her lap and said not to be afraid. She assured me it would be over soon, and that you had to go through a lot of pain for me to have a little brother or sister. Papa was nervous and pacing back and forth. I heard him say, 'If it's a girl again, she will be deathly disappointed.' Mama, I've always known what a disappointment I was to you. I apologize for the pain I caused you for not being a boy."

I searched her face for some indication that she accepted my apology. There was none, so I continued, "All the grown-ups were seated in rattan chairs on our veranda. At 4:30 we heard the cry of a baby. Dr. Levi stepped out of your room and announced, '*C'est un garçon!* (It's a boy!)' Everyone clapped. Right at that time, the air raid siren sounded, so we all ran to the bomb shelter, except papa, who went into the bedroom to see you and the new baby."

As I was telling of Max's birth, mama smiled contentedly. She said, "Yes, I finally had my son, exactly four years after you. He was born in the afternoon of Christmas day. Even though I was not Christian, I still felt it was a lucky day because so much of the world celebrates it. It was so dramatic. I had so many people outside my room waiting for his first cry! He was such a beautiful baby, perfectly formed with a full head of hair, and very soon he started to smile."

As mama was gushing about how wonderful my brother's birth was compared to the grief I had caused her, I could not keep from remarking, "Even though Max was born in the concentration camp, I've never heard you say *he* came at an inconvenient time." Inwardly I felt I was sticking my tongue out at her.

With a twinge of irritation she said, "He was my miracle baby *son*. Can you imagine our excitement to see arrive a new life while we were in the oppression of a concentration camp? The adults lavished attention on him. They delighted in watching him grow, change, and develop. He was our beacon of hope. The poor boy did not have the good food you had, no powdered milk, no daily baked apple, or banana. Nothing nutritious was available for him. I nursed him myself and was told that was best for his health. I had Ah Jie put him in a cradle next to her in your room. When he cried she brought him to me to nurse."

I replied, "Yes, I remember him being the center of attention." I have never harbored any bad feelings toward my brother. In a way he saved me by deflecting my mother's disappointment, anger, and resentment (photo 7). "Who gave him the name Max?"

Mama smiled, "It was Consul General Yin. His wife loved Max Factor pancake make-up and was bemoaning the fact that she had run out. He joked that by naming the new baby Max, he hoped to call forth the ability to purchase cosmetics again—a frivolity that would symbolize that life was again good. I gave him his Chinese name, Lu-yueh. I thought it was a brilliant choice because the Chinese character *yueh* is made up of two parts that mean prison at the foot of a mountain. After the war, your father changed it to Lu-liang—*liang* meaning 'forgiveness.' He did not want Max to carry the association with the concentration camp in his name. He said that part of our life was over and we needed to move on."

At that moment papa interjected, addressing me, "I changed your name too. When you were born, my father gave you the name of Lu-sui—*sui* meaning 'follower.' When I watched you play with the other children in the camp, I realized you were a leader, not a follower. So I named you Lu-zhu—*zhu* meaning 'bamboo,' which symbolizes flexibility, determination and humility. By making the change, I put meaning and purpose in your name to bless your life. Of course you know that Lu is the middle name of your generation in the Shen family. Later you'll understand how important that generational middle name is in society. If you or your cousins make a name for yourselves, other people will recognize your family by virtue of your shared middle names. For example, Tsu-hai Shen, whom you call Uncle Haigo, is a well-known architect in Taiwan. He designed and built many government offices, along with the Taipei railroad station and the Taipei Hilton. During the three years I lived in Taiwan, sometimes when introduced by my full name of Tsu-hsun Shen, people would ask me how I am related to Haigo—then I would respond that he is my younger brother. I enjoyed a measure of credibility due to his success."

"Thank you, Papa. I really like my name," I said. "You gave me important virtues to strive for. Courage is the other virtue I work to develop, because without it nothing gets done."

"You are very right," papa commented. "Consul General Yin was an example of what courage can achieve. Despite being in the oppressive circumstance of that camp, he had the courage to demand a certain measure of safety for all of us. In the latter months of 1944, Phu Luong was frequently bombed by the Allies because it had a large detachment of the Japanese army. So Yin requested that the French government negotiate with the Japanese to move us to a safer place. Because of his courage, one morning before sunrise, three plain horse carriages came to pick us up. They were typical Vietnamese carriages, flat bottomed boxes with no seats, so we had to sit cross-legged. We were crowded in with eight people in each carriage."

"Oh yes, I remember," I interrupted. "Mama complained that she was terribly uncomfortable sitting like the natives and that her legs were numb. And I remember my legs felt like they were being pricked by a hundred needles. Papa, you said we were going to a rice plantation in the country for safety. But on the way, just at dawn, planes flew overhead and began bombing all around us. We jumped out of the carriages, and when Ah Jie pushed me into a ditch I got a mouthful of dirt. To this day I hate the smell of dirt, especially after a rain."

Mama explained what happened next. "After the bombing stopped and things calmed down, we stood up and yelled out, 'Is anyone hurt?' We were relieved that out of all 24 of us from the consulate, plus the three carriage drivers, not a single one was injured. We got back into the carriages and made our way to our new home at the plantation. Our quarters there were crowded and primitive compared to the Phu Luong camp, where we had running water and flush toilets. The Japanese had confiscated that house from a rich Vietnamese man who had several wives. In the country we stayed in the workers' *paillottes* (grass shacks). Mei Jie had to draw the water we used every day from a common well. We had to share an outhouse. How disgusting! You were the luckiest one—you never had to use the outhouse. Ah Jie had potty trained you with a white enamel potty I had brought back from Shanghai. She made sure to carry it with her when we were moved to the plantation."

I smiled at my good fortune for Ah Jie's care. "Oh yes, I remember that potty. It had a dark blue rim and a handle." Then I recalled another memory from that time that had left an indelible mark on my young mind. "Do you remember that I started playing with the Vietnamese landowner's daughter, Xuan? She was a couple of years older than I?"

My parents both nodded. "One day, out of nowhere, planes suddenly appeared and dropped bombs near where we were playing. Even at our age, we knew to immediately crouch down on the ground. Suddenly, I felt warm liquid on my left side, hair, face, arm, leg...all over. After the sky was silent, I stood up and discovered I was covered with blood. Xuan did not stand up. I screamed. Ah Jie ran toward me, yanked me up, terrified that I had been seriously wounded. She shouted, 'Where do you hurt? Let me see!' I replied, crying, 'I don't hurt, I don't hurt anywhere.' She assumed I was in shock and did not believe me. She carried me next to the well and dumped a bucket of ice cold water on me to clear away the blood, and stripped me naked to better examine me for wounds. Eventually she saw that I didn't have a scratch. She said she had never been so scared in her life. I was drenched in my friend's blood, but I was not hurt at all.

"The next day, Ah Jie got permission from the Japanese guard to let us go to my little friend's house. There I saw her body in a box. She was so pale, nearly white, and so still. Her mother was sobbing, seated on a stool next to her. Other people were chanting prayers. White candles and incense lit the room. That was the first time I had seen a dead body. Ah Jie told me she was no longer in her body and that she couldn't be my playmate anymore. Just as we were about to leave, her mother gave me Xuan's tin cigarette box filled with the shiny glass beads that we had played with. The lid of that box was decorated with a picture of the head of an English sailor, surrounded by a lifesaver and ropes. It smelled of tobacco. I treasured that gift for years. It reminded me of my little friend who died while I survived, covered with her blood. Along with being in shock, my main feeling was bewilderment. I felt a kind of survivor's guilt, and I developed a death wish. Since I always thought of myself as worthless and ashamed of being a girl, I felt she was the lucky one to have died. Now she would have the chance to come back as a boy. When I was watching her mother sob, I wondered if you two would have cried had I died that day, and if you would have given my stuffed giraffe away like her mother gave me her beads." Glancing at papa, I said, "Did you realize I felt that way?"

Papa hastily replied, "Of course we would have cried! B-be, how could you think otherwise! We would have been devastated. You are our precious little girl. Don't be so hard on yourself. There must be a good reason for you to be born a girl this lifetime and to have lived through those bombs. You must have a destiny that you will realize when the right time comes."

Mama was noticeably silent. Soothed by papa's remark, I continued, "Walking back from my friend's house, Ah Jie told me that since my friend lived a very short life, and because she died so suddenly, she would probably return quickly as a baby in another family." That was my first lesson of life after life. It made a strong impression on me. Even though Ah Jie was the only person with whom I shared my feelings in those days, I did not tell her that I had envied my friend's chance to come back as a boy.

Eventually mama spoke and admitted, "I had totally forgotten this incident until now. I remember seeing you all bloody. You scared me so much that my legs were too weak to run to you. Ah Jie had the presence of mind to wash the blood off of you, and thank goodness you were not wounded. You could have been crippled—that would be worse than being dead." I was quite aware of mama's discomfort around people who have physical or mental challenges.

Papa continued, "Those were terrible times. You had to learn about death so soon in your life. Do you realize that we were at that rice plantation only a couple of months? On March 9, 1945, Japan ousted the French colonialist government, assumed full control of Vietnam, and installed Emperor Bao Dai as its puppet ruler."

"No," I said, "I didn't understand the political situation, but I remember the night some Japanese soldiers who were not our guards burst into our grass shack at the plantation. They tied you up and one of them beat you in front of us with the butt of his riffle. Papa, I can still see the blood coming out of the gash on your forehead. They kept asking you questions and you repeated that you did not know. Mama, I saw you put on the jacket which had your jewelry sewn into the lining by Mei Jie. I also watched you kick under the bed the silver bowl that Ah Jie used to feed me.

"The soldiers searched and ransacked the few possessions we had right in front of us. Then they put us in a big army truck and took us away. When we arrived at a place in Hanoi, the women and children were put in a big room, joining others who were French. One woman came to speak to you, Mama. You found out she was the wife of Dr. Levi, who had delivered Max on Christmas day. She told you that they were there because they were Jews. The men were kept somewhere else and we did not see them for many days. We had to sleep on the cold ceramic tile floor and we had very little to eat. Once a day, the guards brought in a large flat basket of rice with a few morsels of salty fish on top. We ate what we could grab from it with our hands. In that concentration camp I learned how it felt to be hungry and not know when my next meal would come.

"I remember that a Japanese soldier came to see me every day. Mama, he asked for your permission to carry me outside for a walk. From his gestures, you surmised that when he left Japan, he had left behind a daughter my age and he thought I looked like her. He was kind, sometimes bringing a little food for me, half of a banana or a small ball of rice, and he always made me eat it before he brought me back. Before leaving, he would hug me, but I hated that because I could feel the stubs on his face."

At this point papa picked up the story, "Eventually, we men were reunited with our wives and children. We were in that place only six weeks, but didn't it seem a lot longer? Then, for unknown reasons, we were taken back to the camp in Phu Luong. On the way there we were actually allowed to stop by the rice plantation to gather whatever was left of our belongings. Your mama told Ah Jie to retrieve your silver bowl from under the bed. She was really brave and cool-thinking the night we had been taken away."

I smiled at mama and said, "Do you remember you gave me that bowl when I went away to college? I will always keep it with me in remembrance of your bravery."

"It was strange," she said, "that we felt relieved to be taken back to Phu Luong. At least we were with our own people instead of being in a room full of strangers. I finally understood what your papa meant that, live or die, it was better for us to be together than separated. I worried so much about him while we were separated in the camp in Hanoi. I noticed right away, upon our return to Phu Luong that our meals were slimmer. Still, they were better and more regular than at the other camp."

As we were speaking, another incident slowly came into focus in my mind, but I hesitated to share it because I did not understand it. After a good while I said, "Mama, do you remember the time after we returned to Phu Luong when bombs came in the middle of one night with no warning?"

She replied, "Yes, I do. That was the night the ceiling plaster fell on your bed and you were buried under it."

As if finding the right piece of a puzzle, I ventured, "So it did happen! I remember hearing a very loud noise first, then the house shook, and suddenly the ceiling fell on me, breaking the wooden sticks that held up my mosquito net. I saw Ah Jie jump out of bed and grab Max, who was crying, and take off for the bomb shelter. I saw you and papa run to my bed to free me from the rubble. I didn't feel anything, but I heard you scream at papa, 'You are pulling on *my* arm, not B-be!' Finally, he got me out from under the debris and I started to cry because my head hurt. I had plaster in my ears, nose—everywhere."

Mama looked at me, incredulously, and said, "You couldn't possibly have seen us run into the room, you were completely buried!" She paused and gave papa a questioning look, then continued, "I did say to your father that he was pulling on my arm. How could you have known that?"

I knew that I had been buried, but I actually remember *seeing* my parents run through the door from the other room to my bed. We all noticed that something didn't quite line up but we couldn't figure it out, so we shrugged it off. My parents offered no other explanation, but at least they confirmed to me that this incident did occur.

After this, little pieces of plaster would sometimes fall from the broken ceiling, so Ah Jie moved my bed. That ceiling was never repaired the rest of the time we were there. Once again, Ah Jie was the one who paid attention to my emotions and taught me valuable lessons. She took me aside and showed me how to offer prayers of thanksgiving. She helped me to understand and be grateful that the mosquito net had deflected some of the falling plaster and kept it from crushing the life out of me.

This happened to me before I turned six, yet it wasn't until nearly fifty years later that I would finally be able to piece the puzzle together and understand what had happened.

In the early 1990s I heard a lecture given by a Native American about her near-death experience. I remember gasping and nearly jumping out of my seat. Suddenly I realized that the reason I had been able to see Ah Jie carrying Max, and my parents rushing from one place to another—even though, as my mother had correctly recalled, I was completely buried under the rubble—was that I, myself, had been hovering between life and death. My parents called me back to life.

As if to dispel something he couldn't explain, papa moved on, "In the summer of 1945 the harvest was bad, and severe famine struck Hanoi and the surrounding areas. One day in August, *Bep* (the cook) came back to our camp from shopping, highly excited. He was not supposed to transmit news from outside our walls—but he could not contain himself. He told the servants that he heard the Americans had dropped one huge single bomb on Japan which burned up an entire city, and that the Japanese were panicked. A few days later, *Bep* reported that the Americans had dropped a second huge bomb on another Japanese city, which also had been leveled. Of course he was talking about the atomic bomb, but we didn't even have a word for it at that time. No one had ever heard of a bomb that could annihilate an entire city.

"People were anticipating that the Japanese were going to surrender. We finally heard that they had done so, unconditionally, on August 14, 1945. There was so much noise outside our gates—screaming, yelling, celebrating. We were amazed to see how quickly things could change. One of the Chinese consulate men, Yueh Bing-han, ordered the Japanese guards to let him out—which they did, surprisingly. Yueh was the nephew of the family who owned the famous herbal pharmacy in Beijing, called Tong Ren Tang. He was the most talkative and exuberant person in the camp. A few hours later he came back with many stories. Consul General Yin scolded him and ordered him, as well as all of us, to remain in the camp. He explained that the Japanese government may have surrendered but the soldiers were still armed. He warned us they might lose all control and start looting, raping, and killing. He absolutely forbade us to leave until we were officially liberated. We understood the wisdom of his thinking and complied."

I inquired, "Then when did we finally get out of the camp?"

Papa added more historical details, "Unbeknownst to us, the Allies divided Vietnam in half at the 16th parallel. On September 2, 1945, Japan signed the surrender agreement on the American battleship USS Missouri, anchored in Tokyo Bay. Immediately after the official surrender, the Chinese Nationalists moved in north of the 16th parallel to disarm the Japanese. British troops took responsibility for disarming the Japanese in the south. The fact that it took the British eleven days to finally move in caused great chaos and violence to occur in the south—just as Consul General Yin had warned."

Excitedly I interrupted, "I absolutely remember the day the Chinese soldiers arrived. It was early one afternoon. You had eaten lunch and were in your bedroom for a nap. Ah Jie had fed me. I was playing on the veranda with pebbles that had been warmed by the mid-day sun. I was waiting for Ah Jie to finish her lunch so she could put me down for my nap. Suddenly I heard lots of noise outside the walls—shouting, clapping, even drums. I didn't dare run to the gates to see because that was forbidden. I ran toward your room to call you, but you were already coming out. Soldiers were at the gate with big Chinese flags. They ordered the gate to be opened, gathered all the Japanese guards and had them throw down their weapons in front of them. By this time all the other families had come to our veranda. They were jumping up and down, crying. Papa, I heard you say, 'Thank Heaven, thank Earth, we are finally free!' I looked at your rosebushes—they were both in bloom. Ah Jie was crying, too. I saw her wipe her tears with her sleeve. She ran back to our bedroom to get a little dress to slip on me because I was only wearing a pair of panties. Cloth was scarce, so even the green dress she got for me had been cut from an older dress of mama's. It was made of thin gauze with little white dots and thin black lines in triangular shapes."

Mama chimed in, "That green dress was so thin and comfortable for the hot weather in Vietnam. I am amazed you remember so much. What you don't know is that the Chinese troops that came to liberate us came from Chang Sha of Hunan province. The commander's name was Zheng Jye. He wanted to hear all about our years in the different concentration camps, three years and nine months in total. When I told him I had given birth to Max on Christmas day, during an air raid, he said, 'That calls for a poem.' He asked for a sheet of paper and immediately composed it."

Years later, in 2003, when mama was 90 and her memory was failing, her physician asked me to encourage her to speak of her past, of events and people she could remember. She mainly spoke of her childhood in Beijing. When I brought up the days in the concentration camps, she said, "I don't want to remember that time." But when I spoke of Max's birth, she not only elaborated on it, she even recited that poem. I asked her to write it down so I could give it to Max.

With the close of World War II, our life at this last concentration camp had finally come to an end. Once again I heard the whistle blow. Children and servants gathered in the dining room where the adults already were. This time we were not counted by Japanese soldiers, but by Chinese, to prepare transportation for our departure. The grown-ups were seated instead of standing, and they were all talking with great excitement, this time to the Chinese commandant.

My parents, Ah Jie, and Mei Jie gathered our few belongings. Two days later, all of us were off to Hanoi in the back of an army truck—with the Chinese national flag blowing in the wind to lead the convoy. Bystanders on the road cheered us as if we were heroes. We were lodged in a little Chinese hotel. The Chinese community organized a welcoming party with music and long speeches by several people. We received gifts of food, packages in cones made from layers of newspaper pasted together. In those cones were things I don't remember seeing before: peanuts, candies, cookies, and an orange. I heard Auntie Da Hung say, "My orange is over-ripe. Hew! It's spoiled, I can't eat it." I thought to myself, "I have never seen or tasted an orange. How would I know whether mine is spoiled or not? I'd better ask Ah Jie before I eat it."

The whole world was new and noisy. There were so many things I had never seen, heard, smelled, or tasted before. Very soon mama received a visit from a woman whose sister had been mama's classmate in Beijing. She had married a Chinese man from Hanoi, whom she met in Hong Kong during the war. Her husband's family had a business of canning pickled vegetables. She invited us to her home. Her driver came to pick us up and we drove through her courtyard, passing rows and rows of earthen pickle vats. Even though they were sealed, the whole place stank.

At lunch, I had never seen so much food on a table or tasted so many delicious and new things. To this day, I delight in having plenty of good food. Experiencing this abundance of food after having so often gone hungry surely contributed to my eventually owning and operating three Chinese restaurants in my 40s and 50s.

This friend of mama's also gave me several dresses that her two little girls had outgrown. Ah Jie washed and mended the clothes, replacing missing buttons with new ones she now had the freedom to go to the market and purchase. When I noticed that the buttons did not match, she said to me, "There is no shame in wearing older clothes as long as they are clean. Mending and patches are also all right, but tears and holes are not—they are signs of laziness and lack of self-respect. As long as I am the one who takes care of you, you will always be clean."

Just two days after we arrived at that Chinese hotel, papa and Consul General Yin flew to Chonqing in an army airplane. They needed to make a full report of their time in the concentration camps to the Ministry of Foreign Affairs, and receive orders for the future of the Chinese consulates. China had been devastated by the eight years of war with Japan. The government was overwhelmed by all the situations that needed attention. Consul General Yin convinced the Ministry that the Chinese consulates needed to be resumed in Saigon and Hanoi, for the sake of the many Chinese who lived in Vietnam. Papa was promoted to vice-consul, second in command under Yin.

Our week of free accommodation at the Chinese hotel was coming to an end. Since mama had no money, she didn't know what to do. She was hoping father would bring some money back from Chonqing. Auntie Da Hung took charge on behalf of all of us. She approached Chen Shu-tong, director of the Chinese Bureau of Information. He had recently requisitioned the big house that had served as the Japanese Information Center, called *tong meng sheh*. In those days, any information center was a powerhouse, a nerve center for the region. Auntie Da Hung proposed that we move into his big house and that our servants would take care of the cleaning, laundry, and cooking for him and his staff. It became a win-win situation for all of us.

That house had been occupied by Japanese news people, so there were a lot of household items made in Japan—porcelain plates and bowls, black and red lacquer serving trays, chopsticks, and *bento* (lunch) boxes. Director Chen said to Mei Jie, "Clear out all these Japanese-looking things and destroy them." Everything Japanese was regarded with spite. When he had Mei Jie clean out the dining room cupboard, I happened to be around. I asked him if I could possibly have the little silver toothpick holder with Mount Fuji incised on it. He gladly gave it to me. I still keep it on my dressing table. It reminds me that my life after the concentration camps is a gift and that I need to live it with purpose, and be a beneficial presence in the world.

Chapter 6

NEW LIFE IN SAIGON

In the second week of October 1945, papa and Consul General Yin returned from Chonqing with the good news that they had orders to reopen both the Saigon and Hanoi offices. The men assigned to Saigon left and almost immediately found a good location for the new office—a free-standing house at *47 rue Pellerin*. Papa quickly rented a house for our family at 104b *rue d'Arfeuilles*, where we would live for 13 years. It was almost a month before we could move in because the residence was housing Japanese soldiers awaiting repatriation after the war.

In the meantime, a Chinese family, the Tihons, took us in. They had two boys, and a girl named Suzanne, who was a year older than I. The two families quickly became good friends. So, as was common practice, I referred to the parents as auntie and uncle. Uncle Tihon was the manager of a large, fancy French-style furniture store called "Foinet," which was big enough to have its own factory on the outskirts of town.

Before we moved into our future home, Uncle Tihon went to inspect it to see what furniture he could provide. When he looked at the beds he told Ah Jie to throw away all the mattresses: "The thought of your sleeping on mattresses formerly used by Japanese soldiers is disgusting. I can do something about it. I will have my truck bring you new ones." He also ordered for my parents the first queen-sized bed we had ever seen—we thought it was beautiful. Uncle Tihon had total say-so in the furniture company because the French owner was an opium addict who did not take care of the business.

Suzanne (photos 9, 27) was the one who, years later, while I was in college, helped me find my first summer job in Washington, D.C., as a waitress in a Howard Johnson restaurant. And the following Christmas, she was the one who drove me to visit Chinese Ambassador Yeh, who took me to the White House.

Early in 1946, Air France opened air routes to serve Saigon, Hong Kong, and Shanghai. The general manager gave our family round-trip tickets which would allow us to visit our relatives. That spring we arrived in Shanghai and stayed in the home of mama's older brother, whom I called *Jiu Jiu* (Uncle), and his wife, *Jiu Mu* (Auntie). For the first time in my life that I could remember, I met relatives. Mama told me that their opinion of us was most important because we have common ancestors. If ever we did anything to shame ourselves, it would also bring shame on them. She emphasized I must never "lose face"!

In *Jiu Jiu's* house were also my maternal grandfather, *Wai Gong,* and grandmother, *Wai Po,* and three cousins who were older than I by a few years: two girls, *Siao-Mao Jie* and *Siao-Mei Jie,* and one boy, *Jiu-Yu Ge.* I was also taken to meet papa's two stepmothers, two half-brothers, and three half-sisters who lived in Shanghai. His two married sisters lived in another city; I was not to meet them until I returned to China in the 1980s. All these relations seemed so complicated to a six-year-old—I couldn't keep them straight. What I remember most is that papa told his brothers and sisters, "Now that the war is over, you have to resume your education and I will pay for it."

Papa and mama left Max and me in Shanghai while they went to Fuzhou to attend to the burial of *Yeh-Yeh* (paternal grandfather), who had died during the war. The family had waited so long because it was papa's duty as the first-born son to conduct the ceremony. Shortly afterward, papa went back to work in Saigon. Mama, Max, and I stayed in Shanghai. *Jiu Mu* hired another maid to take care of Max and me. *Wang Ma,* as we called her, spoke with a thick Yangzhou accent that was difficult for the two of us to understand.

One day after lunch, while I was seated in an armchair, Max ran past me with a little Chinese flag. He tripped on my feet, fell on top of me, and the flag poked into my left eye. I screamed and cried. *Jiu Mu* picked me up and forced my hand away from my eye to examine it. She called out to a servant, "Call a taxi! We have to take her to an eye doctor—it's serious."

Mama held Max and I heard her say to him, "Don't be afraid. It was not your fault. Your sister should not have stuck her big feet out and tripped you. She caused the accident." Later, I was told that the cornea had been torn and shoved out of place. I learned that if *Jiu Mu* had not responded so quickly I would have become permanently blind in that eye. I was bandaged and kept in a darkened room for a couple of weeks. From that experience I developed a special respect and admiration for blind people who learn to become productive and engaged citizens in society.

Auntie Yo-Yo, papa's fourth younger sister, came to see me while I recuperated and brought me my first colored pencils, and my first coloring book, *Snow White and the Seven Dwarfs*. She stayed and kept me company, telling me fairy tales. The first time I was allowed to go outside I had to wear dark sunglasses, which cousin *Siao-Mei Jie* had given me.

Another aunt took mama, Max, and me in her chauffeur-driven car to a fancy Western-style tea room, called *Sha Li Wen*. She ordered cream-filled cakes and vanilla ice cream served in silver goblets— so cold, sweet, and delicious. She bought Max a chocolate treat—a car with a tiny bear driver. She told me I could choose a chocolate creation for myself, so I selected an airplane because it had a rabbit in it, my Chinese Zodiac sign. Having so recently come from the concentration camp where I often had little to eat, suddenly tasting and being able to choose all these goodies dazzled me.

As my aunt and mama talked, I heard mama describe what had happened to my eye, "If that accident had left her blind in one eye on top of her *chou ba guai* look, there would be no hope for this girl to find a husband." I noticed my aunt protested, so I guessed that mama had used a not-so-nice word. After we got home I asked mama what *chou ba guai* meant, and she told me, "So ugly that you scare people. Like in your coloring book, Snow White's stepmother turned into a hag. It means hideous, worse than ugly."

Timidly I asked, "Mama, am I so hideous?"

Her answer was, "*Chah bu tuo le.*" (That's about right.)

This was the image my mother had of me—hideous. But I refused to hide away as Quasimodo did, in the bell-tower of *Notre Dame*. I thought to myself, "I may be hideous, but I can still do something useful." Throughout my life, whenever I hear of women who are bulimic or anorexic, I understand and feel compassion for their distorted self-images and the struggles they go through.

Parents must realize the enormous impact of the words they use to scold, correct, or describe their children. Words can inflict deep wounds and cause an indelible imprint on children's self-image that can affect them the rest of their lives.

After a two-months stay in Shanghai, Mama, Max, and I returned to Saigon. I was six years old and should have been starting school. Since there was no Chinese school in Saigon, mother decided that I should be sent to Cholon, the nearest Chinatown, which was about half an hour away by car. There was no way for me to commute because gasoline was difficult to come by so soon after the war—it could be obtained only with government-issued ration coupons combined with money. There was no boarding school facility for a child of six, so mama went to several schools looking for a place to board me. Finally she persuaded the music teacher at *Kun De* Elementary School to take me into her apartment above the schoolhouse. She had a kind, soft-spoken husband. I was to call them Auntie and Uncle Quach. They became my godparents when I was baptized just after my 13th birthday (photos 22, 23). They had two small boys, Robert and Pierre, and a girl, a little younger than I, named Helen, whom I called Mimi (photo 10).

About eight years after I had stayed with the Quach family, mama helped make the initial contacts to find sponsors to enable them to immigrate to Australia. Little Helen Quach would grow up to become a noted conductor of the Sydney Philharmonic Orchestra. For a time she trained under Leonard Bernstein in New York. In the 1980s she became conductor of the Taipei Philharmonic Orchestra. Mama thought Helen was talented and beautiful, and often emphasized the huge contrast between Helen and me. She said that I made nothing of my life except mistakes, causing her to lose face in front of her friends and relatives, whereas she was proud of Mimi. Mother would show her off to friends—buying extra tickets to invite them to attend Mimi's concerts in Taipei.

Auntie Quach's apartment was small and hot. There was no air conditioning in those days. A small electric fan was our luxury. I shared a bed with Mimi. Only a curtain separated her parents from us kids. There was no running water or flush toilet in the apartment, so we had to go downstairs to use the common bathroom. I was allowed one bath a week, with cold water in a dark wooden tub. It was disgustingly slimy, as if it had never been scrubbed clean.

At that age I was shy and ill-at-ease with new people and never knew what was expected of me. I felt lost and abandoned. It was a horrible experience, having just come out of nearly four years of concentration camps where I was with my parents daily, knew exactly what I needed to do, and where I could consistently count on Ah Jie's care and attention. In Saigon, she never gave me a cold bath—she would boil a kettle of water to add to my tub so that the bath would be warm and pleasant, every evening before bedtime, something that had not been possible in the camps.

I was in the first grade. Classes were mostly boring to me because I had already learned all the characters being taught, thanks to papa, back in the camp, with paper flash cards. But I did enjoy learning to write them with a pencil in my notebook, luxuries I had not had in the camp. I was careful when I made the different strokes, in the correct order, so that I did not waste paper or pencil—and so that I could receive praise from my teacher.

Often I saw, outside my classroom window, a woman whom I deemed to be ancient, since she had white hair. She sat on a wooden stool and worked on fine embroidery in a large, rectangular, free-standing wooden frame. One day as I came out of class I asked her why she was there. She said she had never been taught how to read so she sat outside my classroom to listen to the teacher and learn with the first-grade children. She mentioned that the principal was very kind and allowed her to *pang ting* (audit). Later when I learned that embroidery was her livelihood, I understood why she was always working. Once in a while I saw her stop work and massage—not rub, but carefully massage—her eyes. I told her I had been injured and sometimes had trouble seeing, so she showed me her massage technique and exercises, which I could use to help my eyes feel better and also to improve my vision. In the 1980s, when I was a tour director in China, I saw grade school students do this kind of eye exercises. It reminded me of that old woman—and I blessed her for what she had taught me.

Kun De—which means "female virtue"—School was founded by Auntie Quach's great-aunt from Guangzhou. I never knew her name because everyone addressed her as *Xiao Zhang* (principal), her proudest role. She was from the old generation, when the feet of little girls of high birth were bound so that they would be more submissive—and therefore desirable—to their future husbands. Foot-binding was an inhumane practice that subjected girls at the age of three, or a little older, to a painful process that deformed the foot into a tiny doll-like shape. It caused extreme pain because all the toes except the big one were broken and turned under, pressed to the bottom of the foot and bound tightly. This kept the feet from growing larger than ten centimeters, or three-point-nine inches. After two or three years the feet would actually shrink to fit into shoes that were only three inches long. The term "lily feet" was used to describe these tiny feet because they were thought to be beautiful, a symbol of gentility and high class. In reality, however, bound feet kept women subjugated because, for the rest of their lives, the pain was so intense that they could not walk even short distances without assistance. In the upper class of old China, a good marriage could only be arranged if the young woman had tiny feet. This exclusively Chinese practice lasted about a thousand years. Thank God it was outlawed in 1911, when the Republic overthrew the last imperial dynasty.

It was difficult for *Xiao Zhang* to move about, but I often saw her hobbling around to visit and inspect different classrooms. We would stand up immediately when she arrived, as we did whenever any grown-up entered the room. After a moment, our teacher would wave her hand, motioning us to sit down. The principal would chat with the teacher and look at our work. She believed that only through education could a person succeed and become a beneficial member of society. I don't know when she founded the school, but it had to have been many years before I went there in 1946.

Xiao Zhang must have considered her spirituality important, given that she maintained four small altars in the schoolyard. All of them had statues or some Chinese writing to denote the deities they represented. For example, the altar placed on the ground at the foot of an enormous old tree stood for *tuu di gung* (Earth deity). Incense sticks on each altar were lighted daily as a sign of gratitude for the life we live and as a petition to the spirits to protect the people and the purpose of the school. I loved standing in the shade of that huge tree because I believed it had been there long before the building and it had seen many human events—I thought, "If only it could talk, it would have many stories to tell."

I also remember that across the narrow street in front of the school entrance, behind a wrought-iron gate, was a large fish pond and a nine-dragon spirit wall in bas-relief, made of beautiful multi-colored ceramic tiles. I did not know to whom they belonged, but I admired them every day and noticed that the small enclave was always swept clean of fallen leaves—no small feat with several big trees around in a tropical climate. On my first trip to Beijing, in 1981, seeing a huge nine-dragon spirit wall in front of one of the gates of the Imperial Palace was a déjà-vu experience that took me back to my Chinese school days.

On Saturday afternoons, *Anh Hai*, our Vietnamese chauffeur, would pick me up at school. Ah Jie would give me a bath and wash my hair as soon as I got home. One afternoon she cried out, "My Heavens, *So Beng* ('shortcake' in Cantonese, her endearing term for me), you have lice in your hair! How terrible! I've worked so hard to keep you clean. Do you remember that I cut your hair very short in the camp to prevent lice?"

Ah Jie immediately went to the pharmacy to buy medicine, washed my hair again, soaked a towel with the potion, and wrapped it around my head like a turban. When mama came home from playing *mah jong*, she took one look at me and exclaimed, "What in the world is going on?"

"*So Beng* has lice in her hair," Ah Jie said. "I've already taken care of it. Another washing and she will be all right."

Then, to my astonishment, Ah Jie continued, "*Madame,* I've bitten my tongue all this time, but I can't help myself anymore. What's the idea of sending her away *so young*? She is only seven years old! She's very frightened to be far from home. It's almost as bad as the old Chinese child-bride system. She cries every Sunday afternoon before you send her back to school. She told me her papa has already taught her all the characters and numbers they are teaching now, and she can recite her multiplication tables all the way to the nines. Why should she be forced to endure this—especially given that she isn't learning much new? You are too *hard-hearted!*"

I had never heard Ah Jie talk to mama in such a tone. In this class-conscious society, as a servant she was not permitted to scold her mistress. Mother was shocked by this insolence and did not answer. She only mumbled, "How disgusting—lice in her hair. How embarrassing! Lose face." Arrogantly, she walked away.

When I was alone with Ah Jie, I asked what she meant by the child-bride system. She said, "I'll explain to you later when you are more grown-up; you are too young to understand."

Sunday afternoon came and I was hoping I could stay home. No such luck. Mama ignored my tears and *Anh Hai* drove me back to school.

A few weeks later I came home with a high fever, rash all over my body, and a terrible headache. Mama took me to the doctor. I had the measles. At last I got to stay home. Ah Jie had heard that measles could settle in the weakest part of the body, so she was afraid the disease would damage my eyes and make me blind. Therefore, she kept me in a darkened room until I was well. For years afterward, I would have a headache after seeing a movie, especially if I came out of the theater into the sunlight. Even now, some 60 years later, driving at night and facing the headlights from oncoming traffic hurts my left eye.

Mama made me feel guilty about "giving" Max the measles—even though the French doctor told her that it was much better for him to go through the childhood diseases at an early age because they would be less severe and leave fewer lasting effects.

Mama complained to papa that Ah Jie had been disrespectful, so he wanted to get to the bottom of the confrontation. When he found out how scared I was to be away from home, he decided I should not be sent back to Cholon. Since he was a career diplomat specializing in French colonies, more than likely he would always be working in French-speaking countries. So he decided that his children might as well take advantage of the French educational system, which was well-known for its excellence. He also wanted us to learn Mandarin. I remember hearing him say to mama, "I hope you will take it upon yourself to teach the children Chinese at home. It will be a great advantage for them to be multi-lingual." To my recollection, mama never gave me Chinese lessons consistently. To say she gave me even ten lessons in all my growing-up years would be a stretch. She finally told papa that she was too impatient to teach me because I was stupid and hard-headed. At that time Max was only three years old and not ready to learn Chinese characters.

I spent the summer preparing to start French school that fall. Mama found a first-grade teacher, *Madame* d'Argence, who agreed to give me private lessons in her home. She taught me my French ABCs. One day I proudly went to my lesson with a brand-new invention—the ball point pen. She said, "No, no, no! You must learn to write and practice to improve your handwriting with a *pencil*. If you start with a pen so hard and inflexible, you will stop improving and freeze the looks of your letters as they are now. Use a pencil now. Later you will work with a dip pen and ink. You will learn to make the thick and thin strokes and your handwriting will be beautiful." I followed her advice and, thanks to her, I did develop a calligraphic style of penmanship.

Years later at a country auction in the U.S., I bought several items. When I received the bill, I said, "I don't have enough cash. May I write you a check?" The man studied me and said, "I'll have to see some ID." I wrote the check and handed it to him. As I was reaching into my wallet for my driver's license, he looked at the check and stopped me: "With handwriting like this, I don't need your ID."

In the school year of 1947-48, I entered Saigon's *Lycée Marie Curie*, as a second-grader—what the French call eleventh year, because they count the grades backward, meaning that one must go eleven more years to complete high school. I was in a classroom of 42 students, which was a typical size. As was customary in the French system, every month I received a grade and a rank report. The first month I was sixteenth in my class. When I took this report to my parents, papa said to me, "It is acceptable since this is your first month, but you must work harder to improve your rank. I expect you to achieve first place soon. I am confident you can do it. Chinese students have a reputation for excelling. Consul General Yin has no children, so at your school you represent the first Chinese family. Make our country and me proud of you." That was quite a tall order for a child of seven but I improved little by little through the first year.

The following summer Auntie Quach decided to switch Mimi to French school because her piano teacher was French. She found a French tutor for Mimi, and I joined the class. Our summer teacher was a Vietnamese woman. Class was held in the home of her brother, a physician. Close to the front gate was a separate building which served as his clinic, always full of patients. *Mademoiselle,* as we called our teacher, had ten students around a long dining table, three of whom were her brother's children. She grouped us by level and taught for three hours a day, three times a week. She was always organized and had something for each one of us to do. Her tutelage greatly improved my French.

Mademoiselle was Catholic, so she knew that a priest came to teach catechism once a week at the *Lycée Marie Curie.* She encouraged me to take the class. With my parents' permission, I did so year after year. The priest who conducted those classes was Father Paul Bardet, a kind and gentle man from the *Missionnaires Apostoliques de la rue du Bac* in Paris. He taught me that I was created by a loving God who thought me so worthwhile that He sent His Son to die for me. *What a new concept!* This Jesus did not just appear on earth—instead He was born of a woman. The Catholic Church assigns great importance to the Blessed Mother as intercessor for our prayers, which introduced me to the image of a caring mother—so different from what I was experiencing at home. There were also stories of women saints, whose courage and compassion moved me to embrace Catholicism. Father Bardet's kindness and his lessons deeply influenced me and lifted my self-image and self-respect.

By the first month of my second school year, in the class of a beautiful blond teacher, *Madame* Hoeg, I finally ranked first, and did so nearly every month for the next four years. Through the sixth grade we had one home-room teacher, who would instruct us in all subjects except physical education and music. Beginning with the seventh grade, each subject was taught by a different teacher, and students moved from room to room, thus ending the monthly competition for numerical rank.

Students would then choose different subjects, in the classics, sciences, or vocational courses. Foreign languages were introduced. I chose Latin and English, then later added Spanish. I studied very hard because I was focused on getting excellent grades. Academic success was the only criterion with which I could demonstrate my worth to my parents—especially to mother, who frequently called me stupid. Papa was proud of my success at school. I heard him say to friends, "My daughter is very diligent. She took first place in her class again this month." Because of his encouragement, I strived even harder to do well.

At the beginning of my third year, 1948-49, mama took Max to Shanghai again to visit her family. I was happy to stay in Saigon. While there, she decided to bring my cousin *Siao-Mao Jie* back to live with us. I was told she did not get along with her younger sister. *Siao-Mao Jie* was 14, six years older than I. She was beautiful and talented. She had chosen for herself the name Lily (photo 8).

Mama lavished attention on her in the form of pretty clothes and birthday parties with bakery-decorated cakes and catered food. Lily continued piano and ballet lessons which she had started in Shanghai. Mama found her the best ballet teacher in Saigon, a woman who had been a famous ballerina in Paris. One day when I went with the chauffeur to pick up Lily, I got to watch part of the lesson. Her teacher held a thick wooden stick. When I asked if she was ever hit with that stick, my cousin answered, "No, stupid—she pounds the stick on the floor to emphasize the rhythm." How was I to know that?

My cousin lived with us for two years. I often wondered why mama couldn't treat me half as well as she did Lily. When I asked mama if I could take ballet lessons too, she said, "Not with that teacher—she is too expensive for *you*." The following summer I did begin ballet lessons and continued for many years with a less expensive teacher, who was also one of the physical education coaches in my school. She made us work hard, but she carried no big wooden stick. Throughout the year, she gave her students many chances to perform for the school, which I enjoyed doing several times.

In early March 1949, mama received a telegram saying that her mother had had a stroke and was paralyzed and unconscious. Despite widespread political unrest at that time mama flew to Shanghai. Her mother looked at her briefly when she arrived by her bedside, then lapsed into a coma and died, on April 4. This was the day before Tombs Sweeping Day—similar to Memorial Day in the U.S.—when Chinese families visit the graves of the departed and offer prayers, candles, incense, flowers, and fruits. From then on, our family dreaded the first week of April every year, because mama would be extremely moody, crying over her mother's death, and her regret that she was not present at the funeral. She did not get to attend because as soon as *Wai Po* died, her brother insisted that she return immediately to Saigon. Uncle *Jiu Jiu* knew the Communists were ready to enter Shanghai and told her, "Get out of here *now*! It's too dangerous for you." Later we learned that the Air France plane mama took was the next-to-last flight to leave before the arrival of the communist troops. Only two weeks later the Communists took over Nanjing, the capital of China. I never once heard mama say how fortunate she was that she left in time. Had she not heeded her brother's advice, as the wife of an official of Chiang Kai-shek's party, she likely would have suffered terribly under the communist regime. Jiu Jiu endured much hardship and many years of "re-education" in labor camps simply because he had worked for a foreign firm—the British-American Tobacco Company.

I often thought that mama never learned to count her blessings.

I remembered that papa was troubled throughout 1949. From the month of *Wai Po*'s death, in April, and for the rest of the year, in city after city, the soldiers of the Chinese Nationalist Government lost to the advancing communist troops.

The history of twentieth century China was shaped by the fall of the last Chinese imperial dynasty in 1911, which left the northern part of the country under the control of several powerful warlords. The founder and first president of China, Sun Yat-sen, had turned to Western democracies to seek aid, but he was ignored. So, in 1920, he reluctantly went to the Soviet Union, which had recently gone through its own revolution. The Soviets decided on a dual policy of support for both Sun's Kuomintang (KMT) and the new Chinese Communist Party (CCP). By the early 1920s the KMT, which was anti-monarchy and pro-democracy, counted over 150,000 members, while the CCP had only some 1,500. Soviet advisors helped set up China's political and military institutes.

In 1923, Sun Yat-sen sent one of his most trusted lieutenants, Chiang Kai-shek, to study in Moscow for several months. After Chiang's return, he participated in the establishment of the Whampoa Military Academy outside Guangzhou, based in part on the Soviet model. The next year, Chiang became head of the academy. He rose to prominence as Sun's successor and head of the KMT when Sun died of cancer in 1925. So the early Republic of China was very much patterned after the early Soviet Union. Both countries had just overthrown their absolute monarchies and were pioneering new ways of governance.

Chiang became commander-in-chief of the National Revolutionary Army, known as the First United Front. They set out against the Northern warlords and conquered them within nine months. By 1926 the Chinese government became divided into right and left wings. The communist left faction grew rapidly. By early the next year the KMT/CCP rivalry had split the revolutionary ranks that had brought down the dynasty. Chiang's success against the warlords emboldened him to use his forces to try to destroy the CCP. He established an anti-communist government in Nanjing in April 1927, and began an intermittent civil war that was interrupted by the Japanese invasion in 1937. At that time the two warring parties joined to form the Second United Front against their common foreign enemy.

Japan's defeat in 1945 marked the end of World War II in Asia. It was reported that on the evening of Japan's surrender Chiang sadly said to his entourage, "Our real trouble starts now." Full-scale civil war resumed in China in 1946. It lasted over three years, resulting in countless deaths, heartbreak, and suffering on both sides. The CCP rapidly gained the following of the population because of its promise of land reform that would benefit the masses of poor, landless downtrodden farmers. They conquered region after region.

On April 23, 1949 the KMT government retreated from its capital city of Nanjing and went west to Chengdu, then again farther to Chonqing, then several weeks later was forced south to Guangzhou, and finally crossed the Strait to Taiwan, in December 1949. More than two million Nationalists landed in Taiwan—one of history's largest diasporas. Many were highly educated or wealthy, which led Taiwan to rapidly rise to prominence in the global economy. On January 1, 1950, Chiang Kai-shek declared Taipei the temporary capital of China and sole legitimate authority of the country.

Even before the KMT had left the mainland, Mao Tse-tung had declared the founding of the People's Republic of China, on October 1, 1949. He made this pronouncement from the balcony of the Imperial Palace to a huge crowd that had gathered at Tian-An-Men Square in Beiping, now renamed Beijing. Losing his homeland to communism was papa's greatest sorrow.

In the midst of all the turmoil, the Chinese consulate in Saigon retained its international standing, because Vietnam was still a French colony, and France maintained a diplomatic relationship with the Chinese Nationalist government on Taiwan. In December 1949, Consul General Yin and papa were invited to the civil and military offices of the French Union in Vietnam for secret talks and negotiations. They traveled to northern Vietnam and remained there for several days. Papa told our family he couldn't talk about what he was doing at that time.

Four months later I heard him tell a real piece of history. One evening, he gathered us and related what had been held in such secrecy. "All this time, what I couldn't tell you had to do with the defeated Nationalist army and many other Chinese who were fleeing the communists. Remember when Consul General Yin and I went to Hanoi? Well, the crisis we were faced with was that tens of thousands of Chinese who were escaping the communist armies wanted to cross the border into Vietnam. The majority were Nationalist soldiers under the leadership of General Huang Chieh (photo 18), a hero of the Sino-Japanese War, from Hunan province. Instead of surrendering to the communists he led them across the mountains that separate China from Vietnam. Along the way, ordinary citizens, families with farm animals, local police forces, and all kinds of people who did not want to live under communist rule joined the exodus. As you can imagine, the French colonialist government was not sure how to deal with this mass of humanity, most of them on foot.

"That's when the French authorities invited Consul General and me to help strategize. Chou En-lai, the Premier of Communist China, objected to the colonialists giving assistance to the refugees. But instead of sending a direct message to the government, he used a radio broadcast to suggest that they stay out of the situation. At the border, the French decided they had no choice. By legally allowing the Chinese to enter Vietnam, they would gain the authority to disarm the troops. This provided safety and security for the local Vietnamese population. Otherwise these country-less and homeless people, many with military armament, could likely turn into bandits simply for survival. In total, 33,400 Chinese crossed the border. Imagine the economic aspects and logistics of feeding that many people even one meal a day, much less dealing with the emotional and physical needs of the injured and traumatized among them. They had lost their country, their homes, their land, their families—everything.

"In March, 1950, the French authorities finally decided to use their Navy to transport all these refugees to the island of Phu Quoc, off the Vietnam coast (photos 19, 20, 21). They would remain there until they could be moved to Taiwan three and a half years later. The Chinese Consulate in Hanoi got involved with registering the refugees—all 33,400 registrations had to be done by hand. But the majority of the work assisting all the people on Phu Quoc and dealing with the French government is still going on at our office in Saigon. We are overwhelmed!"

Father took a deep breath and continued, "I prayed for help. A couple of weeks later it came in the form of a Chinese young man, Ting Mao-shih, who had just finished post-graduate studies at the University of Paris. He came to my office looking for work because the Central News Agency in China, where he had been employed before going to France, no longer exists in the same way. He was unwilling to go back to China and work under a communist regime. I thanked God! Our office has been given a Chinese journalist, fluent in French and loyal to the KMT, who can serve General Huang Chieh as assistant, interpreter, and translator—all rolled into one.

"The Chinese troops and the non-military people who had fled the communists had been moved to Phu Quoc, but the General had to remain in Saigon in order to continue negotiations with the French government. Consul General Yin applied for Ting Mao-shin to have the honorary title of Vice-Consul at the Consulate, in order to allow Ting to obtain authorization to reside and be employed in Vietnam. An immediate security check was made and he entered the employ of the General. By then Huang had established a small residence in Saigon that he occupied with his fourteen-year-old niece, Shih May Chan (photo 14), and an aide-de-camp, Mr. Heh, who both had followed him in the exodus."

We were speechless. We had known something serious had been happening, but we had no idea of the enormity of the situation. Finally we understood why papa had been working such long, stressful days and weekends. He was further exhausted because his health had been compromised ever since he had contracted amoebic dysentery in the camps. The tenacity of this parasite weakened him the rest of his life.

With Ting's arrival, the general decided it was not proper to keep his niece May in a house of three men, so he asked mama to take her in and be her godmother. My cousin Lily had recently gone back to her family in Shanghai. So again another girl would take precedence over me in our home. During the week May stayed in a Chinese boarding school, *Ling Nanh*, in Chinatown, Cholon. On weekends we spent time together doing things girls like to do. I admired her sewing, drawing, and beautiful painting. She made clothes for the two of us so we could be dressed alike. She was like an older sister to me. Sometimes May, Max, and I went to the movies with Ting, who was romantically interested in May. Max and I became their "light bulbs"—the Chinese expression for chaperones.

May told me some of the hardships she endured during her flight through the mountains. She said, "My father is also an officer. He was very busy directing his troops as we fled so he assigned his trusted aide-de-camp to watch over me. During the turmoil we became separated from my father's unit when it was overtaken by communist soldiers. I struggled to try to rejoin papa. But the aide-de-camp grabbed me and forced me to go forward, to my uncle's unit. He even carried me on his back part of the way. I am so grateful to him for saving me. At least I am living in the free world. My poor parents—I have no idea what has become of them." May was especially fearful because her father was an officer in the KMT army.

Most families found themselves split on both sides of the "Bamboo Curtain" which separated communist China from the free world. There was little or no communication during the time of the communist advancement. For many years afterward, family members who had escaped feared they might put those left behind at risk. So there was little direct knowledge of their circumstances.

In June 1950, the Korean War began. Later that year the U.S. government appealed to Taiwan to use the Nationalist troops on Phu Quoc to join in the fight. The Chinese officers objected to serving under the American military, so they went on a hunger strike that drew international attention to the situation. The proposal was dropped.

A few days after mama, Max, and I returned from our trip to Hong Kong in the summer of 1952, papa took us and May to Phu Quoc to see first-hand how the 33,400 Chinese had fared on the island. He was, of course, aware they were doing well but needed to make an official inspection and report.

It was amazing to see how much they had done in a little over two years through focus and diligence. Using only rudimentary tools and local materials, the refugees built thousands of orderly wooden and bamboo houses with thatched roofs made from palm leaves. They had established schools and work centers; market-like exchanges where vegetables and fruits of all kinds could be bartered; tennis and basketball courts with players and spectators; and auditoriums with seats and scheduled performances. Since there was no currency the people accomplished all this entirely through barter.

We saw a couple of acrobatic shows, stand-up comics, and a Peking opera. The fancy costumes could not be embroidered as they would have been traditionally, since there was no embroidery thread, so artists painted on the cloth to make them look like the real thing. We were there for two days. Everything we ate came from their own farms. Papa gave high praise to the community when he addressed audiences before the stage performances that we attended. The military continued their daily exercises with "guns" carved out of wood. As we departed for Saigon, we knew we would always remember our experience in Phu Quoc, because we were so deeply inspired by what these people had accomplished. Today when I see the words Phu Quoc on bottles of fish sauce in oriental grocery stores, I fondly remember those people and that time.

On May 23, 1953, the first group of three ships arrived to transport the temporary residents of Phu Quoc to Taiwan. It took several months and many shiploads to complete the transition. General Huang Chieh, who had led their flight out of China, carried out the French orders to move them to Phu Quoc. He had negotiated the resources and logistics for them to develop a subsistence on the island, and then oversaw their resettlement in Taiwan. Because the refugees, while on Phu Quoc, felt they were in a sort of captivity, they dubbed General Huang "Su Wu on the Sea." Su Wu is a historical figure of 143 to 60 B.C., a Chinese emissary who spent 19 years in captivity among the Huns.

General Huang rose in military rank to become chief of staff of the Taiwan armed forces. In 1969, he became the secretary of state—Chiang Kai-shek's most trusted "gate-keeper." The last time I saw the General, in the early 1990s, he was in the hospital in Taipei. As I walked into his room, he smiled and exclaimed, "Where are your pigtails, B-be?" extending both hands as he addressed me by my early nickname. We reminisced for a while—both aware that we were honoring the profound connections we had shared during those challenging years in Vietnam. General Huang went to his final rest in 1995.

Ding Mao-shih followed General Huang when he moved his troops to Taiwan. In 1958, he left the General's employ to enter the Ministry of Foreign Affairs. He married May and became Special Envoy to the United Nations, later serving as ambassador to several countries, including South Korea. He became the Taiwan senior representative to several more countries, one being the United States. Ting also served as head of the Government Information Office and head of the Security Council. In 1987, he was promoted to the position of Minister of Foreign Affairs. In his 80s, he is one of the major players in the Cross-Strait talks between Taiwan and China. More than 50 years after having served as Ting and May's "light bulb," I usually visit them and have lunch in their home whenever I travel to Taiwan.

In the midst of the turmoil of the Chinese Civil War, we continued our daily activities in Saigon. One Sunday afternoon in 1950, papa announced, "We are all going to see an American movie. It is playing at the Lido in Cholon. The theater owner is Chinese; he shows foreign films with Chinese subtitles." The movie was *The Wizard of Oz*. Through the years, I have seen it many more times on American television—with no subtitles. As we watched the film that day, my parents were deeply moved by the movie's well-known catchphrase, "There's no place like home." Since they had chosen to align themselves with Chiang Kai-shek and the democratic, free China, they believed that as long as China remained under communist rule they could not go home. I think papa understood better than he wanted to admit that it would be a formidable task for the Nationalists to return to the mainland.

When I was born in 1939, because papa was a diplomat in Saigon he was not required to register my birth with the local authorities. Instead, he had registered it through the Chinese Ministry of Foreign Affairs, at that time in Chonqing. When the Nationalists moved to Taiwan, my birth record was lost. Since Max was born in the concentration camp he was not registered anywhere. In June 1950, unbeknownst to mama, papa had the attorney for the Consulate, Mr. Anh-A-Pan, apply to register our births. So on August 7, 1950, our birth registrations were officially completed in the French Union, providing us with genuine birth certificates. In 2009, when giving a talk at the National Archives in Kansas City, I used this personal story of a missing record to illustrate how valuable record-keeping is to our lives and our history. If my father had not found a way to replace that missing document, I could have had expensive and protracted legal problems. When I applied for Social Security retirement benefits, the official who did the paperwork noticed the discrepancy. I had to sign an affidavit explaining why it had taken eleven years for my birth to be reported and recorded. This type of situation has happened to many immigrants who have come to this country without proper documentation, ultimately causing them many difficulties, even deportation.

In 1953 Consul General Yin had a stroke that paralyzed his right side. Because it did not affect his mind, the Ministry of Foreign Affairs in Taipei decided that papa would run the Saigon consulate and Yin would remain the chief officer. Every day after working in the office papa would go to Yin's home to give a report and consult with him.

Because Saigon's noonday sun is extremely hot, it was customary for schools and offices to take a two-hour lunch break and siesta. As a family we always had a sit-down lunch together. Papa would ask Max and me, "What have you learned today?" We had to have some kind of sensible answer. "Nothing," was never acceptable. His questions made me more aware of what I was learning. He used to say, "Reporting to me sets what you have learned more deeply into your mind. Pretend that you are teaching me, because you learn best what you are called on to teach."

Max is four years younger than I, so papa's questions were usually directed to me. One day I went on and on reporting something I had learned, all in French. Papa stood up, took me by the hand, walked me over to an armoire with a full length mirror and gently said to me, "You see this little Chinese girl in the mirror? No matter how good your French is, nothing will ever change your Chinese face. So, at home you will always speak Mandarin to your mama and me. To Ah Jie, you will speak Cantonese only. I know that some of my colleagues' children who grew up in foreign lands cannot speak Chinese at all. That is such a shame! You don't have the opportunity to study in a Chinese school now, so take advantage of your French education. Some day you may have the chance to go to America to perfect your English. But always remain Chinese in your heart. Love the country and the culture of your birth." I was 12 years old when this happened.

I really took papa's lesson to heart. It's the reason I chose to retain my Chinese family name and not to take my husband's last name. Knowing how to speak several languages has served me well and made my life richer. Thanks to papa's insistence on keeping all my languages current, in my 70s, I am called on to interpret for medical personnel and patients at local hospitals. Imagine what a relief it is for non-English speakers in a medical emergency to have someone who can help them communicate their symptoms, understand the treatments recommended, and be more at ease with all the procedures they go through.

My favorite assignments are in the labor and delivery rooms— counting and urging the women to "push" in French, Mandarin, or Cantonese, and being present at the miraculous moment of birth. But one of the saddest moments I experienced as an interpreter was in the winter of 2009, at the birth experience of a recent immigrant from mainland China. During her 13-hour labor, when people asked the couple if they knew the gender of the baby, her husband acknowledged it was a girl, but the woman herself was in denial and said she didn't know. After the girl was born, the nurse offered to show her the baby—before and after she was cleaned up—twice the mother refused to even look at her newborn. How sad that such deep gender discrimination continues to this day and that women themselves perpetuate this on their daughters. Out of concern, the nurses reported this to Family Services. The next day I was called in to interpret for a representative of the social service department, who questioned the mother about whether she wanted to take the baby home and whether she had prepared for taking care of her—such as having a crib, diapers, clothing, and infant formula. Even though the mother said she was prepared, we all felt concern for the welfare of the little girl.

Again, thanks to papa, my language skills also enable me to be a substitute teacher in a French charter school, Academie LaFayette. Students see me in stores and love to show off their French away from school, *"Madame Bambi, Madame Bambi!"* I can't possibly remember all their names, so I call the girls *"Ma Belle"* (My Beautiful), and the boys *"Mon Grand"* (My Big One). So many immigrants lose their cultural heritage as they adapt to their new homelands. I often share the story of my father's wise counsel with parents of different ethnic and language backgrounds to encourage them to keep their mother tongue and culture alive in their children.

In Vietnam, at the end of World War II, the Chinese and the British disarmed the Japanese and returned them to their homeland. Both China and Great Britain were supposed to stay out of Vietnam's internal affairs, but they did not. They each took sides in the dispute over continued French colonial rule over Vietnam. The communist Chinese helped the Viet Minh, a group of Vietnamese communists founded in 1941 to both oppose French rule and to fight the Japanese occupation. The British, being colonialists themselves, were sympathetic toward the French in this regard, so they moved to reinstate France's control. Even after the five-year Japanese occupation ended, Vietnam remained in turmoil because of the desire of the Vietnamese to shake French colonialism. The resulting struggle lasted nine years, from 1945 to 1954, and is known as the First Indochina War.

On September 2, 1945, Ho Chi Minh, leader and founder of the anti-colonial movement, issued a Declaration of Independence, patterned after the American Declaration of Independence of 1776. He hoped to gain America's support, given that the fight of the Vietnamese was similar to the Americans' fight against the British during the American Revolution. But both the U.S. and France ignored his declaration. When the Chinese and the British withdrew from Indochina at the end of 1945, France reclaimed its colony with the aid of American money, weapons, and strategic advice. President Truman's foreign policy was focused on rebuilding Europe and preventing the Soviet Union from expanding communism in the world. The U.S. believed that helping France fight the Viet Minh would reduce the threat of communism in Indochina. Truman also thought France would play a greater role than Vietnam in international politics, so he gave France higher priority.

The French Union forces found that fighting the Viet Minh was more difficult than expected. The Vietnamese were fighting for independence, whether their ideology was communistic or not—they wanted to be free from colonialism. Even though I was just a teenager, I understood the dynamics on a personal level—some of my friends were Vietnamese and some were French, children of the colonialists. By virtue of my father's post, I was a diplomatic guest resident in the country. I was caught in the middle and couldn't take sides. I saw both aspects of colonialism, the good and the bad. Most of the ugly colonialists were the ones who were uneducated yet had been given a position of authority. I witnessed a rubber plantation foreman actually kicking some Vietnamese workers—reprehensible! At the same time I observed the progress that the colonialists brought, including elevated education standards, roads, electricity, water and sewer systems, and more.

By the early 1950s, the French could see that the days of colonialism were numbered, yet they were determined to retain their presence in Vietnam. In 1953, General Henri Navarre took command of the French Forces. He recruited and trained local anti-communist Vietnamese with the promise to negotiate greater independence for their country in exchange for support against the Viet Minh.

The U.S. provided financial assistance and equipment to help the Navarre Plan to prepare for a major offensive. The main objectives were to stop the Viet Minh flow of personnel, weapons, and supplies between Laos and Vietnam, and to destroy them with superior fire power from land and air. General Navarre established a group of fortified posts in the village of Dien Bien Phu and the surrounding hills. The Viet Minh were able to defeat these strongholds one by one, in guerrilla fashion. Monsoon weather in March, with high winds and heavy rain, kept the French from replenishing supplies by land or air. When the weather finally allowed Navarre's planes to fly, Viet Minh anti-aircraft guns brought them down. As a result, the troops were stranded. On May 7, 1954, the French Union forces surrendered. It was the end of colonial rule in Indochina.

Meanwhile, a peace negotiation conference had been set up to be held in Switzerland, beginning May 8. It was called the Geneva Conference and several countries participated. The objectives of the conference were threefold: to arrange for an end to hostilities between France and the Viet-Minh, to achieve Vietnam's independence from French rule, and to create separate plans for the three countries that had until then made up Indochina—Vietnam, Laos, and Cambodia.

In the negotiations India and Canada were assigned to represent non-communist southern Vietnam, and Poland was to represent communist northern Vietnam. Not surprisingly, the two sides rarely agreed. Because the Conference happened to start one day after the Viet-Minh had defeated France at Dien Bien Phu, they had a much stronger negotiating position. An accord was finally reached in July, which temporarily divided Vietnam into two countries at the 17th parallel. The conferees also established the International Commission for Supervision and Control (ICSC) to implement the treaty. The Vietnamese were permitted to move freely between north and south until May 1955. The treaty ordered a general election for both sides to be held in July 1956, under the supervision of the ICSC, in order to re-unite the country. The intended election never took place.

During this time of unrest and negotiations I watched papa become glued to his radio every evening after he returned from his office. He sat in front of our shiny brown Phillips radio, with his forehead right against it, listening intently to the reports. This was his way of learning the points of the negotiations that would greatly affect his work and our lives.

The point of the treaty I remember best, since I heard of its impact daily, was the part that permitted the Vietnamese to move freely between the north and south. By that time papa had assumed the role of acting Consul General, because Yin's physical condition had deteriorated. The government of Taiwan sent ships to transport Chinese and North Vietnamese who did not want to live under communist rule to Saigon. Papa took me to welcome the first few ships. Before we went to the wharf he explained to me, "The refugees' situation is very sad. They had to leave everything behind—homes, possessions, friends, and even families. All they could bring was what they could carry. They have to restart their lives from nothing. I want you to have compassion for them, but behave with dignity in public—keep your emotions in check. Do not cry in front of these people—instead, admire their courage. Their freedom is more important to them than their possessions."

"Yes, papa," I acknowledged, "you've always insisted that I behave appropriately—no tears, no unbecoming attitude in public—even with those nasty Japanese soldiers in the camps. Don't worry, I'll behave."

The arrival of the shiploads of people to Saigon was one of the most moving scenes I have ever witnessed. Most knelt down and kissed the ground as they came ashore. They were of all ages, from babies in their mothers' arms to grandpas and grandmas who had difficulty walking. Papa worked with them from that day forward for years, day in and day out—replacing lost documents, visiting resettlement camps, connecting refugees with different business people who could help them restart their lives, working many late nights and weekends. It really took a toll on his health. Not only was his work heavy, he was often preoccupied and worried about his own family members who had been left behind. No telling what they were suffering under the communists. Years later, he heard that his elderly stepmother had been interrogated. When asked about her son in Saigon, she said, "I am not sure what he is doing. I think he is a merchant of some kind." The communist official retorted, "Don't lie to us. We know he is the Consul General working for Chiang Kai-shek. Just know that we are keeping an eye on *you.*"

Perhaps the most memorable assistance papa gave was to a band of Buddhist monks. One day, over lunch he told us, "Today a dozen Buddhist monks from Fuzhou arrived at the consulate, tired, hungry, and tattered. They were pitiful-looking. The Chinese communists had destroyed the altars and statues in their temple, chased them out of the monastery, and taken over the buildings. The master monk had heard that the Chinese Consul General in Saigon was from the city of Fuzhou. Having nowhere else to go they hoped desperately to find help from me. They walked nearly all the way here. It took them about three months. Along the way, they begged for food. They said they were treated kindly by many Vietnamese who were Buddhist.

"I, myself, had no way to effectively help them. So I was inspired to call the president of the Fukienese-Chinese chamber of commerce in Cholon. I was lucky that I was able to reach him immediately. Within an hour, he was in my office with other members of the provincial organization. Together they vowed to take care of the monks and build them a temple. I was amazed to watch the brotherhood come together, so willing and ready to help. I felt the whole incident was directed by Heaven. It was incredible!"

The Fukienese community rallied around the monks and, within a short time, had a temple built, with a large dining hall where the monks could cook and serve vegetarian meals to big groups (photo 25). This was an effective way for them to earn a living. It became a popular gathering place to celebrate births and business successes, and to hold funerals and prayers for the dead. The notoriety of this temple exploded by word of mouth with the story of prayer answered. A prominent Chinese businessman's wife gave birth to a long-awaited son after having made a vow at this new temple. She had been barren for nearly twenty years! The future of that temple was assured .

Every year to celebrate Buddha's birthday, papa was invited to this temple to be the first person to ceremoniously pour three spoonfuls of water onto a small statue of a Buddha seated on top of a porcelain lotus. The water trickled down and was collected in a basin beneath the lotus. It was considered holy water with miraculous properties. Who can say for sure that it was not miraculous? It was surely imbued with the people's faith. Papa always took me to this ceremony because he said it was important that I keep in touch and learn my Chinese culture. Being thoughtful of Ah Jie, who was a devout Buddhist, I always brought her a tiny bag of ashes from the temple's huge incense pot. I understood its importance to her, as the ashes represented the fervent prayers and the merits gained by many believers.

From the end of World War II to 1958, papa kept his post as second-in-command at the Saigon office, even when it changed status from consulate to embassy, after Vietnam achieved independence and became a nation. The routines of our lives in Saigon which were the result of papa's remaining in his position, gave us some sense of normalcy over the years. Nevertheless, from concentration camps, to living in a country in conflict with French colonialists and communist aggression, to the civil war in China which forced the Nationalist government to Taiwan, our family felt that we had never lived in a world at peace. The incessant slogans in Taiwan, "To re-conquer the Mainland," and in China, "To reunite Taiwan with the Motherland," only deepened the official hatred between brothers and sisters. The hero to one side was a traitor to the other and blood flowed freely in defense of one's loyalty. The eventual deaths of the leaders of both sides—Chiang Kai-shek and Mao Tse-tung—provided historical opportunities for some kind of healing and reconciliation to take place. Instead, their eventual deaths became just two more occasions to perpetuate and deepen the rift, and become further entrenched in their conflicting ideologies. I saw this patriotism close up when a military basketball team from Taiwan visited Saigon for a tournament. I remember seeing all of the players show off the tattoos on their backs and chests, which proclaimed their sacred oath in large characteres.

The polarization and name calling continued—"communist bandits," or "running dogs," depending on who was speaking. It lasted until the normalization of relations between Washington and Beijing on January 1, 1979, the chant changed on the communist side. The National People's Congress of Communist China sent an extraordinary message to their "beloved compatriots on Taiwan to end our disunity." The Taiwan government dismissed the overture in no uncertain terms and continued to hold out against the power of over a billion just a few miles away.

Although my father served the Nationalist government all his life, as an Overseas Chinese, I find myself in an odd, neutral position. Since I never lived in China or on Taiwan, I was not caught up in the emotional aspect of the dispute. In the 1980s I became a tour director, taking groups of American travelers to mainland China and to Taiwan, just to enjoy the beauty of the sights and the richness of the ancient culture. With the same Chinese blood coursing through our veins and our common ancestry, I wish I could say to both sides, "Come on good people, can't we just get along and share this planet?" I realize this is an over-simplification. No one is all good or all bad. Only the future will tell what the solution is for mainland China and Taiwan, and for all the Chinese people, who account for one fifth of the entire population of the earth.

Papa was often invited to officiate at weddings of Chinese couples, since the local authorities of Vietnam recognized the validity of his signature on marriage certificates. Therefore we, as a family, were invited to many weddings (photo 26), frequently held in restaurants, where the feasting could continue seamlessly after the marriage ceremony. One day as Ah Jie was helping me get ready for such an event, I asked her, "Remember the day you argued with mama to keep me at home instead of sending me away to school? You said something about some child-bride system, and you told me you would explain what *tong yang sih fu* means when I am older. Don't you think now is a good time?" With a deep sigh, Ah Jie explained, "Yes, I think you are old enough to understand. It means 'raising a child-bride.' You see, when I was only about twelve years old, my parents sent me to the home of my future husband. He was three years younger than I, as it was the custom of those days to match child-brides with even younger husbands. So I was there to take care of him, as if I were his older sister, and to learn all the household and farm chores from my future mother-in-law. It's worse than being a *ya tou* (slave girl) bought by a rich family—at least a *ya tou* could have better food and maybe the chance to obtain some education, even possibly the freedom to choose her destiny after becoming an adult.

"I was stuck there with no hope of a better situation for the rest of my life. In my case, it became a nightmare about two years later, when my future husband became sick and died. Of course he was too young to have been my *real* husband, so I had not yet given birth to a child, much less a boy-child. Because of this, I was not considered part of his family, so I was told to return to my own people. The family discovered that I had been born under the sign of the tiger. This was considered the worst for a girl, because it was believed that a 'tiger bride' would be too powerful and would dominate her husband's life force. When my marriage was being arranged, my mother lied about my age, saying I was a year younger, as if born under the sign of the rabbit. After my future husband died, believing in that superstition, I felt so guilty that I confessed my mother's lie. My mother-in-law said I was 'bad luck'—that my life force snuffed out her son.

"I was too ashamed to return to my own village, so I joined a sisterhood of women house-servants in a Buddhist temple. We made a vow to remain single and to look after one another. Soon after our training, we all immigrated to Vietnam. There I became employed by your father and his two colleagues. The other two men were transferred to another country, and I stayed with your father, who soon married. Then, after you were born, I became your nanny."

Shocked by her story, I said, "Poor Ah Jie, you have had such a sad life!"

She sighed, "It's my fate, my karma this lifetime. If I had been educated I could have had a better life. Treasure your opportunity to be in school and learn all you can, Little Miss. Given the social etiquette of that time, she always addressed me by this formality, or by the nickname she gave me, "Short Cake." No one can take that away from you. You will never have to 'bow your head' against your integrity. As I watch you receiving all this Western education, and living away from China, I see you developing a frightfully independent streak. I wonder if you could ever fit in the shoes of a submissive Chinese wife."

I giggled at her old-fashioned concerns and replied, "It will be many years before I can get married. I have to go to college first. Then who knows where life will take me? Mama doesn't think I have much chance of finding a husband anyway, so who cares?"

Ah Jie made a gesture to button my mouth, "Don't say bad things. Remember I taught you the importance of the power of the word? What you say, even in jest, may well stick to you. Don't let your mama's prophesies rule your life! Shake off her words like a duck shakes off water. With an education and good health you can handle anything. Be true to the goodness of your heart and you will be fine."

1. Bambi's parents' wedding, Shanghai, February 1, 1939

2. Bambi with parents, Saigon, 1940

3. With mother, Bambi's first birthday,
Shanghai, December 1940

4. Bambi on the veranda in Kontum, 1943, about the time of the elephant ride

5. Mother at Yenching University, 1936—Auntie Sophie gave Bambi this picture when she first arrived in the U.S., 1958; mother's signature is still visible

6. Bambi in Kontum, first "protective residency," 1943

7. Brother Max and Bambi, Saigon, 1948

8. Mother with niece Lily Kuo, Saigon, 1950

9. Bambi (with braids) with friends, Suzanne Tihon on her right, Peter Tchan on her left, Saigon, 1950

10. Helen Quach, age 10, after a recital, Saigon, 1950

11. Dr. Porte, father's physician in Kontum, on his wedding day, Saigon, December 6, 1950

12. Max, Bambi, and mother; picture taken for paperwork to travel to Hong Kong, summer 1952

13. Mother and her cousin, Siaoti Kuo (age 18), Hong Kong, 1952

14. Bambi and Shih May Chan in costume, in front of Peking Opera scene, Phu Quoc, 1952

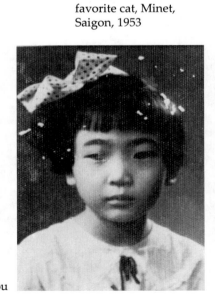

15. Bambi with her favorite cat, Minet, Saigon, 1953

16. Bambi's uncle Tsu-tong Shen

17. Uncle Tsu-tong's youngest daughter, Lou-Lou

18. General Huang Chieh in our living room, Saigon, 1952

19. General Huang speaking to residents, Phu Quoc, 1952—note the bamboo gazebo with thatched roof

20. How rice was served on Phu Quoc

21. Part of the 33,400 Chinese who followed General Huang, Phu Quoc, 1952

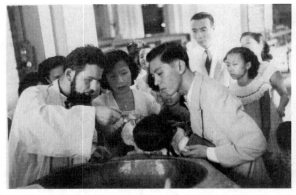

22. Bambi's baptism by Father Paul Bardet; Uncle and Auntie Quach are godparents, Saigon, December 27, 1952

23. Brigitte Luong and Bambi's confirmation, Saigon, December 20, 1953

24. Archbishop Yu Pin with Bambi, Saigon, 1955

25. Monks from Fuzhou, in front of their vegetarian dining hall, Cholon, 1954

26. Father with Bambi in her first Chinese dress for attending weddings, Saigon, June 24, 1955

27. Bambi and Suzanne Tihon, New Year's Eve ball, Saigon, 1955

28. Bambi in school play—Lycee Marie Curie and Jean-Jacques Rousseau High Schools combined, Saigon, 1956

29. Bambi dressed for another play, Saigon, 1957

30. Celebration party after the Bac, Saigon, 1958—if you recognize yourself, please contact me

31. Shen family portrait before Bambi left for the U.S., Taipei, 1958

32. Miao family: K.K., Uncle C.T., Auntie Pearl, and Raymond, Flushing, New York, 1958

34. Bambi with Elvis Presley, the week after he completed filming *Blue Hawaii*, Memphis, 1962

33. Bambi at St. Catharine College, going to a ball, her leg in a cast, 1960

35. Bambi's Siena College graduation yearbook picture, Memphis, 1962

36. Parents with Bambi, the day she arrived in Tahiti, May 1962

37. Mother and Bambi, on the island of Moorea, Tahiti, 1962

38. Bambi's parents with the Chinese community, Tahiti, 1963

40. Daddy Mac, Nana Sue, baby Michael, and Gregory, Noel, Missouri, 1967

39. Michael and Gregory, Butler, Missouri, Christmas 1969

41. Bambi with Michael, Simon with Gregory

42. Father, Ambassador in Niger, with Taiwan's Agricultural Technical Team, 1965

43. Father's sisters and their mother (2nd from right)

44. Bambi's art show, sponsored by *China Post* (co-founders Y.P. Huang and Nancy Yu Huang, back row far left), Taipei, 1980

45. Mother, Don Hinshaw, and Bambi, World Miniature Park, Taiwan, 1983

46. Ah Jie and Bambi, Hong Kong, 1983

47. Bambi as tour director, at Ming Tombs, China, 1985

48. Shen family reunion, Kansas City, Christmas 1991, when cousin Lyushun Shen (back row far right) was Director General of the Taipei Economic and Cultural Office in Kansas City

49. Husband Gene Foster and Bambi, Kansas City, 1998

50. El Salvador Ambassador Francisco Berrios accepting the funds for three houses from Zonta Club Taipei II, for the victims of the 2001 earthquakes, to be built by *Homes from the Heart*

51. Members of Zonta Club Taipei II with Ambassador Berrios, Taipei, 2003

52. Family who received one of the houses from Zonta Club Taipei II and *Homes from the Heart*, Soyapango, El Salvador (Zonta plaque on wall)

53. Mother's 90th birthday party with her Zonta Club Sisters; seated on mother's right is the wife of El Salvador's Ambassador Berrios; Max is standing in the back; Taipei, 2003

54. Bambi in her home in Kansas City with son Michael and his girlfriend Lara. The painting on the wall is the cover of this book, 2008

55. Father officiated at this wedding of five couples at the Chinese Chamber of Commerce in Cholon, 1950s

56. Administrators and professors at the University of Beijing, 2002; Bambi is holding the arm of Professor Hou, her mother's history professor in the 1930's.

57. Bambi at Edgar Snow's gravesite, University of Beijing, 2002

58. Gene with Bambi fulfilling her vow made 50 years earlier to celebrate the 150th jubilee in Lourdes, 2008

59. President Chiang Kai-shek and father, with the letter of credentials appointing him to the post of Ambassador to Ivory Coast, Taipei, 1963

Chapter 7
DREAMS OF OLYMPIC GAMES

Thanks to my nanny's love, support, and faith in me, I navigated through high school enjoying lots of extra-curricular activities and fun. For my 14th birthday I asked my parents for and received my first bicycle. With it, I found the freedom to come and go without having to depend on Papa's car and chauffeur. As long as I told Mama or Ah Jie where I was going, what I was doing, and when I would be back—and stayed true to my word—I never got in trouble with them.

The two French government-supported schools in Saigon were the *Lycée Marie Curie* for girls, and the *Lycée Jean-Jacques Rousseau* for boys. All the classes and other activities were segregated, with the exception of the theater. The co-director of our school plays was also my Latin teacher. I was chosen for the female supporting role in three plays (photos 28, 29). During theater rehearsals and while at the swimming club off-campus, I became friends with many boys—French and Vietnamese—and was invited to many dance parties. The songs my friends and I danced to included Doris Day's *Secret Love*, The Platters' *Smoke Gets in Your Eyes*, Henry Mancini's *Three Coins in the Fountain*, and—of course—*all* of Elvis Presley's music, which we adored. We invented fancy steps to the cha-cha-cha. With my ballet training, I was not afraid to allow the boys to flip and toss me around for dancing rock and roll. I knew how to help them lift me by jumping up at just the right time, enabling me and whatever partner I danced with to make the most advanced moves look good. My full skirts and layers and layers of multi-colored nylon crinoline would swirl as I twirled. I was the favorite partner of the showier boy dancers. What fun!

All these joyous memories came rolling down on me one steamy lunch hour in Kansas City, Missouri in August 2007. Over a cool Caesar salad I was sharing some time with my Chinese friend, Da Sao, who revived a buried dream. As we discussed the upcoming Beijing Olympics, just a year away, I learned that her son was the basketball coach for a team in Qingdao. It was her hometown, and also the place where the Olympic sailing competition would be held. The most natural question from me followed, "Are you going back for the Games?"

She replied, "Of course! It's a once-in-a-lifetime opportunity."

Feeling a little envious, I said, "Lucky you, I have wanted to go to the Olympics for over 50 years, but they are so expensive!" For a while we were both silent, lost in our thoughts. Suddenly she exclaimed, "Bambi, why don't you apply to be an interpreter? They really need people like you, who can speak several languages. Go!"

As I was considering whether to apply to be an interpreter in Beijing, I remembered the year I first became aware of the excitement and international importance of the Olympic Games. I was 16. It was 1956, and the Games took place in Melbourne, Australia, from November 22 to December 8. It seemed a bit late in the calendar year for "Summer Olympics," but since they were held in the southern hemisphere for the first time, the scheduling reflected the south-north reversal of seasons. It was the beginning of my third year in high school at the *Lycée Marie Curie*. Every afternoon, at the end of the school day, several of my classmates and I rushed on our bicycles or Vespa scooters to the swimming pool at the *Cercle Sportif,* the French athletic club. Seated on rattan chairs, we listened attentively to *Monsieur* Vatin, our swimming coach, as he read the results of the Olympic competition from the previous day and shared his comments as an insider of the Games. He had been an Olympic swimmer for France in Berlin in 1936.

Our attention was focused on news of the French athletes' performances—even though we were living in the newly established independent nation of Vietnam, there were no Vietnamese participants to support or to follow, and our city, our school, our friends, and our surroundings still had the air of being a French colony. In those days televisions did not exist, so the only way we could see a little of the action of the Games was to wait a week and go to the movies to watch the black and white newsreels that were shown before feature films. So just listening to our coach read and explain the results the very next day was exciting. Even though the three top medal winners—the U.S.S.R., the U.S., and Australia—received a combined 207 medals, we were extremely proud of the four gold, four silver, and six bronze medals won by France.

There was a time when the competition was not between nations; quite the opposite. The Olympic Games were created as a period of truce during which athletes could come together to compete solely on merit and without any political overtones. The ancient Greeks took this to the extreme by having the athletes compete in the nude so that clothing could not betray the men's ethnic or national origin. Only men could be competitors or spectators. Olympic legend tells the story of the mother of one of the competitors who disguised herself as a man to watch her son perform. She was discovered and was sentenced to be stoned to death, but since her boy was that year's champion she was spared.

The Greeks held the first Olympic Games in 776 B.C., dedicated to Zeus, god of thunder and war. They took place every four years for 1,170 years until they were halted in 394 A.D. At that time the Byzantine Emperor, Theodosius II, banned the competition because the Mediterranean world was becoming Christian and the Games were considered to be a pagan rite. A 19th century French educator and sportsman, Pierre, Baron de Coubertin, revived the Games. The first modern Olympics were held in 1896 in Athens. That's why, even today, at opening and closing ceremonies, the Greek flag and team of athletes enter the stadium first in the parade of nations. De Coubertin designed the flag for the modern Olympics with five interlocking rings—blue, yellow, black, green, and red—to stand for the five continents: Africa, the Americas, Asia, Europe, and Oceania. Together with the white background, the six colors include the colors of all the world's flags, making this the most inclusive international emblem. Even in the modern Olympics, the competition ignored national borders under the ancient motto, "Swifter,

Higher, Stronger." This continued until the 1920 Games in Antwerp, Belgium, when athletes began to perform under their country flag and the emphasis shifted to competition between nations.

The 1956 Olympics in Melbourne saw several politically motivated acts. They were the first Games to be boycotted. The Soviet invasion of Hungary, on October 23 of that year, provoked protests from several European countries and caused Spain, Switzerland, and the Netherlands to withdraw. Egypt, Lebanon, and Iraq also refused to participate in protest of the Franco-British Suez intervention, which began July 26. Imagine the disappointment of the athletes who had trained for years, only to have their hopes dashed just weeks before their chance to compete.

Due to my Chinese heritage, what touched me most was that the People's Republic of China refused to take part because of the presence of Taiwan. I grieved that all Chinese could not look at one another as sisters and brothers without political animosity. I wished they could have taken a lesson from the success of the International Olympic Committee which managed to bring together the two Germanys, East and West, in a combined team (EUA), competing under one black, red, and yellow flag featuring the Olympic rings, with Beethoven's "Ode to Joy" as their anthem. It took seven more games—28 years—before China and Taiwan competed on the same fields in Los Angeles, 1984.

That year China participated in defiance of the Soviet-led boycott, and Taiwan's athletes used the official name of "Chinese Taipei."

The 1956 Games were also marked by an innovation in the closing ceremony. At the suggestion of John Ian Wing, a young Chinese apprentice carpenter living in Australia, all the athletes mingled on the field to symbolize friendship and world unity, a tradition that continues today.

In this atmosphere of Olympic Games fever, my track coach, *Madame* Bachet, spoke to me one sunny afternoon by the pool, "You have very strong legs from your ballet lessons and you are my best high jumper. *Monsieur* Vatin and I think you have a chance at the next Olympic Games in Rome. He and I are willing to coach you. But the work and faithfulness to practice have to come from you.

Are you willing to strengthen your legs by swimming 20 laps every morning with a cork board, and also to practice high jumping three days a week after school?"

I was stunned by her offer. Oh yes, I was flattered; but also scared. I thought to myself, "What am I getting into? The Olympics are not some intramural competition; I've already done that. It is serious business. And what country would I be representing? Taiwan? France? Vietnam?"

Finally, with my eyes on my bare feet, hot from the sun-beaten concrete pool side, I ventured, "I will have to ask for my father's permission. I am not sure of his response. Am I really good enough to even try?" I did not want to ask him until I was sure I was worthy. Then, hesitantly, I dared, "What if you train me until Easter, and then, if you still think I am good enough, then I will ask his permission?" Papa had recently said that he doubted Taiwan would be invited next time if the International Olympic Committee thinks it is more important to have mainland China's presence. "What country would I represent?" I asked.

Madame Bachet said, "*Monsieur* Vatin thinks that since you are in a French school you could represent France." They had an answer for all my concerns. So I was willing to go through the difficult training to prove to myself I could do it before getting up the nerve to face my father.

For four months, faithfully and painstakingly, I trained. Every morning I made myself leave the house on my bicycle by six o'clock to do my 20 laps in the Olympic-sized pool. *Monsieur* Vatin was rarely ever at the pool at that hour, so that part was totally up to me. I counted the laps one by one, without fail, grasping the cork board, beating the water until my legs ached.

At home, the only person I confided in was Ah Jie. Although she kept my secret, she didn't fully understand nor approve of what I was doing. She thought I was crazy to get up so early each morning to go swimming. Nonetheless, every day she rinsed and hung my swim suit up to dry. During that time the hair on my legs grew thick and black—I always wondered if it was from all that swimming. Since my nanny thought this was unladylike, she helped me remove the hair by using a painful Chinese technique. She kept one end of a string taut between her teeth while she twisted the other end between her thumbs and index fingers, and ran it up and down my legs to pull the hair out. Ouch and ouch! For centuries Chinese women have used this method to remove facial fuzz they deemed unsightly. What girls put themselves through for some notion of beauty!

One memory of that time that still makes me smile is of my boxer dog Beta. She always accompanied me as my "bodyguard," running next to my bicycle and then sitting by it outside the pool. A friend of papa's, Wu Yong, had brought Beta back from a kennel in Paris. His wife and small children thought Beta was ugly and fierce-looking. They were all a little afraid of her black face. One afternoon when I was at their house for a birthday party, Beta came to me, put her muzzle on my lap, and would not leave. Mrs. Wu said to me, "It looks like Beta has chosen you. If you want her and if your papa says it's ok, take her home, she is yours. It is a sign of good luck when a dog chooses you." Thus Beta became my pet and my mascot. To my knowledge she was the first boxer ever brought to Vietnam. Because people were not accustomed to her looks, they feared her even though she was very gentle. She and I became inseparable.

Madame Bachet was my real trainer. She met me at the high jump sand pit on the appointed afternoons. She coached and yelled, corrected and fussed, pushed and encouraged and cajoled. Over and over I heard, "Again…once more…straighten your legs…take off stronger…." She was demanding and tough. We must have made an odd-looking pair, because she was tall, and her skin was so blue-black that it seemed to shine. She strutted erect, like an African queen, her hair finely braided in rows close to her scalp, with the beautiful legs and derriere of an athlete. She wore very short shorts, red or white, to show off her legs, *a la* Betty Grable. And there I was, 110 pounds of willingness, a short, submissive Asian girl, whom *Madame* Bachet was determined to shape into an Olympic contender. Every day I agonized over the possibility of "to go or not go?"

Then came the moment I had to face my father. Time and time again, I had rehearsed my speech, using every positive argument from my coaches and the good results of four months of training. By that time I was confident in my qualifying to compete. I was able to regularly make the height of the female world record of those years, 5'2".

"Absolutely not!" was his stern answer. "Just last week you received the promise of a two-year full scholarship for St. Catharine in Kentucky. Education has to come before any athletic dreams. You are to start college in a year and a half. The Games in Rome are four years away. What would you do with the glory of a medal, even if you did earn one? We are no longer in the ancient times when Olympic winners returned to their villages to be honored and taken care of for life. Furthermore, it is unacceptable that you even *think* of competing for another country. Are you forgetting that I am a diplomat here in Vietnam? End of discussion!"

My disappointment was deeper than tears. Despite my initial broken heart, I understood the wisdom of my father's words and I submitted. I look back today and see that all the sweat and all the hard work were worth it, for the discipline I learned, the memories I treasure, and the story I get to tell.

Over half a century later, I decided to take my friend DaSoa's advice and applied to be a volunteer interpreter at the 2008 Games in Beijing, the cradle of my parents' youth. As I thought of the excitement of the Games, I wondered what my parents would say to me now that I hoped to at last go to this world event—not as the high jumper I had secretly trained to be, and which papa vetoed in one breath—but as an interpreter, helping in whatever capacity needed.

I researched and reflected on how far the Olympic competition had come since 1956. In Melbourne, 3,184 athletes, representing 67 nations, competed in 147 events, in 17 sports. Beijing will play host to 10,500 athletes who will compete in 28 sports, divided into 302 events. In 1956, my classmates and I could not watch but only hear the results read by our coach. In Beijing, some 20,000 media representatives were accredited to share the Games with the world!

I completed my application to volunteer on-line. A week later,

I received a reply asking my clothing size for the uniform and assigning me a tracking number. I was thrilled and felt I was a likely candidate. After that communication I never again heard from the department of volunteers, despite my several follow-up inquiries. Since I was not chosen to be one of the interpreters I did not make it to Beijing. I was, of course, disappointed not to be there, but I did enjoy the competitions on television, in the comfort of my home, with a far better view than if I had been there.

The opening and closing ceremonies in 2008 were amazing—undoubtedly the most spectacular displays of skills and discipline in such huge groups of performers the world had ever seen. The shows were admired and lauded all over the world as unsurpassable. They were directed by China's famous movie director, Zhang Yimou, whose award-winning 1991 film, *Raise the Red Lantern*, was a memorable depiction of the decadence in a rich family compound in 1920s China. When I made an eight-week trip through the mainland in 2007, my husband Gene and I visited the house that had served as the setting for this film, in the outskirts of Pingyao. It was a complex of 313 rooms built in the 18th century by Qiao Guifa, a merchant who made a fortune in tofu and tea. During that trip I told Gene how 45 years earlier, in papa's office in Tahiti, I wished and predicted that I would one day be able to freely travel through China and climb the Great Wall—a dream that came true.

I think my parents would be in awe at how the world has changed. When papa died in 1969, he never would have dreamed that the athletes from Taiwan would be invited to take part in the Olympic Games held in Beijing. My parents would see this as a positive sign that healing is taking place among the Chinese people, demonstrating to the world that we *can* fulfill the Olympic vision and live in a world of peace.

So long ago, I wrote these words—may they speak to all Olympic competitors of all times:

Spirit of all Generations,
Sacred Vision of the Olympic Games,
In the competition that goes on,

I ask but a field that is fair,
A chance that is equal,
And the courage to dare.
If I should win, let it be by the code,
With my head and my honor held high;
If I should lose, let me stand by the road,
And cheer as the winners go by.

Without papa's permission to participate I discontinued my training and concentrated on my next hurdle, the French National *Baccalaureat*, simply called the *Bac*. In the French educational system, no diploma is given after the completion of 12 years of school. In order to apply to a university, one must pass the *Bac*, which is the equivalent of a university entrance exam. Testing starts with several grueling days of written exams, which, if passed, would allow one to move on to the oral portion. My *Bac* began on June 9, 1958. Over 50 years later I can still remember the questions, as well as a fair amount of my answers. Since I was a member of the literary division in my last years of high school, the subjects I was tested on were French literature, Latin, math, history, and geography. Each test was four hours long, in essay form, answered with multiple hand-written pages of well-argued expose or defense. In addition, for three hours each, I was tested on my two foreign languages, English and Spanish, with points for translation, grammar, and vocabulary.

The secrecy around the material and questions of the exams was tight. They came directly from the Ministry of Education in Paris, in envelopes that were sealed with red wax, broken in plain sight of the candidates moments before the exams were administered. Students received an I.D. number and an assigned classroom and seat. To ensure greater objectivity on the part of the examiners, the grader saw an exam paper with only the I.D. number; all identifying material was stripped away. Aside from demonstrating mastery of the material, the only advantage a student could gain would be using beautiful handwriting. The year I took the *Bac*, to further prevent bias, my teachers in Saigon went to the *Lycée* in

Pnom-Penh, capital of Cambodia, to serve as examiners, and we were tested by the teachers from that school. The examiners were given a week to grade our papers.

Because the tests were not standardized, I wondered, "What if my opinions and points of view differ from those of the examiner? What if he or she was especially tired or irritated?" I felt tremendous pressure. I already had received confirmation of my scholarship to St. Catharine, and I thought, "What if I don't pass my *Bac*? Would the American college accept me anyway, on the strength of my good TOEFL (Test of English as a Foreign Language) scores?"

I had taken and passed the TOEFL at the U.S. Embassy in Saigon. Papa accompanied me to apply for a student visa before he left in April 1958, for his new post in Taiwan. I remember that day as if it were yesterday. When we arrived at the imposing building guarded by armed security personnel, Mr. Helm, one of the Embassy officials whom papa knew, greeted us and showed us to his office. He knew the purpose of our visit and said, "Before I can give your daughter a student visa, she has to pass the TOEFL, that's the English proficiency test for foreigners entering college in the U.S. I'm going to give her some books to study and she can come back to take it in a few days."

Papa answered, "Could you give her the test now? If she doesn't pass it the first time, can she take it again? It would be good to see how well she is prepared with the English she has learned in the French school. How long will it take? I'll send my car back for her." Papa had that kind of confidence in my academics, and fortunately, I passed with a high score.

Going to see whether my *Bac* number was on the list of successful candidates was a nervous time, to say the least. Although I knew I was a good student and well-prepared, passing the scrutiny of several examiners was still a hurdle. I saw my number—wow! I had passed the written part of the *Bac*. What a relief! Many of my friends were also at the gate of our school to look for their results. We jumped on our bicycles and went to the swimming pool snack bar to celebrate with a Coca-Cola poured on a slice of lime and ice cubes—that was the way we liked to drink it to cut the sweetness of a Coke, a fairly new import in Saigon. We commiserated with those who did not pass and discussed how they could study for the chance to take the *Bac* again next year as a *"candidate libre,"* without affiliation to a school.

Next, the oral portion was on the same subjects. Each candidate was given 15 minutes to prepare and the same amount of time to speak on the questions, drawn randomly from a box of printed slips of paper flown in from Paris. I still remember that for my orals in English I drew a text called *Spring on Campus*. I had to read it, translate it, and come up with all the definitions I could think of for the word "spring," as a noun and a verb, and to make complete sentences with the different meanings. All went well. I passed everything! We had a dance party to celebrate our shared milestone (photo 30). Now I could prepare to go to college in the U.S.

The first leg of my journey was to travel on Air France through Hong Kong, with mama and Max, to get some winter clothes for each of us. On the airplane mama and Max sat together and I was taken to a seat a few rows away. Soon after we took off, the Frenchman seated next to me and I started chatting. Since we were departing from Saigon, he wasn't surprised that I spoke French so fluently. He asked the flight attendant to request that the captain allow me to visit the cockpit and see the ocean of clouds from that vantage point. It was an unforgettable sight. From the pilot that day, I learned to wish people who are flying, *"Heureux atterissage"* (Happy landing). Come to find out, my seat companion was himself a pilot, going to Hong Kong for his vacation; that's why he so freely suggested to the stewardess that I be given such a treat. Nowadays it is impossible to visit the cockpit of a plane in flight. How lucky I was.

We were in Hong Kong for two weeks of appointments with tailors, and shopping. I had no idea what the weather would be like in Kentucky and what clothes would be required for the cold, since I had lived all my life in the tropics. A cousin of mama's, Aunt Daisy, was a great consultant and a help during our shopping trips. She talked mama into buying a set of three suitcases for me—I chose a beautiful carmine red. After all the purchases we made, mama said to me, "I've spent a lot more on you than I had intended. You might as well consider all these things your *jia juang* (wedding trousseau). There is no more coming to you even if you should be so lucky as to find a husband. Since you have the chance to go to America with your scholarship, you'd better make something of yourself. It's really not such a bad idea to hide you away in that convent with those Catholic nuns—maybe that's where you are supposed to stay." Once again, I felt worthless in her presence.

Whenever friends or relatives made remarks of admiration, or sometimes even of envy, that I had the chance to go to the U.S. to further my education, mama always retorted, "Good thing she got that scholarship! She would be hopelessly incapable to continue her studies in Taiwan because she is an illiterate in Chinese." Even though I could speak Mandarin fluently, I could only read and write about 300 characters that papa had taught me. Mama loved to hone in on this and call me "illiterate"—a grave insult to the Chinese, who value education as an important privilege. She enjoyed putting me down in front of others. I never understood what satisfaction she gained from belittling me. Most parents brag about their children rather than drawing attention to any shortcomings.

One day in Hong Kong, Uncle Siaoti brought a copy of Alexandre Dumas's *Le Conte de Monte Cristo* when he came to visit. We discussed this long tale of a man wrongly accused and sent to prison, his escape, and his new life. As we talked I saw similarities in my own life: I was about to escape my mother's negative prophesies and would have the chance to make choices for myself.

After completing the shopping in Hong Kong, mama, Max, and I flew to Taipei. I was there for only three weeks, to see papa, before taking off for the U.S. He was working for the first time in the headquarters of the Ministry of Foreign Affairs, where he had been promoted to Director of the Asian Division, by Minister George Yeh. The city of Taipei did not have the feel of opulence, like Hong Kong. It had been only eight years since the Nationalist government moved to the island. Even though there was construction everywhere, and an air of progress, people seemed to be living frugally, as immigrants do in a new country.

Our relatives looked upon us as being "very Westernized," by our mode of dress and, I supposed, even by our actions. In particular, I dressed like a French teenager with spaghetti straps, décolleté dresses, and short shorts. I realized very quickly that I needed to look more conservative to fit in with all the relatives I was seeing. I connected with three girl cousins—Margaret, Linda, and Irene, daughters of mama's favorite playmate, *Ba Gu*. Years later, when I went back to Taipei to take care of mama in her last years, Irene was my only friend for many months. She was aware of my mother's resentment and tried to buffer me from it by coming to visit, spending time with us, and occasionally taking me out for lunch just to get me out of the apartment. During that summer visit, I felt like a fish out of water even though I was able to speak Mandarin fluently. How I blessed papa for having insisted that we speak Chinese at home; otherwise, it would have been embarrassing not to be able to communicate.

On August 24, 1958, I left my childhood (photo 31) and crossed the big Pacific Ocean, with stopovers in Guam and Honolulu, and arrived in San Francisco to meet an unknown destiny.

The Uncrushable Rose

Chapter 8
FLY, FLY TO AMERICA

Somewhere between Guam and Honolulu breakfast was served, and on my tray was a small waxed cardboard box. The label said it was milk, but I had never seen milk served this way. Trying to follow the directions, I made the first tear, but could not figure out how to open it. Seeing me struggle, the woman next to me reached over, took the carton, separated the flaps—which were unusually stuck—pushed the sides in, and poured the milk on my cereal. I was embarrassed but I was grateful for my first lesson in this new culture.

The layover in Honolulu was long enough that old friends of the family, Frances and Jimmy Hsia, picked me up and took me out to breakfast. It was so early that the sky was still dark. While we ate I saw the sun rise over the ocean. What a beautiful place! I thought, "So, this was the island that the Japanese bombed, at Pearl Harbor, on December 7, 1941. What were they thinking to attack a giant such as the United States of America?" In a way it was lucky for me that the U.S. entered World War II in the Pacific. Otherwise, my family and I might not have survived the Japanese concentration camps.

After breakfast my friends' little boy handed me a small piece of red Dentyne chewing gum. I took it from him even though I rarely chewed gum—papa deemed it unladylike, saying it was like "an old cow ruminating." Dentyne gum tasted odd to me since I had only experienced Wrigley spearmint gum, with its green arrow logo—the only flavor known all over the world at the time. Jimmy drove us around and showed me a little of Honolulu. I promised myself that someday I would return to Hawaii, a promise which would wait 42 years to be fulfilled—in 2000 I attended a convention in Honolulu with the Zonta International Club, an organization of business and professional women executives.

My next stop was San Francisco. The Chinese named it "Old Gold Mountain." In the early days of Chinese immigration, the image of Old Gold Mountain was that money—lots of money—could be made there. As my plane landed, I thought, "Is America the land of my destiny? People who are able to come here rarely want to leave. Opportunities are said to abound with success assured as long as one is willing to work. My parents gave me a one-way ticket; there is no going back. Live or die, kid, you are on your own." I felt daring. I was only 18, yet I knew, somehow, that I would make it—because I had to.

A former classmate of mama's, Auntie Sophia, and her husband Honki, picked me up at the San Francisco airport and took me to their home in Oakland. I carried a letter from my parents to them. Auntie Sophia read it and told Honki the content since he could not read Chinese. This was the case of many overseas Chinese who had no opportunity to study their mother tongue. Before we went to the house, Uncle Honki drove to a Western Union office to send a telegram to my school to say I had arrived in the country and needed instruction to get from the Louisville airport to St. Catharine. In those days long distance phone calls were much more costly than today. It would have been an expensive call, so Honki chose to use the telegram.

St. Catharine, Kentucky was such a small town that it did not show up on any map I had consulted. In their home, Uncle Honki was finally able to find it on a Kentucky state road map. He told me it was some 60 miles south of Louisville. I was relieved that this place really existed.

The next day a telegram came in my name: "Greyhound bus leaving Louisville 4:30, arriving St. Catharine 6:10. Classes started yesterday. Come promptly." It was signed by Sister Jean Marie, the same person who signed my scholarship award letter. I had no idea what "greyhound" meant. I took out my dictionary, looked up the word, and, to my puzzlement, read that it was a type of dog frequently used for racing. My first thought was, "Surely they don't use dogs! Would I travel on a bus that also transports this type of dogs? What a strange country!" I was totally confused but too embarrassed to ask Auntie Sophia what "Greyhound bus" really meant. I thought, "My plane ticket for Louisville is not until the day after tomorrow. Maybe she'll say something that will help me understand."

That evening after dinner, before Auntie Sophia went upstairs to read to her children, she handed me two copies of the *Saturday Evening Post* and said, "This is a magazine that deals with life in this country and American views on world events. It will help you understand the culture and the people's attitudes. So much will be new to you. Your transition from a French style of living to an American life will be less of a shock to you than when I came to the States to marry Uncle Honki after the war. You are younger and you will be in school with American girls. You will have much to learn, but it will be easier for you to adapt."

Uncle Honki went to his study to work on his stamp collection. He was a kind and thoughtful person, but not very talkative. My English was limited, so I was happy to settle on the living room sofa and flip through those magazines. I remember papa had many copies of the *Post*. When I was in high school and studying English and Spanish, I used to search and cut pictures out of that magazine to make my vocabulary notebooks. The teachers said that we would remember the meaning better if we had made the effort to look for a picture to represent each object, instead of using just the word translation. In our notebooks, only pictures—cut out or drawn by us—were allowed. I recalled looking for two *papillons* to represent "butterfly" in English and *mariposa* in Spanish. Even 60 years later I recall those exact images when I think "butterfly" or *mariposa.*

As I sat on Auntie Sophia's couch and turned the pages of the *Post,* suddenly I came upon a full page advertisement of an ideal family of four—mother, father, a boy, and a girl with a doll in her arms—traveling on a long, shiny Greyhound bus. I had never seen a bus so big and comfortable-looking. Oh, the relief on my mind! I thought, "So this is what I will be riding on from Louisville to St. Catharine. Wonderful!"

The next morning Auntie Sophia showed me how to make a bed, realizing that I had never had to do that before. She said, "You will be with Catholic nuns. They are the most disciplined, neatest, and demanding people in my experience. For a short time I worked as a nurse in a Catholic hospital in Shanghai. Let me show you how they would probably want you to tuck the sheets." She had me sit down and she demonstrated. "They call them 'hospital corners,' and they make the bed have a finished look."

At lunch time Sophia fixed a fresh fruit plate with cottage cheese. I watched her peel a cantaloupe at the sink. To my horror, I saw her shove the peeling and seeds into the drain. I thought, "Why is she doing this? She is going to plug up the sink!" Then I saw her reach over and turn on a switch; a whirling motor noise came on and the sink was cleaned of all she had dropped in it. Seeing the stunned look on my face, she explained, "This is called a garbage disposal. When you turn it on, be sure your hands are out of the drain, and that cold water is running to help move the garbage out and to keep the motor cooled. There are some things you cannot put in, such as the shucks and silk of an ear of corn; they are too fibrous for the grinder and could overload the motor." In the two and half days I stayed with Sophia she taught me several useful things that would serve me in my new life.

The other thing that impressed me was the way Sophia spoke to and cared for her two children, Leslie and Alberta. They were about 10 and 8 years old. When they came home from school, Sophia had milk and cookies for them in the kitchen, which they shared with me. Then from the vestibule coat closet she took out two large plastic circles and we all went out in the front yard. The children showed me how to work the "hula-hoops," which were the rage in those days. I watched the whole scene in amazement and thought, "Mother never played with us like this." She had bought us toys from the French department stores, at Charner or Courtinat in Saigon, but she rarely spent time with us and she surely never played with us. Sometimes she would take a moment to look at the structures Max had built with his metal Meccano set—a precursor of today's plastic Legos—only because he asked her to buy additional pieces to make larger and fancier designs. Other than that she rarely paid attention to our interests.

I thought of my most memorable toy—a blackboard. I had asked for it because I liked to play school. Mama decided to take me to the Courtinat store to buy me a birthday present. Lucky me! My birthday is the day after Christmas so we could expect that all the leftover toys would be on sale. Even though we were in Southeast Asia, Christmas was celebrated as it was in France. I had seen several blackboards before Christmas and was hoping they were not all sold. Mama chose a small board with the edges painted red. Because it did not stand very tall, I was disappointed. While she was paying for it I dared, "Mama, I like the bigger one, with the yellow frame much better. I really will be a teacher when I grow up. Please Mama, I beg you, get me the yellow one. It's on sale and costs the same as the red one did before the sale." I was not sure mama would pay attention to me, but I knew that, if I did not speak then, there would be no chance to get what I really wanted. To my great surprise and joy, I heard her say to the saleslady, "My daughter likes the bigger one better, so we will take it instead. Today is her birthday." I was eleven. I think that was my first experience of being an "opportunist"—to grab opportunities before they are lost forever. So many years later I still think of that beautiful toy blackboard with great affection. The yellow stand brought it to eye level for me. It had several rows of colorful counting beads and a little drawer for my pieces of white and colored chalk, which were included. Many years later, when I was taking care of mama in her late eighties, I talked to her about old events in our lives to spark her memory. I brought up how grateful I was to her for buying that blackboard for me. She remarked, "Yes, I remember that board, it was pretty." She didn't say whether she realized that it had meant so much to me.

On the morning before Auntie Sophia took me to the airport, we stopped at a railroad station to send one of my suitcases on to the college because I had too much luggage for the domestic flight. It cost $18. Sophia also took me to cash a couple of my $20 traveler's checks so I would be able to pay for bus fare and other expenses, in case the bus ticket counter did not accept American Express checks. Inside I felt a moment of panic, thinking, "Of the $500 I have to live on for the foreseeable future, $60 is gone. How will I manage?"

I was fortunate that an acquaintance of papa's, Mr. Chen, picked me up at the airport in Louisville. He drove me to the Greyhound bus depot, helped buy my ticket, and showed me to the waiting room. After I sat down, I looked up and saw a sign that said, "Whites Only." I saw there were only white people in the room. I was the only Asian, so I picked up my bags and went into the room that said "Colored." An elderly black woman said to me, "Little miss, you don't belong here. You have to go to the other side. This is for colored only." Thoroughly confused I said, "I am not white, I am colored too—I am yellow." Again I thought, "What a strange country! Do people here place you in different waiting rooms according to the color of your skin?"

All my life I had gone to school seated next to black or white French children, yellow Asians, and caramel East Indians. I never really paid attention to the differences. I also played with children from other embassies—from different countries, different races, and different languages, although most of them spoke French or English. I remembered seeing a newsreel the year before, about some black students going into a high school under the protection of several policemen. It was in an American city with an odd name, "Little Pebble," I thought, "or something like that. Oh, I remember, it was Little Rock." It was unbelievable to me that these kids had to be taken to school by policemen and to face an angry mob of white people just because of the color of their skin. Now here I was in America facing the issue of skin color first-hand. It was disturbing. But I did not have much time to ponder. Soon I boarded the bus—with no greyhound dogs—and arrived in St. Catharine as it was getting dark.

One of the nuns, wearing an off-white habit with a black veil, met me at the bus stop, alongside a large red brick building. She helped me carry my two bags. I was embarrassed because they were heavy—this was long before suitcases had wheels. Years later, when I was a tour director and had to deal with a lot of the travelers' luggage, I had a funny thought, "The North Americans put a man on the moon before they put wheels on suitcases."

The nun said, "I am Sister Catharine Gertrude. We have been expecting you. Welcome to St. Catharine. This is the side of the convent. Now we're going to walk to the other side of this building where the college and the academy are."

"Thank you for meeting me and helping with my heavy bags," I said. "I am looking forward to college. Is the academy a different school?"

"Yes, it's a boarding school for high school girls. You won't see very much of them. They are in a separate area. I am the college registrar, so you will come to my office tomorrow and I'll help you choose your classes. For now, I'll take you to the dormitory and Sister John Marie will help you get settled."

We walked through several dimly lit halls, three wide wooden doors, and two sets of imposing staircases, on slick, shiny, hollow-sounding parquet floors. They reminded me of scenes in old movies, like *Rebecca* and *Jane Eyre*. "I'll never find my way back here," I thought. Finally we arrived at Sister John Marie's room. Her door was ajar. She was seated at her desk, correcting papers. The whole place was so totally silent that it was a little eerie.

The two nuns whispered briefly, then Sister Gertrude left. Sister John Marie took me to my room in silence, a couple of doors from hers. Wow, it was a private room! I had expected to have a roommate and was delighted that I didn't have to share. There was a brown metal bed with a mattress but no sheets, a desk, a chair, an armoire, a hand sink, and an overhead light. "Did you bring any sheets and blankets?" she whispered. I had not. Within a few minutes she brought me a neat stack of two sheets, a blanket, a pillow with a case, and a bedspread, and set them all on top of the mattress. "Thank goodness Auntie Sophia had shown me how to make a bed!" I thought. "I'll use her lesson right now."

I emptied my suitcases and began to put away the things I had brought from home, so far away—things that I had chosen carefully, in view of the limited space in my bags. On my desk I found a list of rules and regulations and sat down to read them. I learned that it was so quiet because I had arrived during the nightly two-hour silent study time. I was relieved to learn of this rule because I preferred to study in silence. After reading the rules I noticed that something was under the paper. I lifted it and was elated to discover two letters from Siaoti. Tears came to my eyes. How could he be so thoughtful as to have these letters waiting, to assure me that he was thinking of me? I eagerly read his words of encouragement and of missing me. It felt so sweet to be loved! My parents did not want us to correspond. What was I to do?

After basking in his love for a while, I returned to the task at hand: finishing putting away my belongings. I had imagined being in much more confined quarters. Suddenly, music came on, and voices in the hall and in the room next to mine told me it must be 9 o'clock, the end of study-hours. Quickly I turned off my light. I did not want to deal with my future classmates; "Tomorrow will be soon enough," I thought.

At six o'clock the next morning Sister John Marie knocked on then opened my door and whispered, *"Benedicite."* I was startled awake, surprised to have been addressed in Latin. She whispered that I was supposed to respond with *"Deo gratias."* With my six years of Latin in school and my Catholic background, I had no problem understanding what those phrases meant: "May you be blessed," and "Thanks be to God." Again she whispered to me, "Quickly, get ready for Mass; we keep the grand silence until breakfast. Here is a little chapel veil for you to use this morning," she added, as she handed me a small square of black lace to wear on my head. The sink in my room had hot and cold water. How great that I was able to wash up in the privacy of my room. I got dressed and lined up with the other girls at the head of the stairs. They were all white girls. They smiled at me, but in keeping the monastic grand silence from bedtime to breakfast, no one said a word.

From the dormitory we walked downstairs to another building where the chapel was. Mass was said in Latin by a very tall priest. I found out later he was also my theology professor, Father Newman. How comforting it was to worship with my new classmates and the nuns in the beautiful chapel on my first morning at St. Catharine College. The nuns here were Dominican Sisters, a very old order founded in Italy by Saint Dominic in 1215. This convent of nuns in Kentucky started their first school in 1823 and founded their junior college in 1931. I felt so grateful to Archbishop Yu Pin (photo 24) for placing me there. I would have the opportunity to both get my education and start every day with prayer and meditation. I vowed to take advantage of all this place had to offer.

After Mass we all filed into the dining room and the girls started to chatter. Soon I was surrounded by several others and invited to sit at a table with three of them. The questions started to rain. "Where are you from?" was never an easy question for me to answer. I was born in and came from Vietnam, but I am not Vietnamese. Later, when the U.S. was so sadly involved in the war in Vietnam, I didn't want to say I was from Vietnam; I couldn't blame Americans for being bitter about a war which, to so many, seemed senseless. Yes, I was Chinese, but I didn't come from China, nor had I ever really lived there. My origins and where I belonged were never a simple matter to explain. Sometimes I felt like I had no roots, like I belonged nowhere. As I matured I came to understand that I am truly a citizen of the world, and all of that stopped bothering me.

"Where are your folks?"—I did not understand what "folks" meant. Andrea Preston, a very tall girl and my next door neighbor in the dorm, came to my rescue and told me that "folks" meant parents or family. Some of my classmates had an odd accent that I realized was not the more formal American accent I wanted to learn. I later found out they spoke with what is called a Kentucky accent, one kind of southern accent.

This first meal in my American college was a shock to my taste buds. I was served coffee—or rather, what they called coffee—tasteless to me. I was accustomed to French roast coffee, dark, strong, and fragrant, drunk with creamy hot milk to make it a *café au lait*, served by my nanny with a flaky warm croissant, sometimes with ham and eggs, and occasionally my favorite pastry, *pain au chocolat*. I was introduced to American breakfast cereals, Cheerios—which meant 'so long' to me in British English—Rice Krispies, and Corn

Flakes, which I liked best. When my table companion passed me the glass pitcher of milk, it did not look like the right color for milk, and it turned out to be chalky, thin, and awful tasting. What happened? I had always heard that American milk is the best in the world—fresh, rich, and creamy. I found out later that the nuns had their own dairy farm and, because the butterfat had been skimmed off to make butter, what was left over and served to us was called "skim" milk. The bread we were served was factory-baked, white, soft, and mushy.

I remembered that the first time I experienced such bread was in Saigon. I had spent the afternoon playing with Chrissy Haroldson, one of the children from the American embassy. Her mother, Kitty, had served us peanut butter and grape jelly sandwiches for a snack. It was delicious, but the bread stuck to the roof of my mouth. I thought, "If she had spread the same peanut butter and jelly on a chunk of crusty French bread, it would have been so much better." Kitty also gave us each a candy bar called *Three Musketeers*, a combination of chocolate, nougat, and caramel. I was captivated that an American product carried a French-sounding name that was as familiar to me as Alexandre Dumas' *Trois Mousquetaires*. It turned out to be too sweet for my taste. Before I went home, Mrs. Haroldson gave me a gold foil square package with the picture of a young woman dressed in blue and the brand name *Blue Bonnet*. She said, "I am sending this to your mother. It's American butter, less fattening than French butter. The last time I saw her she said she was gaining weight. This will help her." Later I found out that it was called "margarine," made from vegetable oil and colored yellow. I admit that my French-trained taste buds never accepted it as a butter substitute. It is interesting that what we become accustomed to in childhood affects our preferences the rest of our lives.

Over the next few meals at St. Catharine, I observed that my classmates' table manners were different than what I had learned in French school. Most of the time they kept their left hands in their laps instead of having their forearms propped up on the edge of the table. Every time after they had cut a piece of meat, they put down their knives diagonally, at about "two o'clock" on the plates, with the blades turned inward, then changed their forks to their right hands to carry the morsel of food into their mouths. It seemed like a lot of wasted motion compared to the European way of keeping the knife in the right hand and using the fork in the left. I would have to learn this new way. Papa used to remind me to observe the people around me and imitate what they do. He had recounted how he followed what others did when he attended state funerals, which included Catholic Mass at the Cathedral in Saigon. All the rituals were totally foreign to him, so he took his cue from watching others. Here in America I was concerned about looking ignorant or "FOB" (fresh off the boat). So I adopted the formula, "When in Rome, do as the Romans do."

After breakfast my next event was to go to the college office of this imposing building to meet Sister Jean Marie, dean of the college, whose perfectly scripted American-style handwriting I had seen as the signature on my scholarship papers. She was a petite woman. Her beautiful face, chin, and neck were framed by a tight white wimple topped with a stiff black veil, which draped from shoulder to shoulder and fell all the way past her waist. Her piercing eyes seemed to see right through your thoughts. Briefly she welcomed me then turned me over to Sister Catherine Gertrude, the nun who had met me at the bus stop the evening before. Since she was the registrar, she guided me through my choice of classes for the first semester and showed me to the bookstore. The scholarship I received from St. Catharine was a "full scholarship," which included tuition, room, board, and fees, but I had to pay for the books.

Another nun gathered the books I needed, along with a black lace chapel veil, which was to be uniformly worn to the religious services morning and evening. The total bill came to $82. I felt the blood rush to my head. The shipping of my suitcase from California, the bus ticket, and the books already had cost $140 of my $500 — in just the first week in America! Fear gripped me as I thought, "How am I going to go through four years of college on $500?" I knew I could not ask for any more money from home. Mama had told me over and over again that I had overstepped my bounds when I asked Archbishop Yu Pin for a scholarship. Since he gave it to me, my parents felt obligated to follow through and send me to America. Although they thought that educating my brother was more important than sending me to college, their hands had been forced. For a brief moment I questioned my decision to come. Was it pure foolishness or even the sin of pride? There was no turning back, but, "Surely there will be a way," I thought. "Other Chinese students with little money have come to this country, and they made it to graduation and success, so why can't I?"

With this resolve, I attended my first class—theology with Father Newman. I panicked. I understood very little of what he said. I saw that I needed to read ahead to be able to follow his teaching. It was not going to be easy. Sister Catherine Gertrude only assigned four courses to me, each held three periods a week—theology, algebra, English, and logic. I could see I would have to do at least two hours of study for each hour of lecture. I had taken algebra in high school, so it would not be too difficult, though I never had liked math. Sister John Marie, who was teaching it, offered extra help if I needed it, during study-time in the dormitory. Sister Jean Marie, the dean, was my professor in English 101. She assigned a lot of grammar to review, which would be much easier for me than spoken English.

My greatest challenge came when I was introduced to the course of Thomistic logic, taught by Sister Stella Maris. On the first day she warned us, "Do not make a mistake with my name, it is not Stella Marie. Does anyone know what Stella Maris means?"

No one spoke, so I raised my hand, "It means 'star of the sea' in Latin, Sister." She seemed surprised and pleased that I answered. Although Sister Stella Maris spoke very clearly and distinctly, I had a difficult time distinguishing the differences between major and minor premises, the twists and turns of syllogisms, and deductive reasoning from the general to the specific. She was also the librarian. Her stiff demeanor made her seem unapproachable and severe, but she, too, offered to give me extra help. It seemed they all realized my difficulty with English. At St. Catharine there was no such thing as English as a second language class (ESL) as is common in universities that accept many foreign students. I was the only foreign student at St. Catharine that year.

I got through the first day of class having been bombarded with questions by my classmates. Some had never seen an Asian face to face. I had a terrible time understanding the local accent and they had a hard time understanding me because I had learned British English and spoke with a French accent. What a funny combination! I knew I needed to work at smoothing out my American English. What is language learning but imitating the sounds I hear spoken around me? It was very important to me to find the right American English accent to emulate because I knew that the spoken word is very important when you first meet people and try to communicate.

Fortunately, a few evenings later, as I sat in the social room watching the evening news on television, I came upon the Huntley and Brinkley Report on NBC. Immediately I recognized that theirs was the American English I wanted to learn. From then on, Monday through Friday evenings, faithfully I watched the 15-minute news report. I stayed in the back of the room so I could mimic what they were saying, repeating softly as many words as I could. A lot of the time I did so without understanding the meaning, but I got their sounds into my ears. Chet Huntley spoke the bulk of the news from New York and David Brinkley mainly reported news of the national capital, since he was in Washington, D.C. Their nightly reports became the window through which I saw the world. Their newscast was expanded to 30 minutes in 1963, as life and world events became more complicated. I witnessed the events of the late 1950s and 60s through their eyes and their voices—President Kennedy's inauguration, the Cuban Missile Crisis and Bay of Pigs, the assassinations of John and Bobby Kennedy and Martin Luther King, Jr., the horrors of the Vietnam War, the anti-war and anti-draft protests, and many more events that shaped our world.

In Saigon there was no television. We got the news there by reading the newspapers and listening to the radio in French. The first television I saw was in Hong Kong in 1958.

At St. Catharine there was only one television set in the dormitory social room, just as in most American homes in those days. We gathered around this centerpiece of furniture to receive the news almost like a daily sacrament, with Huntley and Brinkley as its officiating high priests. In the spring of 1962, I was chosen as a delegate to a convention of Catholic colleges and universities meeting in New York, near Saint Patrick's Cathedral. I was walking down the street when suddenly I saw a man who looked like Chet Huntley coming my direction. I don't know where I found the courage or the presence of mind to call out, "Mr. Huntley, is it really you?"

He smiled and stopped, "Yes, the last time I checked."

In a few words I told him that he had been my English teacher since 1958, and that I attempted to imitate his speech during his newscast. He said, "You won't see me next week. I'll be fishing in Maine."

I handed him the convention program I was carrying to get his autograph and pleaded, "Oh, please, ask Mr. Brinkley to mention it when he will be broadcasting alone, otherwise no one will believe that I met you when I get back to college in Memphis."

As he returned my program he said, "You can show them my autograph. Thanks for telling me that I've been your coach."

The following week, as David Brinkley handled the broadcast alone he mentioned that Chet was fishing in Maine. I wondered whether Chet ever mentioned to David that he had met a Chinese student who told him that their nightly reports were her daily speech lessons.

I still remember Chet Huntley's last broadcast, on July 31, 1970, when David Brinkley signed off by saying, "Goodbye, Chet," instead of his customary, "Good night, Chet." After their team broke up, I no longer felt that I could trust the veracity of all that was reported.

I was in Warsaw, Missouri when Chet Huntley died, on March 20, 1974, about the time I sent applications for graduate school to three universities. The news of his passing reminded me of his great influence on my English, which had given me much-needed confidence. It also spurred me on to move through the pains and challenges of a recent divorce, taking what I had learned from him into my future.

David Brinkley died in Houston on June 11, 2003, of complications from a fall. I learned of it while I was recuperating from hip surgery at home in Kansas City. I mourned the death of each of these two giants of television journalism because they had shaped my view of the world almost like father figures. They were the symbols of a generation when news reports were purely factual rather than being sensationalized. Watching television news continues to be part of my daily routine, but I will always miss the Huntley and Brinkley reports. Many Americans of my generation would understand my acute nostalgia for them.

At St. Catharine my schooling went smoothly. Since I was accustomed to a French high school's heavy load of homework, I found classes relatively easy, once my ears adjusted to American English, having been trained in British English. I wrote to my parents and Max once a week, reporting to them what I was doing and what my life was like in the U.S. I did not receive a letter from them during the first four weeks. At first I was disappointed, then I became worried, feeling homesick and abandoned. After a while, I realized I was no longer in my family's field of concern and that, because the direction I had decided to take for my life was totally my responsibility, I would have to shoulder the consequences without them. I had a feeling of being pushed out of the nest like a bird being sent out to fly and become independent.

I thought back to the time I met Chinese Archbishop Yu Pin, when he visited Saigon in 1955. He was there to see his former classmate, Bishop Ngo Ding Thuc, brother of Vietnam's first president, Ngo Ding Diem. Since my parents often organized garden parties for visiting officials, they held a big gathering for Yu Pin and many Chinese community leaders of Cholon, Saigon's Chinatown. When Yu Pin realized I was Catholic, by my knowing the protocol of kissing his ring, he asked if I would like to go to the U.S. to further my education. It had been my dream for years, but without a scholarship it would be too expensive. Yu Pin said, "If you have good grades I will find you a scholarship in a Catholic college. I like to place young women with nuns. They are good teachers and train their students to be useful in the family, workplace, and society. Give me the record of your grades and I promise I will find you a school." I felt my prayers had been answered and kept my hope on his promise.

I received confirmation of the scholarship to St. Catharine in January 1958, a few days before the celebration of the hundredth anniversary of the first apparition of the Blessed Virgin in Lourdes, France, on February 11, 1858. During the commemorative candlelight procession at the cathedral in Saigon, I made a vow, "As an act of gratitude for this scholarship, if my life is good in America, in 50 years I will go to Lourdes to celebrate the 150th jubilee."

In 1858, Lourdes went from being a small village known only in the Pyrenees to being a global attraction, especially to the Catholic world. That year, a 14-year-old peasant girl, Bernadette Soubirous, claimed that she saw, "…in the crevice of the rock, a young girl, surrounded by light, who looked at me and smiled." Seventeen more visions followed during which the "lady" requested that a chapel be built, that people pray, and that Bernadette dig for a spring and wash herself with the spring's water. Many people asked Bernadette who this lady was. She was unsure, and simply called her "the lady." Finally, the apparition declared, "I am the Immaculate Conception," which identified her as Mary, the mother of Jesus. Little Bernadette had no knowledge or understanding that four years earlier the Vatican had pronounced the Immaculate Conception of Mary as a dogma of faith. Bernadette did find the spring, which since then has produced some 27,000 gallons of water per week. Chemically this water has no curative properties, but many faithful believe it to be healing.

In November 2008, four days after Barack Obama was elected 44th president of the United States, my husband Gene and I left on our much-anticipated trip to Lourdes (photo 58). What a feeling of fulfillment and gratitude to be able to complete a vow made five decades before, with the added blessing of making the voyage in the company of my soulmate. Gene and I took an icy dip in the specially made pools, in separate areas for women and men. We undressed in private cubicles and put on the knee-length cotton capes that had been provided. We walked down two steps into the pool, aided by a volunteer. After immersing ourselves, and before we walked out of the water, we were invited to kiss the porcelain statue at the end of the pool if we wished. Then we returned to our dressing cubicles. The capes were dripping wet and we dropped them into a plastic basket. When Gene and I got back together, we talked about how, surprisingly, immediately after removing the drenched capes, our bodies were dry enough to dress without having to use towels.

The Catholic Church is careful to declare only a few of Lourdes' healings to be miracles. Yet it is difficult to explain some of the unusual occurrences there. Bernadette was reputed to have said, "To those who believe, no explanation is necessary; to those who do not believe, no explanation is possible." Lourdes is the second most popular tourism city in France, second to Paris in the number of hotels—almost 300—accommodating some five million visitors a year. I had been to Lourdes many times during the five years I worked as a tour director to Catholic shrines, but my 2008 trip was particularly significant because it was the completion of my vow and an act of thanksgiving for the education I received at St. Catharine. Thanks to this education innumerable doors were opened to me. In the autumn of my life, I want the stories of my experiences and the many blessings I have received from my education to benefit others.

Living in a college dormitory became a problem for me on holidays because, as I suddenly found out, the place shut down and I became "homeless." The Tuesday before Thanksgiving, my classmates took off for home at the end of the school day. Sister John Marie, the dorm mother, explained that I needed to go somewhere, too. I did not understand the situation so I contacted papa's friend, Mr. Chen, the one who had picked me up at the Louisville airport when I first arrived. He said I could stay in his home. So I spent my first Thanksgiving feeling like an imposition on his American wife and little boy. I promised myself that in the future, if I were to make my home in the United States, I would buy a house near the campus of a university and help foreign students get accustomed to their new environment and American culture. I would answer their questions and make them feel at home.

My parents helped me address the problem of being "homeless" during the two weeks of Christmas vacation by arranging for me to visit their classmates from Yenching University, Auntie Pearl and Uncle C.T. Miao, who had been living in Flushing, New York for many years. I thought back to our first meeting, in Hong Kong the summer before, while they were there on vacation and we were there to procure winter clothes. At that time, their daughter K.K. was 16 and their son Raymond was 14. I remember feeling quite awkward because I could not communicate with them well—they spoke no Chinese and I spoke very little English. Right then I really understood Father's lesson that having a Chinese face means we must at least be able to speak Chinese when spoken to. We could never change our ethnic origin, and it would be so much more pleasant and friendly if we could communicate with people we meet from our motherland.

The train trip from Louisville to New York City was my first since the time I went from the Moi village to the Japanese concentration camp in Phu Luong. During the forty-some-hour trip I worried about spending money in the dining car so I did not even go there. Instead I bought only one sandwich from a food cart. The round trip ticket cost $78. Over $200 of my $500 were now gone. An enormous snowstorm stopped the train for hours. Looking out the window I didn't know what to think. I had never seen that much snow. When I finally arrived in New York, Uncle C.T. was there to pick me up. What a relief! He said the train was seven hours late. Again, I felt like an imposition for holding him up because he had to wait so long.

So I spent my first Christmas in the U.S. with the whole Miao family (photo 32), who treated me very kindly. They took me to several parties, including a New Year's Eve dance. K.K. told her mother she didn't want me to wear a Chinese dress because it looked too old-fashioned. So Auntie Pearl gave her some money and told us to go shopping. K.K. took me on the subway to Manhattan. I was incredulous at the sight of the graffiti on the walls and the newspapers and other trash strewn on the floor. "Where is the respect for common property?" I thought. "No one looks you in the eye; they all seem very preoccupied. There is no person-to-person connection." I was glad that even though I had been in the country only three months I could chat with K.K. comfortably in English. The streets, the stores, and the display windows were decorated to the nth degree. I was dazzled by the opulence of the stores and the volume of merchandise. I followed K.K. as she headed for the sale racks at Macy's. There she selected a deep purple, chiffon, spaghetti-strap dress for me and had me try it on. When she asked me if I liked it, I said yes, so she just bought it. I was very impressed at how K.K. acted so decisively and with such maturity. She was only 16, two years younger than I. I admired her and wondered if I would *ever* be so at ease shopping in America, with money to spend. Since I now had less than $300, I held on to it like a miser and simply could not imagine a day when I would have extra money of my own to spend on luxuries.

The New Year's Eve dance took place in the ballroom of a fancy hotel in the city. Almost all the people attending were Chinese, since it was the gathering of some Chinese club. K.K. was with her American boyfriend, Steve. Uncle C.T. invited a young Chinese man to be my date. He was what was called an "A.B.C."—American-Born Chinese. He did not speak Chinese and seemed totally unaware of any world outside of New York. Our conversation was sparse and uneasy. Fortunately, the music was so loud that it made talking unnecessary. He brought me a pretty red corsage that clashed with my purple dress. I thought, "So be it. It is still wonderful to have a fresh flower in the dead of winter," and I considered it to be a sweet gesture, unaware that it was an American custom that the young man was to bring his date a corsage. Steve gave K.K. a beautiful wrist corsage. After the dance she pinned it on the cork bulletin board in her bedroom, where several other dried corsages were trophies of past dances. K.K. and Steve were openly affectionate toward each other in front of her parents and me, behavior that my parents would not have permitted. So much public display of affection was one of many points of culture here that differed from my upbringing.

Uncle C.T. worked in the Chinese division of the United Nations. One morning I rode with him to work. He showed me around the impressive building that I had seen many times in pictures. Since he was an insider, he had access to places off limits to tourists. He took me to the interpreters' booth, even though there was no conference taking place at the time. "You already know four of the five official U.N. languages," he said. "You may want to consider training to become an interpreter or a translator in the U.N. It's a much-needed service and it pays well."

That's when I admitted, "Oh, Uncle C.T., I have so little money left for college. My parents gave me $500 before I left home, with no more to come in the future. I have already spent nearly half of it in my first semester alone. I do have a full academic scholarship for my first two years, but there are a lot of extra expenses. And how am I going to make it through *four* years? Mama said I was foolish to think so big as to dare come to the U.S. But, now that I am here, I *have* to make it." He was the only person to whom I confided the reality of my situation.

He was quick to answer, "Don't worry about money, Bambi. You can get a summer job and earn enough for your next year expenses. You can come back here, and I'll help you find a job." Prior to his reassurance and offer to help, I had been very worried about how I could manage financially, because I didn't know how easy it was to find a job in America if one is willing to work.

I wasn't sure if Uncle C.T. realized how much he had put my mind at ease. When he took me to the train station, he stuck a twenty-dollar bill in my hand and said, "Eat something during your trip." I was deeply touched by his compassion and thoughtfulness, and gratefully accepted his gift. Those were the most unexpected and helpful twenty dollars I ever received in my life. During all the eleven years I owned restaurants I made a conscious effort to pay back his kindness by passing it on. After closing my business for the day I would often stop for dinner on my way home. I would ask the hostess to assign to me a server who was a student, and after enjoying the meal I would leave him or her a $20 tip.

My next bout of "homelessness" was during spring break in

my freshman year. This was also solved by one of papa's friends, Chou Er-hsun, a colleague from their first post in Saigon in 1936. He sent me a round-trip train ticket to visit him and his family—a wife and two teenage children, Cissy and Winston. Uncle Chou was on the staff of the Taiwan Chinese embassy in Washington. During my stay I was able to get in touch with an old friend from Saigon, Suzanne Tihon, whose parents had taken my family in shortly after we got out of our last concentration camp. Suzanne introduced me to several of her Chinese friends, also students. They all promised they could help me find a summer job in Washington, or at some resort, assuring me that it would be easy to make enough money for the next school year.

I decided to go back to D.C. for the summer, both for the promised help finding a job and because I wanted to investigate a scholarship for my third and fourth year at some university there, since St. Catharine was only a junior college. Suzanne told me the easiest job to find was that of a waitress. She gave me some pointers about how to take orders and how to carry a tray, then took me to a Howard Johnson's Restaurant. The hostess, Margaret Peters, interviewed me and hired me on the spot. An added blessing was that she rented me a room in her apartment for only seven dollars a week, while her husband was away in the U.S. army. In those days, because of the military draft, there were a lot of "single-for-the-moment" women with rooms to rent. She also scheduled me to work the same shift as hers so I could ride to work with her. I told her the truth that I had never worked as a waitress, so she taught me all I needed to know—knowledge that I put to good use then and also many years later when I was in the restaurant business. The first table I served was that of a single woman who left me 15 cents. When I told Margaret, she said, "She must have been especially pleased with you because she normally only tips 10 cents." I thought she probably realized I was a poor student needing this summer job and wanted to encourage me. That summer and in my first year in this new country I learned so much that set the tone for how I lived and acted for many years to come.

In Washington I made enough friends that I had several options of places to go the next time the dormitory was shut down. I made plans to continue college in this capital city. But an accident changed my destiny. In March 1960, on an unusually warm day during gym class at St. Catharine, my physical education coach set up the high-jump equipment. I was delighted to see it, as I remembered all the effort I put into training during high school and the satisfaction it brought—it was challenging and fun to push my body to do beyond what was expected, and a real joy when I succeeded.

My classmates and I lined up to take turns jumping. I watched them do the "scissors" as they went over the elastic rope. When it came to my turn, I naturally did the "roll over" as my French coach, *Madame* Bachet, had instructed me to do so many times. The girls were impressed and wanted me to teach them how I did it. Over and over I repeated the moves, to demonstrate, when suddenly I landed incorrectly. I sustained a compound fracture of my left ankle. My classmates screamed! I was horrified by the sound of my bones cracking and then by the sight of them sticking out of my skin. My first thoughts were, "Oh my God, I am going to miss school!" and, "How much is this going to cost?" A nun called the ambulance, and a sister-nurse from the infirmary came and gave me a shot to reduce the pain and to calm me down.

The ambulance took me to Lebanon, Kentucky, a few miles away, where some of the sisters of St. Catharine's convent staffed the hospital. I immediately had emergency surgery. Afterwards I was cared for by a nurse named Elizabeth Browning; we talked about how she shared the name with the famous poet. I was in a cast from my toes to my thigh and had to walk with two crutches. Several women who were hospital volunteers came to visit me with flowers and Easter candy, as it was nearing the holiday, which came on April 17 that year. Mrs. Agnes Williams was one of those volunteers. When she learned I had no place to go during Easter vacation/spring break, she invited me to her home. She and her husband Cy were an older couple with no children. They owned a typical American country general store, in Lebanon, Kentucky, a town of about 4,500. I was amazed at their generosity and gladly accepted their invitation.

Every day during my visit, Agnes drove Cy to work so she could keep their light blue four-door Chevy Impala for us to do our running around. Cy's general store was something I had never seen before. The floor was made of rough wood planks, never stained or varnished, which were swept clean daily. There were so many things packed in, everywhere, that only a narrow path remained for us to walk through. One could smell a mixture of aromas—no wonder, given the diversity of stuff in there. A couple of new saddles hung on the wall. The cash register was decorated with ornate brass and clanked with a distinct sound when a button was pushed to open it. A three foot tall wooden barrel of dill pickles was kept in front of the counter, and Cy always dipped one out for me when I visited. I loved the taste when I bit into it and didn't mind the juice running down my arm. I found it was less sour than the French small *cornichons* I was accustomed to. I saw beautiful oval, copper wash tubs, used to boil laundry, as well as galvanized tin washbasins. Many garden tools and farming implements stuck out of wooden barrels; I had little idea what they were used for or what they were called. Bolts of fabric, mostly plain-colored, some with plaids and small flowers—all very old-fashioned looking—were standing vertically in a row at the end of a long counter. There a yard stick had been nailed onto the edge, and a pair of scissors hung on a nearby hook. Packets of flower and vegetable seeds were neatly displayed on a rack. Other seeds were in huge gunny sacks on the floor, with scoops in them—I supposed these were for farmers rather than backyard gardeners. Some canned goods were stacked on shelves against the wall. Jars of different candies sat on the counter near the cash register where I watched children proudly buy a penny's worth. I observed housewives include in their purchases a stamp or two, at four cents each, the domestic postage rate at that time. This deep fuchsia stamp featured the profile of Abraham Lincoln. Cy served everyone with a big smile and a kind word.

Due to my limited mobility, going to Washington the following summer in search of university interviews and scholarships was out of the question. When I returned to school after surgery, the nuns thoughtfully had moved all my classes to one floor and made a bedroom out of a small office so that I did not have to climb the steps to my dormitory. It was too difficult for me to go up and down the waxed, slippery wooden stairs and corridors. The sister from the infirmary served meals in my room. Everyone treated me very kindly.

I was extremely worried about what to do for school the next year, so I consulted Sister Jean Marie. She contacted Siena College in Memphis, Tennessee, the senior college to St. Catharine, and obtained a one-year scholarship, renewable based on my maintaining a B average. My biggest hurdle had been crossed.

When I went back to the Lebanon hospital for a checkup, six weeks after surgery, the news was bad—my ankle had not healed properly. The way it had knitted, I would be able to walk only if it was re-broken and reset. Instead of agreeing to allow the doctor to do so immediately, I told him I could not miss the last few weeks of school or my final exams. For once, I splurged and made a long-distance call to Uncle C.T. He was quick to help me with a solution, "Arrange to leave most of your things in storage at the college. As soon as school is out, come to New York. We have a good friend, Dr. Yo, who is a physician at Flushing Hospital. I will ask him to arrange to have your surgery done by a bone specialist." What a blessing! (photo 33)

When the orthopedic surgeon in Flushing examined my ankle and foot, he shook his head and declared, sympathetically, "You have a severe infection. Because your care has, unfortunately, been delayed, there is a possibility that I might have to amputate." I was 19 years old—the news of possibly losing my leg shook me to the core. In those days, slacks were not acceptable attire for a proper woman, and wearing a skirt would show that I was missing a leg. My mobility would be greatly limited and I would have to use the kind of crutches that have metal semi-rings to keep them on my arms. I thought to myself, "My education is still more important than my leg. I cannot succeed without an education; I can without a leg. I will find a way."

My good fortune was that the surgeon saved my leg. But that accident forever altered my ability to walk any distance and left me with permanent pain, ranging from tolerable to so severe at times that it is impossible to put my foot down. Nevertheless, I have not allowed this condition to stop me from doing what I have been called to do. In my mid-sixties, a fall caused me so much suffering that I contemplated amputation. The pain medicine prescribed at that time made me so groggy that I felt I was losing my mind, and I also gained an inordinate amount of weight. Fortunately, a Chinese acupuncturist's four-month treatment put me back on my feet. I learned to use magnetic therapy—taping small magnets on the proper meridien points—to lessen the level of my pain. I consider my physical limitation a lesson to teach me greater compassion for the suffering of others. My belief is that there is a silver lining in every cloud and a gate in every wall.

As I recuperated from the surgery, I wondered what I would do for money for my third year of college. I couldn't be a waitress over the summer because of the crutches. But an unexpected opportunity arose when C.T.'s young son, Raymond, came home from visiting a classmate. His friend was disappointed at having to miss her planned study at an exclusive French camp, due to a last minute staff shortage. Immediately, I had Raymond get the name of the person in charge of the camp and I called to apply for the job. Wow, did that fall out of heaven! The camp was *Les Chalets Français* on Deer Isle, Maine. I spoke first with Helma, then Elsa, the sisters who founded the camp. Both tested my French over the telephone, and I was hired even though I told them I was on crutches. Elsa said, "Instead of living in a cabin with 10 kids, you can sleep in the infirmary. You will have the responsibility of staging little plays with the older campers and teaching puppetry to younger ones, all in French." At this camp they did *everything* in French—even teaching tennis lessons, horseback riding, and ballet.

My work with the campers became a case of "fake it until you make it." I had never made puppets or used *papier-mache*, so I consulted the arts and crafts counselor who gave me useful ideas. In order to build finger puppets I collected the necessary materials, including old tennis balls to use for the heads and yarn and fabric to shape and dress them. I helped the kids write the skits and pronounce the French words. We worked feverishly every day and our productions were received with great enthusiasm. Teaching at *Les Chalets Français* gave me enough money to supplement my scholarship, covering my junior year expenses for books and extras. Helma and Elsa were so pleased with my work that they hired me for the following summer.

When I returned to Flushing the surgeon removed my cast. He was pleased with the progress of my healing. I had been in a cast for nearly six months. My left leg was weak and still painful, so I had to walk with a cane. I managed to return to St. Catharine to thank the nuns for their kindness, and pick up my belongings, and traveled to Siena College in Memphis, Tennessee.

Now I was in a large city with more of the hustle and bustle I was accustomed to. Cater-cornered from Siena campus, on Poplar Avenue, was a shopping center with department stores such as Sears and Goldsmith's. The college had more day-students than boarders and classes were larger than at St. Catharine. Sister Sheila was the dean and also my professor of Spanish literature. She had spent many years in Puerto Rico, so her Spanish was fluent, like that of someone who had lived with the language. When I first met her I thanked her for the scholarship that was so essential for my college studies. The following school year I was again thankful that she gave me the final scholarship to complete my senior year.

One of the day-students who quickly took me under her wing was Nancy-Kate Harris. She was a tall, slender, beautiful young woman with fair skin and long, blond, straight hair that flowed loose on her back. One Saturday afternoon she invited me to lunch at her home to meet her mother. Afterward, we went to a play rehearsal at the Memphis Little Theater. Nancy-Kate was working on the set of the upcoming play, *Sunrise at Campobello.* She wanted to introduce me to Harry Dinwiddie, the lead actor who played President Franklin Roosevelt. The story depicted Roosevelt's struggle with polio, showing him in a wheelchair until the closing scene, when he stands up at the podium of the 1924 convention. Nancy-Kate was eager to have me meet Harry because he had learned Chinese through the Carmel Army Language School in the early fifties.

Harry was happy to show off his ability to speak Chinese. I was amazed at his proficiency after only about 18 months of training. He described how he had been totally immersed in the language, spending almost all his waking hours with his Chinese teachers, even taking his meals with them so he could converse and practice the language. His training took place during the Korean War. Harry told me that on numerous occasions he had been awakened in the middle of the night to submit to mock interrogations in Chinese. After the Second World War the Army Language School had the largest language program for American military personnel—the most studied language was Russian, followed by Chinese, Korean, and German. That school led the way with its audio-lingual method, which included the use of the language laboratory.

Nancy-Kate took me to rehearsals on several occasions. While she worked on the set I chatted with Harry during his breaks. One evening he asked, "How do you think I look on stage in my wheelchair?"

I was surprised by the question and said, "Harry, I need to be truthful with you. You are too stiff in your wheelchair. Your legs need to be limp; you should move them once in a while with your hands because you are supposed to have polio and aren't supposed to be able to control them." He seemed pleased with my input and changed his posture accordingly.

The play opened at the Memphis Little Theater, in the Pink Palace, which was the unfinished mansion of Clarence Saunders, founder of the Piggly Wiggly grocery chain. The nearly 300 seats were placed on the sloping concrete of the never-used indoor swimming pool. On opening night, the director of the Memphis Veterans Hospital went backstage to congratulate Harry on how well he had portrayed Roosevelt's paralyzed legs. Harry thanked me for my contribution to his acting.

Shortly after *Sunrise at Campobello* closed, Harry was transferred by his employer, the Cotton Council International, to their New York office. During my visit to stay with Uncle C.T.'s family in New York during the Christmas holiday in 1960, Harry took me to see an adaptation of James Agee's Pulitzer Prize-winning novel, *A*

Death in the Family. The play, named *All the Way Home*, was staged at the Belasco Theater. That show let out a few minutes before other Broadway shows, so Harry took me to Sardi's Restaurant, the famous pre-and post-theater hangout where the walls were decorated with caricatures of Broadway celebrities. The owner, Vincent Sardi, got the idea of decorating his restaurant from Joe Zelli's, a restaurant and jazz club in Paris where internatioinal movie stars' caricatures were displayed. After the maitre d' showed us to the center booth facing the entrance, the premium seat in the restaurant, Harry whispered, "The way you look and the way you are dressed, he has mistaken you for France Nguyen, who is playing in *The World of Suzie Wong* on Broadway. If people nod and smile at you, just nod and smile back." For a couple of hours it was fun pretending to be a star. Shortly after I returned to Memphis, Harry was transferred to Belgium and we lost touch.

Back in Memphis I became active with an International Students Club. One of the sponsors was Mrs. Mildred Newby. She picked me up at the dormitory every Saturday evening for a get-together in the basement of a large church. Mrs. Newby had three daughters: Carol, Patsy, and 12-year-old Ruthie. Carol was a young adult with a life of her own and seldom went with us. Mrs. Newby did not work outside the home because Patsy, who had cerebral palsy, required constant care. Thanks to Mrs. Newby I became involved in volunteering for the Easter Seals programs and in their assisted living homes.

Mrs. Newby occasionally hosted some Indonesian students from Millington's Naval Base, outside of Memphis. It was not always easy to take them to certain places because of the prejudice of the day toward their dark skin. I remember we were once asked to leave a bowling alley because they were not "white."

One Sunday afternoon Mildred suggested we go on a sight-seeing ride. Since I knew that Elvis' home was in Memphis I asked if we could drive by and see the famous white gate with his silhouette. Outside the gate there was a place to pull over. We got out of the car for the young Indonesian men to take some pictures. I saw a man just inside the gate and spoke to him, "Good afternoon sir. Are you Elvis' uncle that everyone calls 'Uncle Vester?' We are foreign students and wanted to see where Elvis lives."

To our surprise, Vester opened the gate and stepped out to speak to us, "Elvis is in Hawaii, just finished with a movie called *Blue Hawaii.* He will be home next week, and plans to have a party Saturday. I arranged to borrow the Graceland school's football field for him and his buddies to play touch football in the afternoon. If you come back then, I'll ask him to say hello. He appreciates his fans."

Of course the following Saturday Mrs. Newby drove us back to Graceland School. It was amazing to see how focused Elvis was on playing the game. In those moments he wasn't the movie star or the recording idol. He was just an American guy having fun with his friends. He was simply dressed in black pants and a black t-shirt, very unassuming, his hair in disarray. The Indonesian boys had their cameras ready and Elvis graciously allowed us some photos with him. We chatted for a short while. Elvis was soft spoken and courteous. I felt fortunate that I got to meet "the king of rock and roll" and that I have a photo to prove it (photo 34).

Mrs. Newby continued to take us to the Saturday evening International Students' get-together, where I met Edwina, the French teacher at St. Mary's Episcopal School. Before Christmas of my senior year, she told me her husband was getting out of the army in a few months so she was planning to move away, and her position would be open for the following year. She said she would mention me to the headmaster, Dr. Hughes, and help set up an interview. During my meeting with Dr. Hughes, I told him that my student visa would expire at the end of the school year. If he intended to hire me I would need to have a signed contract so the Immigration Office would allow me to remain and work in the U.S. He decided to engage me and handled the necessary procedures swiftly. My future seemed to be on track. Since I did not have to worry about looking for a job after graduation (photo 35), I could enjoy taking a summer vacation, in Tahiti, at my parents' new home.

The Uncrushable Rose

Chapter 9

From Doormat To Bulldozer

After my treasured three months vacation at my parents' in Tahiti, I flew back to Memphis for my first professional job. Mrs. Newby picked me up at the airport and helped me find a room to rent in a home on the bus line to St. Mary's Episcopal School. I had saved enough money—from teaching the summer before at *Les Chalets Français* and from tutoring French during my senior year—to pay the $85 that was my first month's rent, which included a bowl of cereal for breakfast and a simple dinner. Mrs. Clark, who owned the house, had a teenage daughter, Barbara, and kept two elderly ladies as boarders. They were all friendly but I had little communication with them because teaching kept me away the greater part of the day and my evenings were taken up with papers to correct and preparation for the next day.

Papa had advised me over the summer, "Since you like to study, go for a master's degree as soon as possible. Don't ever get out of the habit of reading and learning." In discovering right away how much I enjoyed teaching, I took papa's advice and went to Memphis State University (MSU) that fall to investigate their master's program. With a double major in English and Spanish and a double minor in theology and psychology, I thought a master's in education or in Romance languages would be ideal for my teaching career.

The first four years of my life in the U.S. had been in a Catholic environment. Teaching just a couple of months in an Episcopal school made me realize how divisive the Christian churches are in American society. I thought that I had better connect with my own religion when I started school at MSU, so I contacted the Newman Club, the Catholic club on secular campuses with its own house, similar to a fraternity or sorority. I found out their social program schedule and showed up at a get-together on a Saturday afternoon.

Being the only Asian and not yet even a student at MSU, I felt intimidated as I arrived. But very quickly some students, male and female, surrounded me to chat. Again the questions about my origin and background started to fly. So often I became the center of attention in a conversation such as this, where people are curious about where I came from and what I am doing at this time and in this place. One of the young men who came to talk to me was Simon, who was in charge of social activities. He was not very tall and had a fair complexion with a receding hair line—my first thought was, "So young and already balding?" But he was very animated and friendly. He spoke articulately and proposed a couple of future activities for the group to discuss and vote on—supporting the university basketball and football teams by going to the games, and also going on an outing to the Shiloh National Military Park, not far from Memphis. Later he asked if I would take part. I said, "Not the games, I am not much for team sports. I prefer individual performances such as track and field. But I would love to go to Shiloh Park if I can get a ride with someone."

"That's no problem," he said. "When the time comes I can pick you up. Just give me your phone number and your address." I gave it to him then, even though the outing to Shiloh was planned for spring.

"Thank you," I replied. "I'll look forward to it. Isn't it ironic that *shiloh* means 'peace' in Hebrew and that the two-day battle there was one of the bloodiest of the entire Civil War? Thousands of men died on both sides."

Surprised, he commented, "How did you know that?"

"Oh, I read about it not too long ago. I don't know how long I'll be in the U.S. so I try to learn all I can wherever I am. I even remember that the battle started at six in the morning on April 6, 1862. It's easy for me to remember historical dates, especially if war was involved. I have seen some of its horrors first-hand. There truly are no winners."

Simon responded, "I'd like to hear more sometime."

Over the next few months I attended several social gatherings at the Newman Club. I saw more of Simon, always in groups, and even went to one MSU football game against arch-rival, Ole Miss (University of Mississippi). There was so much "rah-rah-rah." The game was like a circus with grown men hurting each other for a ball. I saw pretty girls jump around like acrobats and fans so passionate that it seemed that their lives depended on the outcome of the game. I didn't understand much of it. The whole thing looked like a farce to me.

When Simon took me home, after much celebrating and drinking that evening, I recounted a sports story from Taiwan that I had heard from my father. "The Taiwan government bought a large piece of land from a local farmer to build a project, maybe it was the airport, and paid him a sum of money such as he had never seen. He thought he would not live long enough to spend it so he decided to use it to build a school because he had never gone to one and always had heard about the value of education. He was invited to the ribbon cutting ceremony and celebration, including a basketball game. All the rough and tumble competition just to possess a ball was appalling to him. He whispered to the principal, 'Did I not give you enough money for the school? Please don't allow the boys to fight like this for a ball. They can make better use of their time. I beg you, buy a ball for each boy! I'll give you more money if you need it.'"

Simon laughed and said, "If that farmer knew how much money these games make for American schools, he would *really* be appalled."

At last, on Saturday, April 6, we had our outing to Shiloh National Park, on the 101st anniversary of the battle. I was really happy to be able to go to this historical place, since not having transportation usually limited my ability to come and go. It was eerie to walk on the ground where so much blood had been spilled. The Shiloh battlefield was made into a National Military Park due to the request of local farmers who were upset when their pigs dug up the remains of soldiers who had died during the battle. Several ghost stories are connected to the site. One of them is that of a young Union drummer who did not know how to drum "retreat," so he repeated the drumming for "charge," contrary to his orders. That led to a successful advance by Union troops. The drummer, who was seen as a hero by his comrades, was killed shortly afterward. Supposedly, his drumming can still be heard at sundown when the park closes. Jurisdiction over the park was later transferred from the War Department to the National Park Service. When Simon took me home that evening he asked if he could call me for a date after he returned from spring break at his parents' home in Springfield, Missouri.

Having been educated by nuns in two Catholic colleges had kept me in a cocoon. It seemed that dating a Catholic boy was a good way to stay safe—outside would be dangerous to my religion. I had learned from Sister Eileen Maura in a course called "Marriage and the Family" that before you start a relationship you should analyze and look for similarities in these areas: religious, ethnic, and cultural backgrounds; economic, social, and educational levels; and political views. I could see that Simon and I were not exactly in step in all these areas, but I agreed to let him call me because he was a practicing Catholic.

This was the first time I had even thought of dating since breaking my relationship with Siaoti. My sense of guilt and my pain over our break-up were intense, but since going to Hong Kong to marry him was not an option, due to my parents' strong objection, I had to begin to think of my future. As Sister Maura had said, "Ultimately, you girls are after the 'M-R-S Degree." Part of me thought she was right—it was in my best interest to marry and have a family. But another part was hungry for knowledge and eager for a higher academic degree and the ability to control my own destiny.

Inside me I had two personalities in conflict. My Chinese side was dominated by my mother's voice calling me hideous and prophesying that no man would want to marry me. My lack of self-worth caused me to be passive and self-loathing—perfect material for the making of a "doormat." My French/American side took two lines from Alfred, Lord Tennyson's poem *Enone* as a guide to the freedom to lead my own life:

"Self-reverence, self-knowledge, self-control,
These three alone lead life to sovereign power."

I had seen that freedom in my friend K.K.'s decisiveness and self-confidence when she took me shopping in New York. I wanted to be self-assured enough to voice my opinion, to be assertive, to make my own choices. I wanted the power to control my path. I didn't know what it would take or how long it would be before I got there.

Money was a another big issue I faced. I needed to earn enough to pay for the master's program the following school year. I would have to study on a part-time basis, while continuing to teach, so I planned to look for a position in a Catholic school instead of remaining at the Episcopal Saint Mary's.

When Simon returned to Memphis following spring break, he did call me for a date. I learned that his schedule was very full because, in addition to his full-time university courses, he slept three nights a week at Saint Joseph's Catholic Hospital, where he worked as the X-ray technician on call. Most nights he was awakened to perform procedures. This was the way he earned his living expenses while his grandfather paid for his schooling. I admired Simon's diligence in his work/study program.

When I met Simon's grandfather, Jim, I learned that he had been an auto mechanic in his younger days. Knowing how to manage his money, he came to own numerous rental properties in Springfield, Missouri. He kept busy buying, fixing, renting, collecting, and sometimes selling his houses on contract. Having had just a fourth grade education, he wanted his only grandson to have the advantages of college. He arranged for Simon to spend a year after high school training to be an X-ray technician in order to earn a living while attending the university. I thought Jim's plan was brilliant.

From mid-April on, Simon spent as much time with me as he could. He even drove me to an interview at Saint Agnes Catholic School, where I was hired on the spot to teach the next school year. Two weeks before the end of the school year at Saint Mary's, at the daily chapel service, the student next to me accidentally pulled the kneeling bench down onto my left foot and knelt on it. I heard something crack and felt searing pain in my foot. I was injured again. I was taken to the hospital, choosing to go to Saint Joseph, where Simon worked. I sustained a hairline fracture of a metatarsal bone and some bruised tendons. Even though the injury was not serious enough to require a cast, again I was on crutches for a few weeks.

Having decided to take the job at Saint Agnes, I needed to find a place to live that was on the bus line to that school. Again Simon helped by driving me around. I found a small furnished apartment and he helped me move. Over the next few months we talked a lot and became closer, but kept a respectful physical distance. It wasn't long before he suggested that we should marry. He thought it was a good way to be together and a good way to save money by pooling our resources to pay for living expenses. Although the plan sounded reasonable, I considered it to be too much of a rush. My heart and mind were still with Siaoti. I did not feel the kind of love I thought I should for a husband-to-be, but Simon was so insistent for us to marry before school started again that, in late July, I finally agreed.

In my mind, marrying Simon would put a social and religious barrier between Siaoti and me. According to my church and my culture I could not divorce. Therefore this marriage would serve to cut out all possibility of reconnecting with Siaoti. Maybe this was the pressure I needed to absolutely kill all such hopes and options.

With the help of friends from the Newman Club, we quickly planned a wedding. Father Wallen, the club's spiritual director, was to officiate at his church, Saint Patrick's.

I wrote to my parents to tell my plans to marry Simon. There was no way they could come for a wedding. Father had just received a promotion to open the new Chinese embassy in Abidjan, capital of Ivory Coast, and also serve there as ambassador (photo 59).

When Simon called his mother to tell her he was getting married the following Saturday, she was furious that she had not been informed sooner. Then, when she found out that I was Chinese, all hell broke loose. She stormed in from Springfield. In her state of mind, it was a thousand wonders that she did not have a wreck on the way.

That first meeting between my future mother-in-law, Sue (photo 40), and me was so awful that I have tried to put it entirely out of my mind. It is difficult and painful to recall the things she said because I have done what my nanny taught me to do, shake off hurtful words like a duck shakes water off its back. But some things you never forget. When she arrived she called me every bad name under the sun, including some I had never heard before and did not understand.

She screamed at me: "You foreign whore! You got him in bed and hooked him into marrying you."

I stepped back as if I had been slapped, and protested, "We have never been in bed together. One of Simon's great qualities is that he respects me. It is important to me that I be a virgin for the man I marry. I made that promise to myself years ago."

Because of this humiliating fit Sue had thrown, we settled for a small wedding alone and cancelled the celebration party we had planned to host at the Newman Club. Simon and I simply went back to his apartment after our marriage vows. Our friends were disappointed and we were awfully embarrassed.

The next morning I woke up when the sky was still dark. Tears rolled down my checks. I felt my whole world had disintegrated. Simon was snoring next to me. The night before he had been very unaffectionate and clumsy, and he had hurt me. Floods of thoughts swam in my mind, "Is sex this awful thing? Did I save myself all this time for *this*?" There had been more love and passion between Siaoti and me in our kisses on the sandy beach in Hong Kong than the five minutes of sex with Simon. What horror had I gotten myself into?

While these thoughts were bombarding me, I heard a key turn in the door of the apartment. I jumped out of bed and ran into the bathroom and locked myself in. My mother-in-law burst in, shouting, "How *are* the lovebirds this morning? You said you were a virgin, so I want to see some proof."

As Sue stomped into the bedroom, she yelled at Simon to get up. She threw the covers off the bed and shouted, "I see blood on the sheets, so you did tell me the truth."

Simon yelled back at her, "How could you do this! Can't you leave us alone on our first weekend?"

His mother spat, "I am going to make your lives such a hell that she'll leave you. You'd better not give me any half-breed grandchildren. I sure don't intend to have any little Chinks running around my backyard."

"Mother, you don't have to be so nasty. You know my wife does have a name and it's not 'she,' it's 'Bambi.' And what are you doing here with your suitcase?"

"I am moving back. Need I remind you that I pay this rent and I have my own room? After all, you are my son first, before you are her husband. I am not staying at my friend's house another night when I have my room here."

"Mother, you are being so unreasonable. I am married, can't you accept that?"

"You just watch me. I did not sacrifice all my life for you to see you end up marrying an ignorant foreigner."

"Bambi is not ignorant. She has a college degree. She is a teacher."

"Fake, fake, she is nothing but a fake. She married you to stay in this country."

"No, she didn't. Her teaching position gave her the right to stay and work. Her school arranged for it. She did *not* need to marry me to stay."

"You are so stupid you cannot see past your nose. She married you to stay in this country. I know."

I was still hiding in the bathroom overhearing this horrible exchange. I felt so humiliated and thought, "How could his mother be so coarse as to come check my marriage bed. I am relieved she saw blood. Would that keep her from calling me a whore? I doubt it. She is even worse than my mother."

Simon knocked on the door to tell me he needed to use the bathroom. I let him in. He gave me a hug and said, "Don't worry, she'll come around. I know you'll win her over."

Simon's face was flushed and he held his lips tight. I had never been around people who yelled at each other in anger. My mother used to show me her disapproval with cutting words and disdain but in a controlled manner. All this screaming seemed so crude.

I took a bath to delay having to face her. Eventually I had to come out, and the barrage of insults started again. How I got through the next few hours with her seems fuzzy now. I just remember that I did not scream back at her but softly said, "I so regret you feel this way about me. You have already made up your mind, so anything I would say is of no use. This is Sunday, so Simon and I need to go to Mass. Then I have to pick up the rest of my things and clean up my old apartment before I return the key. Tomorrow is a school day and I did not ask for any time off."

Father had instilled in me that even when we are defeated in a situation, as when we were taken into the concentration camp, we must maintain a degree of dignity and not act like trapped wild animals. How appropriate that he had used that example, because right then I felt trapped like an animal. I tried to ignore her as much as I could. Then Simon and I left for my former apartment.

While we were packing my things and as I started to strip my bed, Simon said, "Maybe you should stay here tonight until Mother leaves. Surely she won't be here many days, as angry as she is. Remember, I go to work this evening from eleven to seven in the morning? I don't think you should be alone with her."

"Simon, you mean we should buckle under and not offer a united front? Do you own up to this marriage? Her goal is to separate us. Is that what you want?"

"No, that's not what I want, but I need to protect you from her fury. I really had not realized how prejudiced she is. I knew the way she feels about blacks from living in Arkansas for a long time, but I did not know she felt so strongly against Chinese."

"Well, she's your mother. You tell me what to do."

I felt sorry for Simon. He hung his head and looked defeated. He decided to drive us back to our apartment. As he was parking, we saw Sue throw her suitcase into her car. Stomping out of the door she yelled at her son, "I will never come back to this place. I consider you dead! And don't expect me to pay next month's rent. You are on your own. Damn you!"

I was horrified by this scene and her words. I asked, "How could she say those things to you?"

Simon sighed, "Don't worry about it. She has cursed me all my life and has disowned me more times than I can count. She'll come around."

I wasn't so sure, "You mean she is like a volcano. She can explode like that and then calm down? I have never been around anyone like that."

The next couple of months are a blur in my memory. Our apartment was not on the bus line to my school. Simon could always drive me to work in the morning, but I had to deal with getting home most afternoons. Even if I knew how to drive, buying another car was out of the question. I had a little money from the previous year's work—out of my $350 monthly salary at Saint Mary's, I was saving $200 a month, earmarked for my master's program. But when I started going out with Simon, I noticed that he expected and waited for me to pay the bills almost all of the time. I dismissed it, assuming he probably thought it was only fair, since I made more money than he did. In retrospect, I see that should have been a clue to me that he was not responsible about money.

As I shared my new life with Simon, lessons from Sister Eileen Maura came back to me in waves: "Your husband will be the source of ninety percent of your joy or ninety percent of your pain. Choose your mate carefully." A concrete lesson she shared on how to create a successful marriage was, "Always make him feel you are happy to see him when he comes home from work—take a lesson from how you feel when your puppy welcomes you home with enthusiasm." She also cautioned, "Never challenge him in the heat of anger—that would push his chauvinist button and back him into a corner where he would act out his maleness." She added, "Believe me—whispering is more effective than yelling. Keep your cool and don't use words you will regret, because you can never take them back."

Most emphatically, she warned, "If you don't remember anything else from this course, remember this: Don't ever, EVER allow him to strike you; because if you do, all you will have to look forward to is the next time, and the time after that. I promise you, the violence would escalate. Your life could be in danger, and also the lives of your children."

I never knew enough about Sister Eileen's background to shed light on her counsel for preventing domestic violence. We girls asked ourselves, "How come she knows so much? A nun is not supposed to have first-hand knowledge of such things. Had she witnessed violence from her father? Had she had an abusive husband or boyfriend?" Although I learned such lessons from her I didn't expect I would apply them in my own life.

On the night of October 30, Simon called me from the hospital where he was working to say he was having a kidney stone attack and was in excruciating pain. He told me to call a cab to get to the hospital. Fortunately, I always kept some cash on hand, so I was able to pay for it. In the meantime, Simon called his mother, who immediately drove in from Springfield to be at his bedside. When she saw me, she hugged me and acted as if I were a long-lost relative, as if she had never uttered a harsh word toward me. I was thoroughly confused—what an about-face! But I was willing to let bygones be bygones and attempt to have a peaceful relationship with this strange mother-in-law.

For two days Simon's urologist tried to get him to pass his kidney stones, but to no avail. In those days the technology of sending shock waves to blast the stones had not yet been invented. The surgeon decided to operate on Simon for fear his kidneys would shut down. Simon's stepfather, whom we called "Daddy Mac" (photo 40), took off from work on the Frisco railroad and joined us at the hospital in Memphis. This was the first time I had met him because Sue had told him not to attend our wedding. During Simon's surgery, Mac took me aside and said, "If anything happens to Simon, I want you to feel free to come live with us in Springfield. You are part of the family now."

I was surprised and I said, "Thank you. You are very thoughtful. I am sure Simon will be fine. The whole Newman Club has a prayer chain going for his recovery. I have my work here and I, too, will be okay. I appreciate your kindness." But inside, I thought, "Not on your life. That would be as putting myself in the mouth of a tigress!"

Sue stayed with Simon day and night, totally focused on his condition. I continued to teach, with Sue driving me willingly—and even kindly—to and from work. Five days after surgery Simon returned to the apartment. Because he was very sore, he asked me not to be in the bed with him, so I slept on the living room sofa.

By mid-November Sue decided that, since I would be gone all day and also because she thought me incapable of taking care of Simon, we had to move into her home in Springfield. I did not know any way to resist this idea except by using the fact that I had signed a year's contract with Saint Agnes School. I hoped that there was no way to get out of it without penalty. Sue went to the principal's office with me to state our case. Unfortunately for me, the nun was kind enough to release me. And she did not ask me to pay compensation to the school. I felt terrible having to break my contract, and having my way of earning money disappear.

Simon had me cash in my savings account and hand all my money to Sue for our expenses in Springfield. It broke my heart to turn over the $2,000 I had so diligently saved over an entire year. That money was supposed to go toward my master's. Daddy Mac took off from work, rented a U-Haul trailer, and moved our furniture and personal belongings into the garage of their house. I was completely under Sue's thumb. I continued to sleep on the sofa, this time in their family room to keep from disturbing Simon. Sue insisted that his bedroom door be left open so that she could hear him and easily check on him during the night.

On November 22, the first day Simon felt strong enough to get out of the house, Sue drove the three of us to shop for groceries. We arrived at home a few minutes after 12:30. While I carried our purchases into the kitchen, Sue rushed in to turn on the television, since she had already missed a few minutes of her daily soap opera, *As the World Turns*. Instead of the expected program, we heard Walter Cronkite announce, "The president has been rushed to the hospital." It was 1963.

Sue exclaimed, "He has been in a car accident!"

I countered, "Presidents don't have car accidents. Their roads are cleared."

"How do you know, smarty pants?" she retorted.

"They ride in a motorcade, don't they? It has to be something worse." For some reason I immediately thought of the assassination of France's King Henri IV, by Ravaillac. And I remembered the strong objection many Americans voiced against Kennedy during the campaign because he was a Catholic. These people feared that if he became president he would be under the directives of the Pope. As for Henri IV, although raised a Calvinist by his mother, in order to prove his readiness to lead a Catholic country he converted to Catholicism, a month before he was crowned king. In the 16th and 17th century, to be a Protestant was a fairly new choice, viewed with suspicion and often persecuted in a Catholic-dominated Europe. In 1598 Henri IV enacted the Edict of Nantes granting religious freedom to Protestants, thereby ending the religious civil war in France. Doubting the sincerity of the king's conversion, a fanatic Catholic jumped into Henri IV's carriage and stabbed him to death some twenty years after he had gained the throne. While I was making these comparisons in my head we heard Walter Cronkite say, "The president has been shot in Dallas."

I quickly put away groceries that needed to go in the refrigerator and freezer and joined Sue and Simon in front of the television. Cronkite was handed a piece of paper. He read it, looked at the clock, took off his glasses, wiped the corner of an eye, steadied himself, and said, "President Kennedy died at one o'clock, central standard time."

Many, perhaps most, Americans alive at that time, remember exactly what they were doing when this announcement was made. For the rest of that Friday, plus three more days, the television networks pre-empted all programs—for the first time in history. They ran nothing but coverage of the president's death: the swearing-in of the next president, Lyndon Johnson; the return of Kennedy's body to Washington; the procession to the Capitol, with the traditional riderless horse following the caisson; John-John's salute as his father's coffin passed; the burial at Arlington National Cemetery; and the admirable dignity and composure of Jacqueline Kennedy. There were no commercials. For four days we were glued to the television, trying to make sense of the President's assasination. The entire nation grieved.

By Tuesday, the pace of life was slowly beginning to return to normal. Since Sue had bought all the ingredients on Friday to make Thanksgiving dinner, she and I proceeded with the holiday preparations. It was probably the saddest Thanksgiving the country had ever known. As an outsider, I marveled as I observed this nation of law, which, in spite of this traumatic loss, could move calmly and seamlessly into the next presidency and the next administration. In most other countries, with an assassination like that, there would be enormous turmoil with numerous factions jockeying to take over, possibly coups here and there, and maybe even more assassinations.

After a lavish Thanksgiving dinner Sue prepared while I helped and learned, she had another one of her fits. She lashed out, "You know Simon is still recovering from his surgery. There is no way he can go to work. How about you? Are you planning to sit on your hands and expect to be waited on?"

"Of course not," I responded. "I had planned to look for a job Monday, but with the death of the president, I didn't think anyone would be in the mood for hiring. Plus, it *is* Thanksgiving week. I promise I'll start looking next Monday. It probably will be difficult to find a job teaching this time of the year, but I can always look for one as a waitress. I know how to do that."

She hissed, "Who do you think is going to give *you* a job? You are a foreigner with your yellow ugly face. I sure wouldn't hire you if *I* had a restaurant."

"In all the years I've been in the States, I've never encountered your kind of prejudice," I said to her. "I am not too proud to do whatever kind of work I can find."

Simon tried to distract her, "I'll make some coffee to go with your pumpkin pie, okay?" And Mac suggested, "Let's go for a ride to see some Christmas lights. I have sure eaten too much." So it was decided we'd go for the drive and then come home for dessert.

Sue had been drinking wine while she cooked. She had a habit of "bad-mouthing" any time she drank alcoholic beverages. When the effect of the alcohol passed, some of her nastiness lifted. Later that evening, she suggested that I could sleep in Simon's bedroom if we kept the door open. I took this gesture as an attempt at repairing the damage done by her drunken, hurtful remarks made at dinner.

On Monday morning, December 2, I called the local board of education, hoping to learn of an opening for a teaching position. I was not surprised that there was none. The person on the phone suggested that I call the Catholic diocese, because there were a number of Catholic schools not under the same jurisdiction. The diocese office gave me the same negative answer and said I could try the different schools individually. In the phone book, the first number my eyes landed on was for Saint Elizabeth Ann Seton School. I dialed. The person who answered identified herself as "Sister So-and-So." I stated my case, "I am a native French speaker and I am looking for a position, if possible, as a French teacher. But I am also a graduate of a Catholic college in Memphis and qualified to teach elementary grades, if necessary. Do you know of an opening in any of the Catholic schools?"

I heard a little cry of delighted surprise, "This is Divine Providence! My niece is *desperate* to find a replacement. She wants out of her contract because her husband was wounded in the army and she needs to go to him as soon as possible."

Holding my breath I asked, "What and where does she teach?"

I could picture the Sister blessing herself with the sign of the cross before she answered, "She teaches French and journalism at Republic High School, eleven miles from Springfield."

It was my turn to bless myself, and to thank my guardian angel "Butterfly," for her guidance. Immediately I called and made an appointment with the principal, Dr. Schatz, for that very afternoon. Sue drove me to the interview and, within an hour, I walked out of that office with a contract for the rest of the school year. Sue had nastily predicted that I couldn't even get a waitress job in Springfield. Yet with four phone calls—all in one day—not only did I get a teaching job, I found one teaching my favorite areas, French and journalism, in a neighboring Missouri town of 8,000, starting two days later, *and* arranged carpooling with Miss Crumrine, the business teacher, who lived only three blocks from Simon's parents. What are the chances of that!

My mother-in-law did not speak to me the rest of the day.

The students of French at Republic High School were immediately receptive toward me as their new language teacher. I had many stories of French life and attitudes to share with them. Classes were small and we had fun teaming up with the home economics classes to cook French recipes in the well-equipped classroom-kitchen. The responsibility of the journalism class was to put out the school paper every two weeks and to work on the year book. By the time I took over the class, the plans and blueprints were in place so it was easy just to follow them. I was insistent that the time their writing assignments were due was treated as their "deadline," just as in the real world of journalism—there was to be absolutely no leeway, because, if late, "news" is no longer news.

Every week I paid Miss Crumrine five dollars for the ride to school and spent five dollars for lunches. I had to ask my mother-in-law for the money. She resented it and lorded it over me, even though I had just given her my $2000 savings. When I received my first paycheck from Republic, just before Christmas break, Simon had me sign over the entire check to his mother. I felt like an indentured servant.

During the latter part of December my menstruation was late. I suspected I was pregnant and shared this with Simon. That evening he told his mother. She was furious and accused me of tricking him into getting me pregnant. I can still see and hear her rage. She screamed, "Get out! Get out of *my* house."

I had no money in my purse, nowhere to go, and not a single person I could call. I grabbed my winter coat and walked out. I was freezing as I walked down the road. I went a couple of blocks before Simon picked me up in his car and took me to the train station. At least it was open all night, and warm. He left me there and went back to his mother's house.

In the station I sat up all night because the hard wooden benches were divided by armrests, so there was no way I could lie down. I was there until the next afternoon with no food. I wondered what Simon was doing and thinking all this time. What was I to do? School was not in session for the Christmas/New Year break. As the hours passed I thought, "I had better find a solution to my situation." I was fairly sure I was pregnant. The baby would be due sometime in August. I wondered, "Could I get a room somewhere in Republic so that I can walk to school and continue to teach until May? At least I have that contract. Then what? I must find a way.I cannot let my parents know what a mess my life has become. It would shame them and me to hear it."

When Mac arrived home from his overnight run to Memphis on the railroad and found me gone, he stood up for me. He told Sue that she couldn't throw me out and he came to the train station to pick me up. I had been there for over twenty hours. When I returned, again Sue acted as if nothing had happened. The same went with Simon. I was baffled. If my existence had to depend on my mother-in-law's mood, it would be like living on quicksand. I didn't think I should continue to do that.

When I received my paycheck at the end of January, instead of giving it to Sue, I suggested to Simon that we find a small, inexpensive apartment not too far away, so that Miss Crumrine could continue to give me the daily ride to school. Even with Simon not working we could manage on my salary alone. We put this plan into action and moved the first week of February. Once we had privacy in our own apartment, without Sue's watchful and critical eyes and ears, I noticed that Simon remained distant. Valentine's Day came on a Friday, two weeks later. I got home from school thinking there would be some sign of romance and intimacy, or at least some affection. There was none. I thought maybe he had forgotten what day it was—sometimes that happens when one is not working. But then I remembered he had watched television at his mother's all day, so he must have known. We went back to his parents' for dinner. When we returned to our apartment I asked

Simon why he had been so distant. He became furious and lashed out, "I did not want to be with you anyway. You couldn't turn me on if you stood on your head. I married you to keep my mother off my back. She accused me of being gay and I couldn't let her find out."

I was horrified, "What are you talking about? I don't understand you. Why did you marry me, then? This is so unfair!"

"You were interesting and I admired your knowledge. But I thought you wouldn't find out or understand, since we agreed to use abstinence as birth control. But you had to push the issue. Now that you know the truth we just have to pretend to have the normal life of a married couple. You have nowhere to go, and you're pregnant, so I guess you're stuck."

My whole world crumbled. What could I say? There was no need to make a scene or cry about it. Simon told me his truth. So this was my fate. I walked into the bedroom and thought, "You cannot make someone love you." I ran a bath and sat in the tub for a long time. "Maybe the water can wash away this insanity and I will wake up from this nightmare," I hoped. But no, there would be no waking up. "I am stuck with him and stuck with this life," I lamented. This is my punishment for rushing into this marriage. I thought of the sobering expression, "I made my bed, now I have to lie in it." When we were dating, I did not allow any heavy petting, to remain pure before marriage. I thought he was just being respectful—how wrong I was! One shouldn't buy a pair of shoes without trying them on; shouldn't that wisdom also apply to taking a husband? I resigned myself, "I'll have to find a way to live with this situation."

Finally, at the end of February, Simon got a job as an X-ray technician at a local hospital on the day shift. On the nights Mac was in town from his job, we had to go over to Simon's parents' home for dinner and watch television with them. When Mac wasn't home, Sue didn't cook, so we ate at our apartment. On those evenings she and Simon would agree to watch the same TV shows and Simon would call her at the end of every show, every half-hour or hour. I thought it was a strange behavior to remain so oddly attached to his mother, but I didn't say anything. I spent most evenings at the kitchen table correcting papers, preparing for the next day's lesson or reading, happy to stay out of his way.

Every Thursday evening, there was a live wrestling match in Springfield. Simon went regularly, staying out until all hours. He would always take a shower before he left. When he returned he smelled so bad of tobacco and other body odors that, after a few times, I told him he couldn't get in bed like that. I was thankful he began to take a shower upon his return. I feigned to be asleep.

One Friday afternoon I came home from school and found the cutest little fluffy puppy in the living room. "What is this?" I asked Simon.

"I got paid and I bought this puppy. Isn't he cute? I named him Happy."

"You bought him? How much did he cost?" I was angry that he had not consulted me for such a large purchase when we had so little money.

"It was $250. I used my paycheck and just a little more from our account."

"Simon, what do we need a puppy for? That's half a month of my salary. I don't even know how much your take-home pay is. I have to start going to the doctor for the baby. We have no health insurance. Don't you realize that as soon as I start showing the school will not allow me to continue teaching? What were you thinking? We have to pay for the doctor and the hospital."

"Oh, you are no fun," Simon huffed as he carried Happy outside, dismissing my concerns.

I had to sit down to catch my breath. He acted like a spoiled child. I couldn't imagine anyone being so irresponsible. We had no savings. This was his first paycheck since November. I had given all my savings to Sue. We had talked about my not teaching for a year after the baby's birth. I could see that I didn't count. I felt like a doormat supreme.

In late April, Simon came home furious, his face flushed, loudly fussing, "That jerk of a doctor complained about my films. He cussed me out and I quit. I'm never going back to work in that stupid hospital. They don't appreciate me." After these words

Simon told me we were going over to his mother's. I suspected he had been fired but I never confronted him about it—I assumed he would deny it, so what would be the use?

I received my last paycheck from Republic High at the end of May, which paid for our June rent. I started seeing Dr. William Walker, an obstetrician, whom I agreed to pay monthly, since I had no insurance. I was still paying for a set of rings Simon bought in Memphis for me. This was my first experience with the concept of buying on credit. I quickly learned it was something I wanted to stay away from—buying before you could afford and paying a lot of interest.

Dr. Walker determined that my baby would be born on or before August 19, which was Simon's birthday. Although at first I was unhappy about getting pregnant, as time went on, feeling my baby grow and kick inside me, I looked forward to this new little person in my life and in my care. Secretly, I hoped for a boy because I was afraid that, if this baby were a girl, I might unconsciously pass on my mother's attitude by belittling her just as it had been done to me, thereby perpetuating on my own child the discrimination toward girls I had inherited. This was a serious, deep concern, even though I had promised myself that I would not let that happen.

Weeks went by and Simon didn't offer to look for a job, excusing himself by saying, "I don't feel like it." I simply couldn't understand that kind of thinking. Before our July rent came due I asked him what we were to do.

"We'll just move back to mother's," he answered.

I was devastated by the thought of it. But what could I do?

We returned into the "mouth of the tigress."

August 7, I went into labor, and 16 hours later we had a beautiful baby boy. We named him Gregory and called him Greg. Sue and Mac were delighted with their first grandson. All of our attention was on this precious new life. Sue was particularly devoted to him and took over his care as if he were *her* baby—rocking, feeding, and changing him. Amazingly, Greg brought out the softer side of Sue. I was happy to see her so taken with my baby because I foresaw that I would have to count on her for childcare. It was obvious that

Simon was not going back to work anytime soon.

Earning a living fell back to me. We had the doctor and hospital bills to pay, as well as the extra baby expenses. It was already mid-August, very late in the year to look for a teaching job. Nonetheless, I called Saint Agnes Cathedral School and spoke with the Monsignor. He immediately conducted an interview on the phone. I later learned that this was because he was hard of hearing and it was actually easier for him to hear me over the phone than in person. We met face-to-face that afternoon, he offered me the position, and I started teaching 16 days after Gregory was born. I thought to myself, "How have I been so fortunate to find a job at this crucial moment?" I taught at this school for two years, while Simon "did not feel like working."

A few days before Christmas, we took Greg to visit his great-grandfather, Jim, who then learned that Simon had not worked since April. He suggested we move into a house he owned and that Simon help him do some of his work as a landlord, such as taking care of some light repairs and collecting rent. We didn't have to pay any rent to Grandpa Jim. Instead, he asked that I cook dinner for him once in a while, and he was always thoughtful to bring extra groceries whenever he came over. Jim kept a bedroom for himself in the house and occupied it only when he didn't want to drive back to his farm a dozen miles away.

Every morning Simon drove me to school and took Greg to Nana Sue's for babysitting. He would also stay there until I got off unless Jim called him with a specific task. Jim was hoping that Simon might show some interest in his rental business so that he could eventually turn it over to him. He was disappointed that Simon had to be pushed every step of the way. After a few months of tugging, Jim quit calling his grandson to work. I couldn't understand a man who had no sense of responsibility to earn a living for his family. He continued saying, "I don't feel like going to work." My early respect for him eroded into contempt.

During the Christmas break in 1965 I came down with the flu. I had a fever and ached all over. I was so thankful that school was not in session. Simon wanted us to go to his mother's, so I said, "Take

Gregory and go spend the day if you wish, just let me stay and rest. I might be contagious and there is no sense exposing everyone."

"No, you have to go. You can lie down at her house," he bossed.

"Why? It doesn't make sense. I will stay here," I insisted.

"No, you will not. She doesn't trust you, and I don't trust you."

"Don't trust me about what? What am I going to do here but go to bed?"

"No telling what you are going to do with Jim!"

"What? Look Simon, you *are* crazy," I replied, and as I turned away from him he jerked me around by the arm and drew back to hit me.

I stepped back, threw his hand off my arm and whispered slowly, "Simon, you *will not hit me*. If you do, don't plan on ever going to sleep because I *will kill you*."

"You would rot in jail if you did!" he screamed.

Looking him straight in the eye, I whispered, "I would rather rot in jail than wait for you to strike me the next time." I turned and confidently walked away giving thanks to Sister Eileen Maura for her most emphatic lesson. I had sensed Simon's anger escalating for months before this incident and had prepared myself for such a confrontation. When my safety was at stake, my survival instinct—combined with my mental rehearsal—enabled me to speak calmly, without stuttering. Simon never again threatened to hit me. Actually, in some ways he became more conciliatory and accommodating as time went on.

During my first three years of marriage all my dreams and expectations of how a marriage and family should be were shattered. Before we were married the one area I thought I could count on Simon for was that he was a practicing Catholic—that was my safety net. After we moved into his mother's home in Springfield we stopped going to Mass on Sundays. The first few weeks were understandable because he was recovering from kidney surgery and could not drive. Eventually, not only did he simply refuse to attend church but he forbade me to do so as well. This became the most painful part of my existence, the disappearance of my Catholic religion, support, and rituals in my daily life.

I had followed the teachings of Catholicism from the time I was eight years old, was baptized at thirteen, went to church every Sunday, and attended Mass every single morning in college. I lived devoutly by Church rules and regulations. But my marriage and daily life with Simon took this constant away. I was shaken in the foundation of my belief. Nonetheless, I attempted to conduct myself in purity and without sin.

In the bed that Simon and I shared, he wanted me away from him as far as possible. If by accident I got too close he would hiss, "You are *breathing on me. Get away!*" I felt stabbed by his voice. Using his most demeaning words, I latched on to the term *breath* and pictured it as the rope that led me to a lifesaver. I recalled what my Buddhist nanny taught me, "When you are troubled, sit still, close your eyes, empty your mind, and focus on your breath. Breathing in, know that you are breathing in; breathing out, know that you are breathing out. That's call *da zuo* (sitting or meditating). It will clear your mind, calm your heart, change the way you look at the situation, and, sometimes, you will receive the solution to your problem."

Because the rituals of my Catholic religion were taken away from me, I found I reverted to a more basic spirituality, one which did not require the dictates or the presence of a physical church. Little by little, the Buddhist teachings of my nanny began to rise up in my memory and they became my support. I pictured the craziness of my marriage and the strained relationship with my mother-in-law as a raging river that I must follow because it was my life. But instead of being pulled in and tossed by the waves, I could walk on the solid bank, and take notes of the situation as an observer. I could even put on an *imperméable* (French for raincoat), then I would not even get wet. I had no control over the movements of the river nor was I attached to the outcome. Believing in Karma, I could look at my difficulties as lessons I needed to learn or reparations I owed Simon and his mother. I was responsible for what happened to me and couldn't expect any outside source to save me. I was to accept my fate. I held on to the belief that I have the power within me to overcome the challenges.

The river I was watching was also the society of mid-America working-class people, with its prejudices and no frame of reference for foreign cultures. I was the first Asian whom Jim, Sue, or Mac had ever spoken to. I was plopped into their midst not of their own choosing. The Vietnam War was going on, so anyone from that part of the world was viewed with suspicion, as if a Communist. I understood some of their difficulty dealing with me and strived to not take it too personally.

When Christmas vacation ended I went back to teach. The winter flu left me with three months of bronchitis, then pleurisy, aggravated by second-hand smoke from Simon and his parents. One day in April, 1966 I fainted in class. The nun-principal called Simon to pick me up. The only physician I had ever seen in Springfield was Dr. Walker, who determined that I was again pregnant. I viewed the next baby as a gift to Gregory so that he would not remain an only child. Since my mother-in-law had grown to accept me through her love and care of her first grandson, when it was confirmed that I was to have another baby I engaged her to be an ally. I asked her opinion whether it was right for Simon not to have worked for three whole years. I pleaded that she encourage him to start looking for a job because by August my pregnancy would be apparent and, as is customary, I would not be given a job teaching. She was well aware of the system and convinced Simon to apply for work. It wasn't long before he was hired by Citizen's Finance Company, one of the companies that made loans to individuals before the credit card system was created. We soon had enough income to move out of Grandpa Jim's house into our own place.

Our second baby came on December 15, 1966. We named him Michael. Because I was able to stay home with him, he gave me the joy of motherhood. Simon worked well at his job and, a year-and-a-half later, he was promoted and transferred to manage the office in Butler, Missouri, a town of about 4,000, some one hundred miles from Springfield. After he had been there a couple of months he found a house and moved the family. We had a seemingly normal family life. Simon went to Kansas City one evening a week, supposedly to watch a wrestling match; but I never probed or questioned.

Being able to be at home with my two little boys was a time

filled with memories I treasure. They loved to dress up at Hallow-een. One year Nana Sue gave Greg an Indian outfit and Michael was the cowboy. They strutted around the neighborhood, proudly displaying their costumes. Later, Simon and I took them around to trick-or-treat. Unlike in today's throw-away society, my boys en-joyed these costumes for many months (photo 39). They were made durably enough to withstand all of their play and many washings. From my present understanding I would not have allowed the combination of "cowboys and Indians" costumes and the scenario of their role playing, now realizing how offensive that is to many Native Americans. This change of perspecitve shows the beauty of how we can grow and develop in our understanding of others.

As a teacher I knew that hand-eye coordination was important for my boys' development so I taught them to cut out pictures from old magazines, learning new vocabulary and spelling as they went. Their kindergarten teachers were amazed at how well they handled the scissors. They enjoyed the stories I read to them, especially the ones about Christopher Robin and Winnie the Pooh. When our neighbor Gail gave them their first dog, Gregory wanted to name him "Tigger" and Michael insisted that it had to be "Piglet." I was surprised that Piglet won out and I always thought that it was comical to be standing outside calling, "Piglet! Piglet!" and it being a dog that answered. Michael's favorite toys were the ones that made music or sounds. At his eighth grade graduation, he was the valedictorian and sang a solo, *The Rose*. Greg loved any toy that had wheels. His first job was washing and parking cars at a dealership in West Plains, Missouri. He continued working in the car business and, at 31, bought his first car dealership.

To subsidize Simon's salary, I spent a dollar on a do-it-yourself book and taught myself how to decorate birthday and wedding cakes. Since there was no bakery in town to make fancy pastries, I was kept busy. My boys participated by placing the tiny toys on many a birthday cake with sports themes or characters from popular culture, such as *Batman and Robin*.

Having had no dental care for years, one day I came down with a severe toothache and swollen jaw. In such a small town, there were only three dentists listed in the Yellow Pages. I randomly picked the name in the middle—Dr. Hinshaw. His receptionist gave me the time slot that was reserved for emergencies. In the waiting room I told Gregory to sit on the camel saddle, which was obviously placed there for children, and explained to him how it was used. Dr. Hinshaw overheard me and delighted in telling me how he bought it in Egypt on his last trip. He enjoyed travelling and sharing his stories. He also told me that he loved Chinese food, so, over my next couple of appointments it was natural that I invited him to our home for dinner and conversation. Years later, I learned that while I was putting my boys to bed that evening, Simon made inappropriate advances toward him. Dr. Hinshaw ignored them, and he distanced himself from further social contacts with us. Thus, we lost the one interesting friendship we could have nurtured.

During the time we lived in Butler my father passed away. I was touched by the kindness of the people of this small Missouri town. Some of them I barely knew came to visit me and brought flowers, food, and words of comfort. After my father was buried I learned that the Optimist Club Simon belonged to had wanted to raise money to send me home for the funeral but Simon had refused without even consulting me.

We were in Butler for a couple of years when Simon said he was tired of the job with the finance company and wanted a change. He found a position with the newly developed federal Office of Economic Opportunity. It required us to move to Warsaw, Missouri, where we bought a house near a lake. Simon started to bring a young man home to spend the night with him, asking me to go downstairs and sleep with the boys. His place of work got wind of it and questioned his behavior. He insisted that I go to bat for him. I did, but I felt used because it went against my integrity. He was fired anyway.

His next job was in Sedalia, Missouri, with E.W. Thompson, a successful businessman who owned several car dealerships. Mr. Thompson had always dreamed of having a hotel/bar and restaurant, so he had signed a franchise contract with the Ramada Inn and hired Simon to help him understand the fine points of the regulations and to get the establishment opened. Being short on help, Simon had me go to work as a housekeeper, cleaning guest rooms. The restaurant chef discovered that I could bake fancy desserts for the dining room and quickly transferred me, paying me the highest hourly wages in the kitchen. That made Simon mad, so he ordered me to quit. I had no choice but to do what he said.

Later, he was promoted to the position of night manager. Late one evening Mr. Thompson dropped by the hotel. Instead of finding Simon running the front desk, he discovered him in the cocktail lounge hosting several young men. He accused him of turning the place into a gay bar and fired him on the spot. Simon's preferred lifestyle, which was surfacing more and more, had now caused him to lose two jobs. I thought I'd better go back to teaching and found work in a second grade in Warsaw. At that time, with Greg going into the second grade and Michael ready for kindergarten, I again became the sole breadwinner.

One day I went to our downstairs extra closet to exchange our summer clothes for winter ones. I discovered a package of dried leaves, the size of a bread bag. I asked Simon what it was. He quickly answered, "Don't you dare bother it! It's dried spinach."

"Sure it is. You really think I am *that* stupid!" I replied.

My next thoughts were for my boys' safety. I could swallow any indignities when they were directed at me alone, but in view of this situation I could not risk my sons' welfare. I thought through a plan. I called Dr. Hinshaw to ask him to get me in contact with Harold Caskey, the lawyer who rented space in his building. I had made my decision to file for divorce but asked Mr. Caskey to wait until my next paycheck to serve the papers.

After I received my monthly salary, I had my neighbor, Gail, who was my boys' babysitter, take me to the local trailer court, where I paid one month's rent for a trailer house. Then Gail took me home. Later, when Simon returned with his partner, Joe, I told both of them to leave with their belongings. I said that I was changing the locks, so if they tried to come back in, they would be breaking and entering.

Simon retorted, "You can't do that to us, we have no place to go."

I handed him a key and the address of the trailer court and said, "Yes, you do. Here is the key to the trailer where you will sleep tonight. Simon, you will be served divorce papers. It's up to you to explain to our boys why you are leaving."

He followed my orders in a daze. I called our sons to the kitchen. Simon sat them both down at the table and said, "Your mama wants me to leave with Joe because I love him more than I love her. She is jealous and she can't take it. I have to do what she says so I can be with Joe, but I still love you both."

Gregory was eight and Michael just five-and-a-half. It was a sad day for our family. I was going against my culture and the teaching of my Church. I deeply regretted that my sons had to continue their lives from a broken marriage. Yet I knew that the way they would come to view their development and their lives would be a matter of their own choice. I was not sure if they would ever understand the necessity of my actions at the time, and was aware they might blame me for making their father leave. Nevertheless, under those circumstances, I chose the lesser evil.

They watched their dad pack some clothes and other belongings. They cried, hugged him, and asked him not to go. I heard Simon say to them, "It is really better for you boys that I leave. I can't stay here with Joe. Your mama will take care of you."

The divorce went through. The judge ordered Simon to pay child support—he never paid a single dollar and I did not press. My deepest regret was that he totally cut off all communication with his sons: birthdays, graduations, weddings, the birth of their babies—all these milestone events came and went without a word from him. I am sure the boys felt hurt but, as the years went by, they refused to talk about him. I am most thankful for Simon's mother eventually helping me watch over our boys while I supported them financially.

I got through the years after my divorce. I survived and made the best of a bad situation. And five years later I married my dentist, Dr. Hinshaw.

The first few months of my marriage to Don Hinshaw were sheer delight. I had never been so relaxed and at ease with a relationship—there were no pretenses and no unreasonable expectations. At 36, for the first time since I was 18, I did not have to count every dollar. We cared deeply for one another, and conversation and daily life flowed easily. Don had a set schedule in which he worked ten-hour days in his dental clinic in Butler, four days a week. We drove into Kansas City on Tuesdays, had a nice dinner out, went back to our individual apartments for that night, and spent Wednesdays on our own. We reconnected for Wednesday evening church services and afterward drove back to Butler for two more days of work. This routine was repeated Fridays after his office hours and we were back in the city for the weekends. He had his friends, I had mine. We navigated easily together and separately, frequently giving parties in his apartment, which was beautifully decorated with mementos of our international travels. We became very active with the People to People International organization, hosting many foreign officers from the Fort Leavenworth Staff College.

Don had asked me to take over the kitchen at his residence back home in Butler. I happily assumed that role, cooking breakfast, lunch, and dinner for both of us. He had set up an unlimited charge account for me to buy whatever I needed or wanted at Jennings' grocery store. I felt I got to *play* in the kitchen, trying all kinds of recipes and baking desserts for the staff of Don's clinic, the office of my former attorney, Mr. Caskey, and the insurance company that rented in the Hinshaw building. I knew it was always smart to make friends with the local butcher, so I went to visit with him at Jennings'. When I approached his counter he exclaimed, "Oh, hello, are you our new doctor's wife?" Since I am Asian he assumed I was married to the Thai physician who had moved to town the week before and set up his practice in the newly-built Bates County Hospital.

I replied, "No, I am Dr. Hinshaw's new wife and my name is Bambi. I would like to know about a cut of meat that I call 'Delmonico steak,' but I am not sure how to ask for it here." With a big smile he told me that the ribeye is the cut I wanted and added, proudly showing off his knowledge, "The fancier name came from the Delmonico Restaurant in New York City."

Once a month I drove to West Plains to visit my boys and Nana Sue for a few days. There I had the pleasure of being with them and also filling their large chest-style freezer and pantry with goodies of all sorts. I gave Sue only $100 a month cash for incidentals. Everything else she and my boys needed was charged at Sears or J.C. Penney's, and a local drugstore—from socks to bedspreads to medicine—and I paid them all. I also gave the boys $36 each for pocket money. After all the bad experiences Sue and I had, her attitude toward me had totally turned around. She was most appreciative of my financial support. We really made a good team for the sake of the boys.

Because Don didn't feel that my old Chevrolet was reliable enough for the four-hour trip to West Plains, he always had me drive his Cadillac. One day upon my return from one of those trips, he said, "I think it's time to buy you a new car. If you could choose any model, what would it be?" Without a moment's hesitation I spilled out what my dream car would be, "Really, you want me to tell you? It would be a white Thunderbird with lipstick red trim and red or white leather interior."

Don chuckled and said, "I *love it* that you are so specific. Let's go look for it in Butler first. If we can't find it we'll look in Oklahoma, since we're going there next weekend to see my mother. Consider it my present to *you* for Mother's Day." That's exactly what we did—we found my dream car in Tulsa. When I test drove it the odometer read seven miles. He bought it and we drove two cars home.

Nine months after we were married, Effie, Don's office manager of over 25 years had a heart attack. Don asked me to fill in for her until she recovered. But it turned out that she could no longer return to work, so I took over her job for the next nine years. In addition to his dental practice, he had a housing rental business with some one hundred and twenty dwellings and a full-time maintenance man. Our life was divided between work in Butler, leisure time in Kansas City, and many overseas trips to Europe, Asia, the Caribbean, and Central and South America. We got along well in all areas.

On one of our trips we went through England, Ireland, Scotland, and Wales. In the Anglican churches we visited, as we sat in the pews listening to the guide tell the history of the place, I would pick up the little cushions used as kneelers, to admire the needlepoint covers. Looking at them, I had a feeling of going back in time and having stitched them myself. Back in Kansas City, I searched out a shop that sold needlepoint project kits. I bought one along with an instruction book and started in as if returning to a lost memory. I wanted to cover an antique foot stool, for which I envisioned a design. Don unlocked a room in his building where he had an art studio from the days when he used to dabble in painting and sculpture. He handed me some old brushes and tubes of paint and told me to put the design I had in my head onto canvas. Two hours later, when I showed him what I had done, he exclaimed, "Oh my stars! Did you know you could paint?" It was a brand new discovery.

An artist friend at the time asked me why I started painting roses, given that they are the most difficult flowers to render. I replied, "No one told me they were difficult." I painted from my memory of a rose rather than copying a real flower. The painting used for the cover of this book is the third one I ever did, one of several dozen (photos 44, 54).

In December 1983, I went to Taipei to spend three weeks with my mother. She had informed me that a 70th birthday was a big deal in Chinese society. I needed to show my filial piety by coming to Taiwan and inviting her friends and relatives to celebrate with a big dinner party. I tried to get my brother Max to participate, but he said he was too busy and couldn't leave his business, so I ended up planning, organizing, and paying for everything. Mama acted as if it was her due and didn't show any special appreciation.

When Don picked me up at the airport upon my return, I noticed a *je ne sais quoi* (I don't know what) indefinable coolness. I was not accustomed to this kind of distancing from him. I just attributed it to my having been gone for three weeks and thought we just needed to get reacquainted. I was happy to be home and chattered away, telling him what I had done in Taipei and also in Hong Kong, to prepare for the tour of American travelers I was to lead in September. We arrived at our apartment building and, very naturally, I unlocked and entered my side. As I started to unpack my bags he asked me to sit down and said, "I need to tell you that I rented the extra bedroom in my apartment to an older student. You and I are gone several days a week and it is not smart to leave this place empty."

"Okay," I answered casually, "if you think that's the right thing to do. How much are you charging him? Did he sign a rental contract? Is it for a semester at a time?" I was speaking as his office manager in charge of the rentals.

"Oh, it's not like that. I am not charging him any money. He is living here in exchange for some light housekeeping and yard work. I want to help him since he is going back to school."

I smiled and added, "It's just like you to be helping someone in need, as you did for me. But *I* insisted on paying you rent at that time. When do I get to meet him? What's his name?"

"His name is Chuck. How about we go out to dinner together? I know you don't want Chinese tonight; you think you would like Houlihan's on the Plaza?"

"That sounds great. Let me take a shower and change first. I'll come over when I am ready. I won't take long."

I first met Chuck in Don's kitchen. He was a Caucasian American about my age, early forties, a bit on the portly side, blond, very meticulously dressed, and mannerly. Our conversation at the restaurant flowed easily, mainly with Chuck and my talking. On Sunday, when Chuck joined us for church and lunch, I started to feel uneasy. He was infringing on my privacy with Don. It was not long before I realized that their relationship was more than met the eye. I kept hoping that I was wrong and that I could still count on Don's word, his promise before our marriage that he would not move in a lover.

In September, for 22 days, I led the trip I had designed and named "The Three Faces of China" (photo 47). Don and I, and 14 other American travelers toured Taiwan, mainland China, and Hong Kong with my leading the group—my first experience as a tour director. Having done my homework, with the help of *Fodor's*

Travel Guide, and with my ability to speak both Mandarin and Cantonese, I communicated easily with our local guides. In 1984, even though tourism in China was in its infancy, our trip went smoothly, to the enjoyment of all.

In Taipei (photo 45), visiting the Palace Museum, which contains the treasures of the past emperors of China, was our highlight. In Guangzhou, a stop at an ivory factory unlocked the mystery of how a Canton ball was carved from the outside in, out of a solid piece of tusk—seven to nineteen layers of concentric balls that could roll independently within one another.

A day-long cruise on the Li River took us between the misty limestone mountains of Guilin, said to be the "abode of the Immortals." Then we were on to Hangzhou, where the hills, pagodas, temples, and porcelain-blue lake inspired Marco Polo to exclaim in the 13th century, "One fancies oneself to be in paradise."

Our pace quickened as we entered Shanghai, the largest city in China—at that time more than twelve million inhabitants. We visited a carpet factory, an arts and crafts center, and the quiet Jade Buddha Temple, where more than 7,000 volumes of Buddhist scriptures are moth-proofed and stored.

In Xian we saw an entire army being unearthed—some 8,000 life-sized terra cotta soldiers, no two alike, with their horses and chariots—which guarded the mausoleum of emperor Qin Shi Huang, who unified China in 221 B.C. This was the same emperor who ordered the linking up of various sections of the Great Wall, reportedly the only human-made structure visible from the moon. Anyone who sees the Great Wall would have to stand in awe of the thought of the human power used and the magnitude of the undertaking to build nearly 4,000 miles of barrier, 35 feet high and 17 feet wide, across the northern border of the country. Officially, it is 12,700 Chinese *li* or 3,946 miles long—more than the distance from Boston to San Francisco. It was completed 200 years BCE (Before the Common Era). It is said that over 300,000 laborers worked ten years to complete it. Five horsemen or 10 foot-soldiers could march abreast, as if it were a superhighway through the rough mountainous terrain.

Long before the trip I hosted a get-acquainted meeting, where I presented the details of the journey and collected all the passports—at that time it took well over a month to complete the visa applications. As I checked expiration dates, I happened to notice the date of birth of one of the women: she was 84. I told her it would be a grueling trip that would require a lot of walking. She assured me, "I come from strong stock. I am still healthy and able to walk some distance. Since I saw the picture of the Great Wall of China in a school book years ago, it has been my dearest wish to walk on it. To tell you how determined I am to make this trip, should I die before we get there, I want to be cremated and to have you scatter my ashes on the Great Wall. Does that show you enough of my resolve? I absolutely would not hold you responsible if there were to be any mishap." She convinced me, so I took her in with great admiration, and she turned out to be one of the most enthusiastic travelers of the group. She had her picture taken, proudly standing on *her* Great Wall of China.

In Beijing, we strolled on the Tiananmen Square, the world's largest plaza, where one million persons can stand side by side. We walked into the former Imperial Palace, also known as the Forbidden City—called "forbidden" because, in the old days, commoners were not allowed inside. An especially exciting point of the trip, for me, was discovering that the calligraphy of one of my ancestors, Shen Bao-zhen (1820-1879), was on display in one of the palace galleries. It was a communication he had sent to the emperor when he was posted as viceroy in Taiwan.

Like a true dual-national, I felt a twinge of homesickness when visiting Beijing University, where both my parents had graduated. I asked to see the grave of Edgar Snow, a noted journalist and native of Kansas City who had taught there for several years. My mother had attended some of his journalism lectures in the 1930s. Before his death he asked that part of his ashes be buried on the Beijing University campus. His manuscripts and professional papers are archived at the University of Missouri in Kansas City, two blocks from my home.

We ended our journey in Hong Kong, with three days of shopping and appointments with tailors. Each of us had an ultra-suede jacket or suit made to measure. We chose the color and fabric on day one, tried on our outfits on the second evening in our hotel rooms, and the finished garments were delivered on day three. Don led the group homeward to the U.S. and I stayed behind to spend a day with Ah Jie, my childhood nanny.

What a reunion—our first in 26 years (photo 46)! We chatted about many memories of all the time she attended to me from birth to age 18. I thanked her for having been the most beneficial influence in my life. When my parents left Saigon in 1958, for papa's new post in Taiwan, Ah Jie chose not to follow them because her younger brother was attending the government medical school in China. She was afraid that her going to Taiwan would interfere with his completing his studies, because, at that time, the animosity between the two governments was intense. When the Vietnam War made Saigon's economy unstable, Ah Jie's sisterhood of house-servants helped her decide to move to Hong Kong to seek employment. During the five years I worked as a tour director, I saw her every time I traveled through Hong Kong, always spending a day with her, eating out and shopping for her. She said she was proud of how I had turned out and bragged about me to her sisters: "My baby came back to see me after so many years."

Back in Kansas City, Chuck was fuming over not having been able to participate in our tour of China. He extracted from Don the promise of a trip during his Christmas vacation. So I accepted the invitation of two antique dealer friends, Gordon and Jimmy, to travel to France and serve as their interpreter while they searched for interesting items for their exclusive shop. Don was happy that I was leaving for a while and asked me not to return home until after the holidays. I agreed, but only under the condition that Chuck would move out of the apartment. I could feel that my life with Don was coming to an end.

After Gordon and Jimmy went back to the U.S., I had over a month to do as I pleased in France. I mapped out an itinerary of places I had studied during my years in French schools, Catholic shrines I had read about, and locations where authors were born or had written their works.

I traveled by train on a France-rail pass. Upon arrival in each city, I went to a gift shop and purchased postcards of the places I wanted to see. Then I hired a taxicab and handed the driver the stack of postcards, asking him to sequence visits to all of the chosen sites. He would tell me how long it would take, and we would negotiate a fee. Usually I treated him to lunch. The drivers were always amazed at my knowledge of the history of the sites and my ability to sometimes quote the words of any relevant authors.

In preparation for an upcoming job as a tour director, I made copious notes on the postcards and mailed them home. My friend Cass White joined me for ten days, visiting the castles of the Loire River valley. At Aix-les Bains, we walked on the banks of Lake Bourget, where one of my favorite authors, Lamartine, wrote about Julie, his lover who had died, *"Un seul être vous manque et tout est depleuple'."* (Only one person is missing and the whole world seems depopulated.)

Toward the end of my month in France after Cass flew in from Kansas City, we visited Lourdes and Madrid. I showed her around my favorite city, Paris. There we met a newlywed couple, Dana and Chris Hambleton, and we spent a whole day together. I gave them a tour of a few of my favorite spots, including the *Marche' aux Puces*, the original term for this, the first European flea market, inaugurated in 1885. We joked about the pests which were transferred at such a place over the century—hence the term "flea market," which has become a world-wide phenomenon. We still maintain contact with the Hambletons, more than twenty years later.

When I returned to Kansas City, the good news was that Chuck had moved out of Don's apartment, but the bomb was that I had twenty days to vacate mine. Don had sold his building west of the Plaza and bought a house in Overland Park, Kansas. His idea was to remodel the house to have a separate entrance and an apartment for Chuck in the finished basement. I vetoed his plan and, feeling betrayed, I confronted him, "Don, aren't you breaking your word? You promised me you wouldn't move someone in. What do you think I should do?"

"I thought you could be more flexible," he huffed. "You have to move to the new house anyway since I've sold this building. I guess

I'll have to figure out something else."

It broke my heart to have to leave my favorite area of Kansas City, the Country Club Plaza.

Back in our office in the country, Don spent several months negotiating to sell his Butler rental property business in its entirety and keep only the few units he had in Kansas City. I was busy with a lot of documentation to prepare for the transaction. When the sale was completed I knew my usefulness to Don diminished that much more. By that time we had moved into our house in Overland Park, but he rarely slept there. One Saturday afternoon, as he was getting ready to go out, I looked at him and shook my head. He exploded, "You always make me feel so guilty!"

I responded, "You feel guilty because you *are* guilty."

Furious, he added, "I don't want you back in Butler anymore!"

"*Fine!*" I walked into my bedroom and shut the door.

The next day was Sunday, so I went to church as usual, but Don chose to attend a different service with Chuck. I went to lunch with a girlfriend, then to visit my antique dealer friends, Mel and Fay, who asked me where I had eaten lunch. I answered, "Across the street at the House of Hunan. You want anything? I'll buy." As I waited in the bar area for their to-go order, I heard the owner, James Hu, receive a phone call and become very upset. His bartender for the evening just called in sick, and he had booked a seventy-person party. He expected a large bar tab, so he was beside himself, knowing he could not handle the orders alone.

Since I had been a frequent customer for years I felt comfortable offering assistance. I said, "*Lao Ban* (Boss), you want me to come in and help you? I know how to mix drinks. If I may take a look at how your bottles are set up, it'll be a lot easier." James was surprised by the offer but happy to accept my help.

I went home, cooked dinner, left it on the stove with a note to Don and changed into a Chinese gown. As I was leaving, Don walked in. "Where are you going?" he said, surprised to see me dressed up.

"You told me you did not want me to go back to Butler, so I got a job and I am reporting to work. Dinner is on the stove if you want to eat." I did not wait to see his reaction. I drove away and didn't return to Butler for twenty years.

Word of my success leading the trip to China had reached a large tour company called Rural Route International of Leawood, Kansas. They hired me to write their brochures, to be the tour director for China, and to design and lead their Catholic pilgrimages in Europe.

My association with the House of Hunan restaurant worked out well. When I was not gone on tours I helped James as a hostess, cashier, or bartender, wherever he needed me. In 1986, an opportunity opened up to lease a small restaurant in downtown Kansas City, Kansas. James convinced me to join him in investing in it. The chef, named K.Y., and I soon bought James out. We simplified the menu and eliminated all pork dishes when I learned that there was a mosque in the neighborhood. We ended up serving a large Muslim population. We named the place Bambi's Kitchen. After three years we sold it and opened a fancy restaurant in south Kansas City, Missouri, which we named the Golden Palace. Both these businesses were successful and the Golden Palace received The Squire newspaper award for best Chinese restaurant two years running.

K.Y. had gone to Taiwan with an uncle at the age of twelve and was separated from his family in mainland China for 44 years. Miraculously, he located his mother in 1993, while working with me. He wanted to return to be with her. It was the right time for me to sell the Golden Palace. I bought back the first location of Bambi's Kitchen, which required shorter hours and a smaller staff. I was happy to have a more personable business and made my faithful "Mexican son," Victor, head chef and manager of the kitchen.

After four years of separation, Don and I divorced in 1987. During the subsequent years of living solo, I learned a lot about managing a business and taking care of finances. Over the course of eleven years, I owned and operated three Chinese restaurants, providing a livelihood for some 30 employees and their families. I often had to make difficult decisions and shoulder the consequences alone. At some point, I realized that I had become the strong independent woman I had so admired in K.K. many years before. By that time, I had become so strong and decisive that my friend, Carol, gave me the nickname "bulldozer." I had come a long way!

Chapter 10

MY WORD IS MY BOND

During the eleven years I owned restaurants, starting in 1986, I arranged to close every year for two weeks, from December 20 to January 4. This allowed me to travel to Taiwan and spend my mother's birthday with her, fulfilling her wish to have me host an annual party with relatives in her honor. She lived in the condo in Taipei that father had bought shortly before his death. Since housing is the most costly expense in that city she was fortunate to benefit from papa's foresight. In 1988, when the twenty-year widow pension she had been receiving from the Taiwan government was about to expire, she informed me that she would have to depend on me for her living expenses. I began sending her $650 a month.

During the next seven years, I also paid for her to take three two-month-long trips to visit relatives in mainland China. This was the only thing she ever thanked me for. In 1995, when mother was 81, she became very ill and required hospitalization three times in two months. Early that December, relatives frantically called me to come to Taipei to make decisions on her medical care. Since my annual late December trip there was already scheduled, I telephoned my brother Max asking him to travel there right away and assess mama's situation. "If she is not in immediate danger I will wait and arrive later, as planned," I said. "At that time I can arrange for a live-in nurse if necessary."

I arrived just after Max had brought her home from her third hospital stay. He needed to go back to the U.S. for his job. After he left, mama started hinting that I should stay longer. It was out of the question because I had a business to run. Even though she was weak, she was able to care for herself. I arranged for an upstairs neighbor, Mrs. Loo, to cook for and check on her daily after I left.

One day she became adamant and begged me, "Move to Taipei and stay with me. I am afraid to die alone. Last month I received news that Auntie Sophia had died in her house in Oakland. Remember, you visited her when you first arrived in America? It was days before neighbors noticed she hadn't been out and called the police. When they broke in, her body was already decomposing. I don't want to end up like her. You don't have a husband, so you are not needed in the U.S. I need you here. You should come and be my 'Filipina maid.' You'd be better for me than a Filipina, anyway. You owe me this. I don't think I have more than a year to live."

I was saddened to hear how she looked at me as if I were only a servant to her, dismissing the value of my entire life in America. Nonetheless, memory of the promise I made to father to take care of her came back to me as if I were sitting in his office in Tahiti. I knew I had to keep my word.

I replied, "Yes, I will come and stay until you no longer need me, but I have to think it through and make some arrangements before coming. Five people depend on me for their livelihood, so I have to help them find other employment. Then I will have to sell the restaurant. I also have to sell my house, because I can't leave it empty or rent it.

"Of course you know that if I don't have an income I won't be able to give you your monthly allowance, as I have done the last eleven years. Since this condominium is in a very desirable location, why don't you consider selling it? You can get a good price, then enjoy the money it will bring you. I need to keep my savings for myself since I have been single for several years. I have to look out for my old age as I am already 56."

Annoyed, she responded, "With all your education you ended up running restaurants. You shame me. You are so commercial. You stink of copper!"—a Chinese insult to those who count money in business, referring to old China's coins being made of copper.

"If I had not been able to earn and share my money," I snapped, "who would have supported *you*? Who would have supported my children, their American grandmother, and myself? Mama, it's too bad that you think I 'stink of copper,' but it's out of necessity. I am one person earning for five." Those were the harshest words I had ever spoken to her. I had been taught never to talk back to my parents, but I was hurt when she belittled all I had accomplished. I was much more offended than all the other times she had put me down.

The paperwork required for me to move to Taiwan proved to be far more complicated than I anticipated. When I was born in 1939, Vietnam was part of the French-Union, therefore Taiwan considered me a foreigner. I was not allowed to be employed because, before I could get authorization to work, permanent residency status was required, but that would only be granted to those who intended to immigrate. Even though I had Chinese parents and wanted to live in Taiwan to care for one of them in old age, it took three-and-a-half years to complete the process of immigrating. In the meantime, I entered Taiwan as a tourist on my U.S. passport. I could stay for only ninety days, then I had to leave the country, even if just overnight; then I could return for another ninety days. Therefore, I went back and forth between Taipei and Kansas City, preparing to sell my restaurant and house and trying to run the business, which was not faring well because of my frequent absence. Airfare was over $1,500 each round-trip!

While I was in Kansas City, Mama sold her condo. She found an apartment in her old neighborhood, near the Taipei domestic airport, for US$1,600 a month, and she signed a two-year lease. When I learned what she had done, I felt manipulated. At the time, she begged me to take care of her and she had said she expected to have only a year to live. She signed that contract without talking to me because she considered negotiating in regard to money demeaning and unladylike, and she knew I would have negotiated for a lower price. She paid all 24 months' rent up front—$38,400! At that rate, how long would her money from selling her condo last? When that lease was up I had her move to a good, safe area in a newer suburb of Taipei, in the Nei Hu district, where I negotiated her rent down to US$500 a month. Again she chastised me for "stinking of copper."

After I made the trip to Taipei to help her move to her first apartment, I came back to Kansas City to handle my own business. Mama became confused in her new dwelling and called me five or six times a day asking me to return. After a week of this I flew back. She was extremely angry, blaming me for having made her sell the only thing of value father had left her. She ranted and raved incessantly during that two-week visit.

Even though I tried to reassure her that all would work out, I realized the enormity of my undertaking. How was I going to survive mother's emotional attacks day in and day out? In Taiwan my cousin Irene was my one and only friend and support. By mid-August I had calmed her down so I returned to Kansas City.

It was on the plane back from Taipei that, emotionally, I hit bottom. Driving home from the airport I scouted the banks of the Missouri River, looking for a place to have an "accident." For the first time in my life I considered suicide. Systematically, I put my affairs in order. I sold nearly all my antique furniture. I wrapped up the medal my father had left me—the one he had received from the Chinese government after the concentration camps—and mailed it to my brother. Before papa died he said he wanted me to keep it because of my memories of those years. The act of releasing his medal shifted my thinking: "In my next life, how could I face him with my cowardice? Where is the courage he taught me? I had given him my word that I would watch over mama. This is no time to buckle—I must find a way."

A short while after that, I created a spiritual exercise which I practiced in my restaurant. At the end of each day, I dropped some coins in a Chinese food carry-out box while affirming, "I Accept, I Adjust to, and I Appreciate the changes in my life." I called it the "Triple A of Change," playing on the American use of the word "change"—coins received back after a purchase. I donated the "change" to Unity Temple and shared the idea with my minister, Duke Tufty. Our church adopted this practice and has used it ever since. Twice a year, on the Sundays when Daylight Savings Time changes, empty boxes are handed out in exchange for full ones. The donations benefit the maintenance and beautification of the Temple grounds, with the volunteer labor of our devoted "Garden Fairies." In Duke's office, I admitted to him how difficult for me this move to Taiwan was. His words of counsel were: "Remember that this, too, shall pass." I hung on to this wisdom along with the words of the first hymn I had heard in that church, "confident living rights every wrong…" as if they were the beams of a lighthouse in a storm.

I sold my restaurant at a great loss. Fortunately, because the man who purchased my house had bought it for investment, I was able to stay and rent from him until my residency papers came through a year later. In the meantime, I volunteered at church, where I encountered Gene Foster, whom I had previously met at a United Nations Association function. We worked on a project together and felt a strong attraction toward one another. Since I was committed to go live with my mother, this new friendship could complicate my life. I argued with fate, "Why should I meet him now after so many years as a single person?"

One day I offered to take dinner to Gene and his 14-year-old son at their home, after a meeting where I volunteered to cook lunch for the group. I planned to have extras to take to Gene's, but had run out of bread, so I decided to stop at the Muehlebach grocery store on the way. There were only a few parking spots in front of that business, and at 5:15 in the afternoon, it was nearly impossible to get one. I asked my angel Butterfly to give me a sign as to whether I should continue my friendship with Gene by asking for one of those rare up-front parking spaces. There were none as I approached, but when I got closer, the back-up lights went on in a car right at the front door. I waited and pulled into the spot. Unreal! I thought, "Thank you, angel Butterfly. Maybe someday the Country Club Plaza will allow me to place a plaque or a statue and create a lover's shrine on that spot in your honor."

When I later told this to Gene, he exclaimed, "What? You would have given me up for lack of a parking spot?" I admitted to him that our meeting seemed untimely and that I felt conflicted, given my upcoming move to Taiwan. For me, it came down to a matter of faith, to trust my angel's guidance.

Four months later, Gene and I were united in an unique ceremony at Unity Temple on the Plaza. It opened with a bagpiper playing *Amazing Grace* for Gene's Irish ancestry, followed by three African drummers beating a wedding call, in honor of my father's many years as ambassador to Ivory Coast, Niger, and Rwanda. The entire choir sang several pieces for us, including one using French lyrics of *Nearer to Thee My God*, which I wrote out from memory. The clown ministry members acted as our ushers, wearing their full costumes and make-up, sprinkling magic dust on our guests. The church teenagers were our attendants, entering the sanctuary clapping and singing *Lean on Me*. One of the girls, Rachel Gaither, broke a strap on her sandal five minutes before start time and asked me what to do. I called out to the young people, "Kick off your shoes, you are all going in without them." No one seemed to care that they were bare-footed. All of our close family members—from near and far—along with their families, joined us for our special day: my brother, both my sons, and my closest childhood friend, Peter Tchan (photo 9), and Gene's son, plus his three sisters and two brothers. All came up on stage with us, participating in the ceremony of the blessing of our blended family. My granddaughter Rachel acted as flower girl and my grandson Ryan as ring bearer. The congregation contributed to a huge pot luck luncheon which followed. Gene and I engaged the legendary jazz band, the Scamps, with Geneva Price as lead singer, and we all danced to our hearts' content. What a party (photo 49)!

Ten days later my residency papers arrived and I left for Taiwan. My relationship with Gene survived nine years of separation with an occasional short visit in Kansas City. We actually deepened our bond in a unique way, through the written word, getting to know one another better, communicating daily. This was accomplished thanks to my son Michael—he forced me, at age 58, to buy two notebook computers and learn to use e-mail and instant messenger. He bought us two tickets to a computer show, walked us through it, and said, "Mama, you and Gene must learn to use the internet. You have to stay in communication while you are separated. I will teach you how." How thankful I am to Michael for "force-marching" us on the communication highway.

The transition to living with mama full time was challenging.

For the first 12 months I couldn't work, so she accused me of agreeing to take care of her only to get at her money. To prove to her that was not my intention I suggested she send my brother the amount she wanted him to inherit, and she did so immediately. Eventually her health improved, to the amazement of doctors, friends, and relatives. I cooked three meals a day and kept her active through her church and two women's organizations: the Zonta Club Taipei II—business and professional women executives, of which she was a founding member, and the World Association of Women Journalists and Writers— known by its Spanish-derived acronym, AMMPE, for *Asociacion Mundial de Mujeres Periodistas y Escritoras*. AMMPE was founded by a Mexican journalist and writer, Gloria Salas de Calderon, in 1969, when the "glass ceiling" of that profession was very low. While in Taipei I had the privilege of joining both groups. This has allowed me to participate in international conferences, where my knowledge of five languages has come in handy. In 2008, I was honored to give a speech in Spanish at the eighteenth world conference of AMMPE in Santiago, Chili. I represented the Taiwan Chinese chapter, discussing the influence of the internet on journalism and professional writers.

In order to go live with mama I had to abandon a comfortable life in Kansas City to spend nine years in Taiwan taking care of her—until she died at 92. During the time I was with her, many of her Chinese friends marveled at my leaving everything in the U.S. to come and care for her. Hardly any young people who live abroad come back to take care of their aging parents full-time. On the other hand, many parents who go to live with their children abroad often end up being babysitters, housekeepers, and cooks for the families of their children.

I served my mother out of duty. She never accepted me, not even to the end of her life. I no longer try to understand her reasons. I just accept that the time I gave her was the repayment of my karmic debt. I can only say that my word was my bond—I fulfilled my promise to father and have no regret.

Once mama was feeling better, I took great advantage of my time there to follow my own interests and dreams. For example,

I attended Normal University, taking Mandarin Chinese classes designed for foreign adults through the immersion technique which was developed by the U.S. Army. At last, at 57, I started formal study of reading and writing the language of my ancestors. After a while my mother no longer called me "illiterate" to her friends. In one of the classes I concentrated on learning medical terms, enabling me later to become an interpreter for patients in Mandarin and English in hospitals in the U.S.

A lifelong interest in Chinese art and culture led me to the Taipei Palace Museum, where treasures of past emperors of China are displayed and stored. Because I wanted to be a docent, my cousin Irene Chang took me to meet the director of volunteers, Dr. Kung-shin Chou. Since I knew there was a three-year waiting list for Chinese speakers to become docents, I quickly revealed my fluency in English and French. Dr. Chou immediately tested my French since she was a graduate of the Sorbonne in Paris. She accepted my application on the spot. My training took over 360 hours and the next several years I guided tours for foreign guests in both French and English. Several years later, Dr. Chou became and continues to be the director of that museum.

To get through the most difficult time dealing with mama, I used to ask myself, "Are you willing to trade places with her?" That question made me realize that if I had been incapacitated, she would have sent me to an institution. Then all my exasperation would vanish, leaving only thankfulness that I was able to serve her instead of the other way around. I ended up with gratitude for the chance to live and learn in a Chinese society.

In the spring of 2001, I returned to Kansas City for a visit. One Sunday, as Gene and I drove home from church, I was surprised to see a for sale sign in front of *the* house I had secretly blessed for 18 years. Every time I had passed it, silently I said, "You are so special; someday I would like to borrow you from the universe." I took down the phone number and the next morning called for an appointment to see the house that afternoon.

I made an unusual request of Gene to allow me to invite my former husband, Don, to view the house with us. Don understood property values and renovation far better than us, from having owned many rentals. It's a real testament to Gene's open-mindedness and generous heart that he agreed.

As we looked at the house I decided, with disappointment, that it would not suit me since there was no bedroom on the first floor and the kitchen was in a separate room. My old high jump injury prevents me from going up and down stairs comfortably. Also, given that it is important to me to do my cooking in the company of my family and guests, the kitchen was just too small. So, I released the idea of using that house as our home.

But the next morning at six o'clock Don called, saying, "I've been up since four and I've redesigned your house so that it will work for you after all. You can have it if you want it." Gene and I went to see his drawings, which showed us how to reconfigure the layout. We were elated. Only 17 hours after we first viewed the house, we signed the purchase papers, fulfilling my long-held secret desire to make it my home. We also discovered that the house is on three registries of historical places: in Washington, D.C., in the state of Missouri, and in Kansas City. It was the original farm house built in 1894, on a large parcel of land purchased by William Rockhill Nelson, founder of the *Kansas City Star*. The world-class Nelson-Atkins Museum of Art was built just a few hundred yards from our home. Streets added later make the museum cater-cornered from us.

Since the campus of the University of Missouri is only two blocks away, all those 18 years I had wished to share that home with international students. Remembering the struggles I went through when I first arrived in this country, I wanted to help other newcomers integrate into a new culture and a new language. Since the universe loaned the house to Gene and me, we have been blessed with students from Taiwan, Bulgaria, Saudi Arabia, France, Spain, Finland, Turkey, Malawi, and China. We have been further blessed to visit some of them in their own countries, making our world richer and far more exciting.

In mid-March 2001, Gene's 17-year-old son, Scott, led us to a new opportunity. Scott's Catholic high school required 25 hours of community service per year of each student. He asked if he could do this in El Salvador at refugee camps of recent earthquake victims, on spring break, as some of his classmates were planning to do. On January 13 and February 13 of that year, two major earthquakes destroyed more than 145,000 homes, damaged 41,000 small businesses, and left 1,500,000 people homeless. Not only did we approve, we helped him connect with a Jesuit priest, Father Francisco Xavier Aguilar, whose church was in Santa Tecla, near the capitol city, San Salvador.

El Salvador, the smallest Central American country and the most densely populated, is one of the countries that maintains diplomatic relations with Taiwan. So, as soon as we decided to make the trip, I called Director General Elizabeth Chu, of the Taipei Economic and Cultural Office in Kansas City. I asked her to connect us with the Embassy in San Salvador and the Buddhist organization, Tzu Chi, to explore the possibility of cooperating on relief efforts. All the connections were quickly made and we traveled to El Salvador.

In Santa Tecla, Father Aguilar sent Scott to work at one of the camp kitchens and took Gene and me on a tour to see the living conditions of the refugees. He said, "Last week three businessmen from Kansas City came to assess our situation. Why don't you get together with them and help raise awareness of our plight? We need your help."

On March 30, Gene and I went to meet the three businessmen: Jack Fisher, retired agent of USAID (United States Agency for International Development); Robert Miller, president of Robert E. Miller Insurance Agency; and Ron Ward, president of Western Forms—a company that makes aluminum forms for concrete that expedite construction. The largest single project that had used this company's technology, at the time, was in Taiwan's Silicon Valley, at the Holland Village Development in the Hsin Chu Science and Technology Industrial Park.

In Miller's office we put our heads together, along with attorney Nancy Jochens, and Othello Evans, manager and construction trainer for Western Forms. The not-for-profit, non-governmental organization *Homes from the Heart* was born. Our mission was to build homes for those in need. Later, Mike Bonderer joined the group and moved to El Salvador to oversee the construction there. His dedication ensured the success of the complex partnership. With Western Forms technology; funds from Catholic Relief Services, Kiwanis, and other service clubs; land from the Salvadoran government; and labor from the recipients, more than 300 concrete earthquake-resistant houses were built. Robert Miller has led several annual fund-raising appeals and the rest of us have found many ways to support the mission.

In El Salvador, I fell on the uneven earthquake-torn terrain, injured my knee, and came back to the U.S. in a wheelchair. I required surgery, so Gene took time off from work to help me. Starting in my recuperation period, we turned our home into a public relations office to publicize *Homes from the Hearts* projects. Scott wrote a report on his community service and visit to the earthquake areas, including pictures he had taken. The Kansas City weekly bi-lingual newspaper *Dos Mundos* published his story in English and Spanish. His article got the attention of the *Kansas City Star* and local radio and television stations.

Homes invited Father Aguilar to visit Kansas City. He spoke to groups at several schools and churches, and to factory workers at Western Forms, many of whom were native to El Salvador. Father received so much attention that Kay Barnes, Kansas City's first woman mayor, honored him with a proclamation. In the City council chambers, a ceremony was held for the Ward Family Foundation to announce their commitment to donate two sets of Western Forms to be used in the construction work in El Salvador. Next, we had to find a way to transport the huge forms at low cost. It was Ron Ward who made the arrangement with the Chiquita Banana company to donate the use of a container that would have returned empty to El Salvador. Gene and I organized a party at the Western Forms factory where the workers loaded the forms and sent them off with cheers, releasing helium-filled balloons. The event was covered by the *Kansas City Star, Dos Mundos,* and local television.

When I went back to Taiwan to care for mother, I shared my experience in El Salvador with the women of the Taipei II Zonta

Club. Out of the purses of six women came donations totaling 6,000 New Taiwan Dollars, which converted to approximately US$200. After I went home from the meeting I thought, "I can send this money to *Homes'* bank account...or I could consider it seed money and make it grow." So I added my own NT$4,000 (about US$140) and went to the Taipei weekend jade market. I found a stall owned by a woman, told her my story, and asked her to give me the most advantageous wholesale discount on the jade purse charms she sold. I spent all NT$10,000 with her. I packaged the charms, adding a label and a card describing the meaning of the symbols. Through the years I have sold these purse charms in many settings to raise awareness and money. I encourage women to attach the charms onto their purses with blessings, knowing they are contributing funds to provide houses for women in El Salvador. I tell them they are "turning jade into concrete."

In honor of mama's 90th birthday, the Zonta Club Taipei II and I raised money to construct three *Homes from the Heart* houses (photos 50, 51, 52, 53). They were built in Soyapango, the largest community *Homes* has built in El Salvador. It is located on reclaimed land which was once an automobile graveyard, and was donated to *Homes* by the local government. I made a display of photos of these houses to share with the women at mama's party. To date, in 2010, Soyapango has 155 houses, all with electricity and running water, plus an eight-room school, a children's playground with slides and swings, a small clinic, a basketball court, a community center, one Protestant and one Catholic chapel, and—the latest accomplishment—a regulation-size soccer field. Soyapango has become a community where several small businesses have sprung up: tiny grocery stores, and shops for sewing and alterations, bicycle repair, and light furniture-making. All of this was accomplished with Mike Bonderer's careful management of the project and funds, combined with volunteer labor. There is still enough land for 50 more houses at this location, awaiting more funds to be built.

During my 2004 visit back to Kansas City, one morning, while walking our dogs, Gene noticed the setting up of numerous tents in Volker Park, next to our home, just across from the Nelson-Atkins

Museum. He found out from the women working on the crew—they called themselves "roadies"—that they were setting up for *O Magazine*'s national tour, "Hi Gorgeous! A Celebration of You."

Since Gene knew my deep appreciation of Oprah's work in raising awareness and possibilities for minority women and all women around the world, he excitedly brought me the news. We decided to invite the roadies over for dinner the next day. They came in groups of four or five at a time, whenever they could take a break. One young woman even sang for her dinner, giving us a heart-stirring rendition of *Amazing Grace*. We also took them ice cold lemonade and home-baked chocolate brownies, some with lavender blooms. They gave us VIP passes that got us close to the stage to see and hear Oprah speak. With a lovely yellow sweater tied around her shoulders, she affirmed that all women are gorgeous"—quite a stretch for me to believe. When the event concluded and the roadies took down the tents, one of the women brought me the bouquet of roses from Oprah's dressing room. I kept one rose and shared the rest with friends, one at a time. I dried mine and still keep it in my kitchen where I can see it, in a fish-shaped vase. In Chinese, the word "fish" and "surplus" have the same sound, so the fish has come to symbolize "abundance." Have you noticed that Chinese restaurants are almost always decorated with an aquarium of fish or, at least, with a painting of swimming fish?

When mama died in late 2005, Gene joined me in Taipei to be my moral support through all the arrangements of cremation, the memorial service, and cleaning up after so long a life. We donated my paternal grandfather's ancient books to my cousin Tung Shen. She is a Professor of Chinese Literature and Dean of International Affairs at the National Taiwan University. Her brother, Lyushun Shen was, at that time, Taiwan's senior representative of the Taipei Economic and Cultural Office in Geneva. He wrote a moving account of my parents' influence on his decision to enter the diplomatic service, which Tung read at mama's memorial service. In 2010 Lyushun was promoted to be the Deputy Minister of Foreign Affairs in Taipei (photo 48).

Max and his wife Ronda went back to the U.S. with mother's

ashes. Before they departed, brother and I made a decision to have father's remains exhumed and cremated, so Gene stayed with me to watch over the procedure. It was done by a bone collector master, who hand-picked and counted each bone, and placed it in a box for the crematorium. The last one was father's skull, which I was supposed to receive from his hands and place with the others. I did so with the greatest reverence. I felt sad about having missed saying goodbye to him in his earthly existence. Gene held father's urn on the plane back to our home in Kansas City, where it remains. Hopefully someday Max will complete our parents' burial according to the Chinese tradition of a son's responsibility—then our father and mother's ashes could lie side by side.

For nine years, Gene and I had not had the chance to function as a normal married couple. I had to learn how to live with my mate, and to be a wife—remembering what Ah Jie had said, "If you can't be submissive, at least respect your husband's opinion and be flexible."

Now that mama had passed, I wanted to write the story of my life. But for a few years could not find the quiet energy or the courage to "stir the ashes."

Gene's passion is golf. I say of him that "he would rather golf than eat." He tried to get me interested by giving me lessons. They didn't take, even though he was an excellent teacher. At least I learned to understand the game better so I can enjoy it when we watch competitions on television.

Gene introduced me to some of his friends. One of them, Lynn Snyder, founded a weekly potluck get-together on Wednesday evenings. Musicians, writers, gardeners, and talkers-of-politics gather around a good home-cooked and sometimes home-grown food. We have a great time sharing stories and capping off the evenings by playing a few rounds of live music. These friends became my encouragers when I finally embarked on writing my memoirs. They often listened to passages and asked questions that helped me tell my story more clearly. Gene and I are regulars, and now host the event once a month.

Shortly after I moved back to Kansas City I adopted a puppy

mill reject. She is a five-pound, seven-year old Pomeranian I named *Chou-Chou* (teacher's pet in French). Chou-Chou and I helped one another heal. She helped me release resentment I held from the day my first husband, Simon, had bought a dog we could not afford. I used love, patience, and time to draw Chou-Chou out of the cage where she had lived all her life—this seemed to have been *her* mini concentration camp. I trained her to meditate and to serve as a therapy dog. Every Sunday she goes to church with me and sits on her own meditation cushion. One day a week she goes to work—her job is to sit on the laps of elderly men and women at the Claridge Court retirement center in Prairie Village, Kansas, a suburb of Kansas City. Chou-Chou keeps them company and the joy she spreads is priceless.

In February 2007, Don's daughter Nancy called to say her father was unconscious in the hospital. She had promised him long ago to get me by the side of his death bed. Immediately I went, taking Chou-Chou, who had done death-watches before. I didn't put Chou-Chou in Don's bed, remembering that Don did not like dogs. I leaned against Don's left ear, the one with better hearing, and said, "Don, this is Bambi, I am here for you. You can let go whenever you are ready. Don't forget to follow the light. We may see each other on the other side. Thank you for everything you have done for me. We have served each other in the way we were supposed to. All is well." He had no verbal response but a tear rolled down his face. For three days Chou-Chou and I did the death-watch with Don's three children. On the third evening, before I left to take his grandson to dinner, I repeated what I had said to him. Three hours later, he passed away. He was 85.

One of Gene's and my greatest pleasures is traveling together. In 2007, we spent eight weeks in mainland China, in the company of UMKC's professor of political sciences, Dr. Robert Gamer, and his wife May, who is Chinese. Dr. Gamer wrote a book in 1998 called *Understanding Contemporary China,* which is used extensively as a textbook in many universities. Going into its third edition, Dr. Gamer felt it was time to update the material, in view of China's recent rapid changes. So on our trip May and I interpreted for him and helped him communicate with local people on the state of their lives compared to a few years ago. We learned how aggressive China is about using natural gas to power all their buses and taxicabs, which we rode a lot during our stay. By special permission we were allowed to visit many areas of Tibet during an eight-day visit, a length of time rarely granted to foreigners. We saw many solar panels installed on roofs throughout China. The most unusual ones were on the *yurts* (tents) of nomads in the high plateau of Chang Tang. On top of these tents made of animal skins the solar panels powered a light bulb and a small television set for the families inside. We returned to Beijing on the sky-train, the railroad which runs at the highest elevation in the world—its boxcars are even equipped with oxygen vents.

In China I reconnected with relatives (photo 43) on both my mother and father's sides, listening to them tell old stories and secrets. The most significant secret to me was a shocker: my parents were first cousins! My paternal grandfather, *Yeh Yeh,* and my maternal grandmother, *Wai Po,* were brother and sister. Even though at the time of my parents' marriage it was not illegal to marry first cousins, the elders did not totally approve. No wonder *Yeh Yeh* had left my papa at *Wai Po's* home on that trip to Beijing when papa was ten—that story now made more sense to me. Suddenly, I understood why my parents were so adamantly opposed to my marrying Siaoti in my twenties, being concerned about the health of potential offspring. I wondered, "Why didn't they tell me the truth?"

Gene and I spent time with my cousin Lily, her son, and his family in Tianjin, where they have a factory that makes high-fashion clothing to be sold in fancy department stores.

In Beijing, we became tourists, visiting sights that Gene was seeing for the first time. At a family luncheon we met the son of Uncle Jin-E—the one who had secured the diplomatic post for papa in Saigon in 1936. I was able to thank Auntie Yo-Yo again for keeping me company, telling me stories, and giving me the *Snow White and Seven Dwarfs* coloring book in 1946, when my eye was healing.

Siao-Mei Jie and Jiu-Yu Ge and their families hosted us royally in Shanghai, giving us the use of Siao-Mei's son's condo with all the amenities of home, in the building just a few yards from their own. How good it was to see my relatives after so many years.

In 2008, Gene took me to Bali to attend the wedding of his nephew Clay and bride Casey. The next year we went to Singapore and Hong Kong and also on a ten-day cruise on the Baltic Sea. Since our ship had only a six-hour stopover in Helsinki we decided not to inform Jakko, the Finnish student who had lived with us the year before. We thought it would be too complicated to schedule a meeting because his hometown was far away. So we focused our visit on the famous, incredibly beautiful Rock Church—*Temppeliaukio.* As we were riding back to the ship, I noticed a pair of holey jeans on a young man boarding our street car. I looked up and it was Jakko! The day before, he had come to the city to visit a friend. He couldn't believe his eyes when he first noticed Gene, then saw me and our Kansas City friends Ray and Clara Hoffman, in whose home he had eaten dinner when they hosted the Wednesday night group. Under the warm June sun of Finland we shared lunch at a side walk café. It was a most incredible encounter. I'll never forget those holey jeans. When Jakko had purchased them in Kansas City, he had proudly shown them to me. I had exclaimed, "Why did you spend money to buy holes?" He defended, "This is the fashion." And we laughed.

In my daily life in Kansas City, I continue to work as an interpreter in area hospitals and remain involved in activities serving several organizations—Global and Multicultural Education (GAME), Sister Cities, and Harvesters community food network.

In 2011 I was invited to be a board member of the Edgar Snow Memorial Foundation. I am honored to serve in memory of the education my parents received in Yenching University, while Mr. Snow lectured on that campus. Mr. Snow donated his professional papers to the University of Missouri-Kansas City, where they are archived in its library, just two blocks from my home. In October 2012 I attended the biennial Edgar Snow symposium in Beijing. It was a joy to visit the city of my parents' youth and to be part of a bridge between the past and the future. (photo 56, 57)

I find ways to support the mission of *Homes from the Heart,* which has continued to serve the landless and homeless poor in El Salvador and is beginning work in Haiti. Is having a house not one of the most basic human needs? How would *we* feel if we had no walls, no beds, no roof over our heads, no stove to cook on, and no water to bathe or wash our clothes? What would our self-esteem be?

I use the proceeds of the sale of my book—now printed in English, Spanish, and Chinese—as one of the ways to raise funds to continue building houses in El Salvador. Working with the victims of the earthquakes there I have become acutely aware of and compassionate toward their plight. It brings to mind my own experience in one of the concentration camps, living with the lack of one of the most basic necessities: a container. Can you imagine what it would be like to live a day without a single container—a glass, a bowl, a plate to drink or eat from? In this light, I've come to understand my special attraction to buying dishes. I recall not having anything to hold the one meal a day we received. All I could eat was what could be contained in the little hand of a five year-old and what my nanny could grab for me and for herself. We felt like we were animals, eating as monkeys do. Where was our sense of dignity at that time?

In the community of Soyapango, El Salvador, the women used to gather every afternoon to pray the rosary at the spot where they wished for a chapel. Now that the chapel has been completed, in 2010, my next step will be to take them life-sized statues of Our Lady of Lourdes and Saint Bernadette. I promise the women that, rock by rock, together we will build the grotto to house the statues. It will be my act of thanksgiving for the education I received through the Catholic Church. This grotto will stand to symbolize my hope for educational opportunities for all women everywhere.

I am developing a workbook, companion to *The Uncrushable Rose,* to use the stories and the lessons from my life to encourage women to empower themselves.

My school in Saigon was named after the Nobel prize-winning scientist Marie Curie. During difficult times of my life I have used Madam Curie's words as an anchor, and I invite you, my readers, to apply her wisdom in your own life:

At times for all of us, life is not easy.
We must have perseverance and above all believe in ourselves.
We must believe that we are gifted to the point of attaining
that which we desire.

Centering Affirmations

Let all things be healthy.
Let all acts be happy.
Let all beings be peaceful.
I count my blessings
at least once a day.
I forgive those who have hurt me
and those who have offended me.
I release myself
from what I have done,
and from what I failed to do.
That which is done,
there is no need to speak about.
That which is past,
there is no need to blame.
I have self-control, self-knowledge,
self-respect, and the courage to dare.
I am tranquil and the Light
of Intelligence will shine.
I strive to make the spot
where I stand beautiful;
then Peace and Harmony will
follow me in all my ways
and through all my days.

Bambi Shen

Poems by Lulu Shen-Chow

I was unable to be at father's side when he died in Taipei in March 1969, nor did I get to attend his funeral. My little cousin Lulu Shen, Uncle Haigo's daughter, 12 at the time, attended and recalled the event, along with her affection for my father, in the following two poems. First published in 2010 in her book of poetry, *Memories of You*, by Lulu Shen-Chow with photos by her son Randal Chow, they are reprinted here with her permission.

Lulu was only two (photo 31) when she first met my father. His western manners of hugging and kissing her on both cheeks, unfamiliar in her culture, meant that the French cologne he wore made a deep impression on her. Thus, she nicknamed him "Uncle Cologne."

Cologne

Greased up hair,
Cigarette in hand.
Tall slim shadow,
Sweet smelling cologne.

Gifts from afar,
Rare and beautiful,
Strands of white shells,
A place called Tahiti.

Strong loving hands carried me,
Smiles brightened my day.
Stories of travel mystified me,
Cologne, the Consul-General.

Rwanda he went,
Time stood still.
Holding strands of white shells,
Remembering that sweet smell.

245

The Funeral

Rwanda flew home in a wheelchair.
Frail and sickly, purple and blue.
Unknown, fever, unknown fate.
Never die in a foreign land!

Saw him sleeping peacefully.
Saw him moving quietly.
Cologne awakes, he's not dead!
Cologne smiles, Silly Girl too!

Hired criers, cried for him.
Cried for his good deeds,
Cried for his life.
Cried for a good man who died so young!

Funeral lasting hours long,
White robe, burlap hood,
Small red paper pinned to the back.
Silly Girl knew Cologne is alive!

Up a dirt road on the hill side,
Carried casket to the burial site.
Monks sent prayers, Priest with blessings.
Incense burning, food on the stone!

Burial was over, what a day!
Bored and tired, nothing else to do.
Cologne hides, Silly Girl seeks.
Scold by First Aunty "Sit and behave!"

Sitting in the chair, trying to behave.
Cologne smiles, Silly Girl too.
Imaginary or for real?
Sweet smell of cologne lingers on!

Epilogue

May 15, 2011

I appreciate the new insights and perspectives brought to me from readers. The perspectives I shared in my book were, of course, those of a child and teenager, influenced and limited by the views of my parents, nanny, teachers, peers, and classmates. My life is continually enriched by the gifts of learning new points of view on how others' lives were affected by the same historical events. Some lived through different phases of the turmoil of the Japanese occupation of Southeast Asia. Others went through the many changes that took place in the years that followed World War II, including the move of the Nationalist government to Taiwan.

Through my book signing events I have connected with former classmates, veterans of the Vietnam wars —both South Vietnamese and U.S. military—and relatives still in mainland China or Taiwan, as well as those who grew up away from Chinese society. I take special delight in some, from the younger generation, telling me that through reading my memoir they have gained a clearer understanding of their own ancestry. They appreciated the way I used my father's voice to explain our family connections to China's 19th and 20th Century history. Even some, from my own generation, have commented, similarly, that my way of telling stories from the 16th through 18th Century—about the opening of China's trade with the Western world, including the financial and cultural exchanges and difficulties that ensued—has helped them connect the dots of their history lessons. One said, "I learned of these events in school as historical facts; but you explained them in a way that helped me really *understand*."

I also want to acknowledge how much this whole process of writing my story and sharing it with my non-Chinese friends means to me personally. It is a *good thing* to get my black and white and caramel-brown friends here in the U.S. thinking, talking, and caring about people and history from the other side of this planet! This experience has enabled me to fulfill one of my dearest intentions: to engage many, many people in developing their understanding of other cultures, thus creating the possibility of expanding cross-cultural friendship and peace.

Many people have commented that *The Uncrushable Rose* reads like a Chinese *Gone with the Wind*—because my family's history played out against the background of the turmoil and aftermath of wars: the 19th Century Opium Wars, World War II in Asia, the 20th Century Chinese Civil War, the Indochina War, and the Vietnam War.

Just as in personal lives, the development and evolution of nations take many twists and turns. Sometimes periods of chaos, conflicts, false accusations, injustice, and lawlessness are part of the process. A spirit of forgiveness can be cultivated which will promote new possibilities for peaceful co-creation of the future.

About the Author

Bambi Shen with her dog, Chou-Chou ("shoo-shoo")

From her complex roots as the female child of a Chinese diplomat in French Indochina, Bambi Shen has navigated vast geographic and cultural terrain to become a businesswoman, author, teacher, international tour director, public speaker, interpreter, and co-founder of a not-for-profit charitable organization. She received a B.A. from Catholic Siena College in Memphis, Tennessee, and an M.A. in French Language and Literature from the University of Missouri, Kansas City. Ms. Shen received the U.S. Department of Labor Women's Bureau 2011 Kansas City "Sheroe" Award.

Bambi makes her home in the heart of Kansas City, Missouri, with her husband, two international students, and three dogs.

She now uses her life and her stories to inspire and empower others to be a beneficial presence in their world. Her invitation to all women is: support and challenge one another, shatter the ceiling of mental and cultural restrictions, raise your sights and expand your horizons, call forth whatever is needed for growth and progress, patronize and promote one another's businesses, and work *together* to help *each other* succeed.

Bambi Shen is available for select readings and talks. To invite her to speak to your group, to obtain additional copies of her book, or to learn what else she's "cooking up," please visit www.uncrushablerose.com, or email: bambishen888@gmail.com.

QUESTIONS AND TOPICS FOR DISCUSSION

I offer the following to help us expand our horizons and promote cross-cultural understanding, thereby enriching our lives and increasing peace and harmony in our human family.

1. Describe three things—cultural, historical, or spiritual/religious—which you learned from *The Uncrushable Rose*. How does your new understanding expand your experience of life?

2. What events, descriptions, or stories moved, surprised, delighted, saddened, angered, or inspired you?

3. Pick one or two of Bambi's challenging experiences that remind you of your own life—e.g. having experienced war; or being in a foreign country, unsure of the culture and language; or either observing or experiencing a racial barrier, such as evidenced by the "colored" sign in Bambi's Greyhound bus station experience. How did you handle your situation(s) and what did you learn?

4. How has your life been influenced by your: gender, birth order, economic circumstances, and the education level of your parents or grandparents? Imagine how your life would be different if you were of a different gender, or class, or...

5. How has your life been influenced by your culture, race/ethnicity, language, or religious traditions? Discuss how your life would be different if your circumstances were different.

6. What is your reaction to Bambi's account of the extreme gender preference in her mother and in Chinese culture? In what ways has your understanding of gender oppression been deepened by her story? Pick a topic of gender oppression that continues in the world today—e.g. literacy rates, land and property ownership,

rights to inheritance, rights to transportation/mobility, rights to drive a car or travel without a male relative chaperon, and the plight of female genital mutilation (FGM). Research that issue and briefly summarize what you learned.

7. In your own upbringing, what kind of favoritism did you and your siblings experience from your parents? Often those who receive favoritism or privilege are unaware of it. Consider how members of your family view this dynamic differently. How does this translate into favoritism and privilege in society at large?

8. Give three examples of the rules and norms of Bambi's family that resemble or differ from those of your own. How have these rules changed over time as your family members have matured?

9. The importance given by Chinese culture to a person's birth sign is evidenced by the description of being a "tiger bride," given by Bambi's nanny, Ah Jie—accused of snuffing out the life force of her young husband-to-be. (page 139) Describe how this view of the Zodiac is similar or different from your own cultural beliefs. Research your own birth sign according to the Chinese Zodiac, and describe two positive and two negative characteristics of your sign that seem to fit your personality.

10. How old were you when you were first aware of faith traditions different from the ones taught in your family? Describe your reactions then and how they have changed over time.

11. What is your first memory of a cultural group or race other than your own? Describe how the prejudices and opinions of those around you—family members, friends, neighbors, and classmates—affected your early opinions of that culture or race. Consider how you would like to grow by stepping outside of your comfort zone and connecting or building bridges with people of other races and cultures.

12. When do you remember first consciously choosing your own personal views and actions, beyond what you were taught? What influences made this possible for you? What did you see in Bambi's development that resembles or differs from your own? Identify a belief system you inherited and describe two of its facets which you have adopted, and two you no longer follow.

13. When Bambi married her first husband she was unaware of homosexuality. How have attitudes toward and rights for gay and lesbian people changed since the early 60s? How have your attitudes changed?

14. Reflect on the book's title, *The Uncrushable Rose*. How has Bambi put her father's rosebush lesson (page 96) into action? In what ways can you apply this to your own life?

15. Bambi leads workshops on five tools of empowerment: self-image, health, education, legal rights, and finances (S.H.E.L.F., page xx). Reflect on and assess your current level of strength in each area, with a rating from 1 to 10, then choose two areas you want to strengthen. Set a goal and an action plan for each. Invite a trusted friend to hold you accountable and celebrate your success.

16. What is your experience with other languages? If you had the opportunity, would you make the effort to learn a new language? What language would you choose and why? If you are from a family of recent immigrants, describe your parents', your own, and your children's attitudes toward retaining the language and culture of your ancestors. On page 46, Bambi said, "...when I spoke French I was not bashful...when I spoke Chinese...more timid and submissive." How does this example shed light on the dynamics between language and cultural values?

17. Given the examples of Bambi's difficult relationship with her mother whom she came to view as her most valuable teacher, are you open to reconsider the people in your life whom you see

to be challenging? Could they be there to teach you something you needed to learn? Name a way you could change your attitude to help the relationship and enrich your life. Based on this new perspective, what steps can you take now to initiate healing, bring more closeness, and create greater harmony? (page 245)

18. Reflect on what else you have learned from Bambi's story that you can apply to your life, such as her philosophy (page 179), "There is a silver lining in every cloud and a gate in every wall."

19. How have Bambi's experiences inspired you to deepen your awareness of and engagement with your passion and purpose?

20. What needs exist in your community where you can be of service? How can you match your interest and skills with those needs? How can you be a beneficial presence in your world?

21. Compare and contrast Bambi's "Triple A of Change" (page 228), with *The Serenity Prayer* by Reverend Reinhold Niebuhr: "God, grant me the serenity to accept the things I cannot change; courage to change the things that I can; and wisdom to know the difference."